THE PROPERTY BOOM

THE
PROPERTY
BOOM

OLIVER MARRIOTT

ABINGDON PUBLISHING
LONDON
1989

First published in 1967
by Hamish Hamilton Ltd.
This edition published in 1989 by
Abingdon Publishing Company
14 Old Park Lane, London W1Y 3LH
© *Oliver Marriott 1967, 1989*

ISBN 1 872317 00 6

Printed in Great Britain
by Butler & Tanner Ltd
Frome and London

Contents

Preface to 1989 reprint

I wrote this book during 1966 and 1967. It has now been out of print in both hardback and paperback for around fourteen years. This present impression reprints the book exactly as it appeared in 1967. Why have I not revised it for the events of the last twenty three years or written a sequel?

There does appear to have been a steady unsatisfied demand for The Property Boom, partly from those within or interested in the property business in its widest sense, and partly from students, for whom it has been a set book on most courses on Land Economics or Management, Geography, Surveying or related subjects.

Since 1966 there has been a further boom, then a prolonged bust, in which some of the leading characters in my Property Boom fell by the wayside, and yet a third and even more sumptuous boom which is still − only just perhaps − going strong. I left journalism in the autumn of 1969 for business, mainly the property business. Often I have considered writing a sequel to The Property Boom. But I have never thought that my subjective viewpoint from within the industry would carry the conviction with the critical reader that a book on current affairs or recent history should do.

It has been a surprise to me that no-one has written a book on the intervening twenty three years. There have been dramas and colourful case histories in plenty. There have been new types of development, new methods of financing, new political constraints, old policies thrown aside, collapses, bankruptcies and new empires founded.

But underlying the sagas and the cycles, the system has not fundamentally changed much in twenty three years and this explains in part why no other book has appeared. Reading again my chapter 3, The System, which was the central description of how property development happened in the Fifties and Sixties, it is curious how applicable that is still to the Eighties and is likely to be for the Nineties. And having myself seen the property business from the inside, I have been able to see that system at work.

The firms of estate agents, architects, contractors, bankers, insurance companies or pension funds, these are all still essential ingredients for the developer to juggle. Some new firms have started up, some old ones have declined. But as development has tended to be larger scale and more complex, so the professionals have been more in demand: and fuzzily defined operators have filled gaps as planners, consultants, marketing men. Yet at the centre of the web with all these professionals revolving around remains the developer. He is the impresario, the conductor, the visionary, sometimes the hopeless optimist, who dreams of what might be done if a whole series of events would fall into place.

I wrongly predicted in the last chapter of my book that the era of the individual was passed and that the institutions would take over the developers role. The institutions have indeed been increasingly busy in direct property development and investment, but equally the individuals have flourished as never before in this latest, Thatcherite, boom.

That prediction was fostered by the all-pervasive corporatism of the Sixties. It was extremely hard to imagine then that governments as fiercely capitalist as those of Mrs Thatcher would return. Indeed one of the lessons drummed in by these twenty three years is that many barely imaginable events can take place — and have taken place — whilst the basic system is mainly intact.

I wrote that 'the Development Levy is never likely to disappear'. It is now forgotten. Few would have conceived of the degree of building obsolescence, that office blocks of the Sixties could be pulled down in the late Eighties: or that Harry Hyams would lose control of his Oldham Estate Company to the Co-Operative Insurance and to MEPC; or that the GLC would disappear and its headquarters, County Hall, become a giant opportunity and renovation project for developers.

The revival of capitalism and the partial dismembering of the corporate state has led to many rich opportunities for developers, chiefly for those younger ones in tune with the unusually long economic boom of the Eighties. Fewer who were successful in the stop go cycles of the Fifties and Sixties and then survived the crash of the Seventies could adapt as well to the lengthy upswing of the Eighties as the younger men, less scarred by experience and keener for risk. Without enough experience myself when I wrote, I did not stress sufficiently the life cycle of the developer himself, as opposed to the business or property cycles. Most developers grew cautious and drew in their horns as they grew older. Jack Rose was a classic developer of the Fifties and Sixties who sat on his developed assets in the Seventies and Eighties, preached caution and did nothing new. And all the while in these last two decades the likes of Stuart Lipton and John Whittaker, Godfrey Bradman and John Hall and the Beckwith brothers, and many others, some not born when Jack Rose began to develop, created vast fortunes starting from scratch. None were doing what Jack Rose could not have done except that they were seizing different opportunities, taking different risks, looking at the future with different coloured spectacles, harnessing different energies from within themselves and from others.

These newer developers of the Eighties were greatly helped by operating in a commercial property market much broader and more active than that in the Sixties, mirroring the far more muscular economy at large. Not only had the institutions plunged in to invest and develop to a greater extent, though somewhat more cautiously than the property world at one point expected, they also came to believe in a less passive approach to their investments, weeding out and selling properties which did not fit in to their portfolios. That in turn threw up fresh opportunities for property companies, private and quoted alike. On top of this overseas buyers, mainly from Japan, Australia and Europe, were keen to compete in the second half of the Eighties for the better quality investments in London. And no longer was the government by so far the most important tenant for office blocks.

The trend among institutions to buy and sell and manage their properties more actively was another facet of this broader commercial property market in which companies and individuals were traders in property both short and medium term, as opposed to being developers. In the tradition of the great post-war dealer Max Joseph came those in the Seventies who specialised in buying blocks of flats wholesale and selling them off flat by flat retail − the break-up merchants − and the same policy was applied to parades of shops and portfolios of properties and all manner of odd lots great and small by such as Manny Davidson or Tony Clegg or Elliott Bernerd and plenty of others; while an increasingly powerful force in this side of the market were those of Asian extraction, particularly East African Asians, one of the chief being Nazmu Virani. In October 1987, in the biggest auction of commercial properties up to then, in which £55 million changed hands in two days, 40% was estimated to have been bought by businessmen from Asian immigrant families.

One further benefaction for the developers of the Eighties was the considerable change in attitude and practice among the planning authorities as the pro free enterprise waves from the government filtered down even to the bureaucrats, turning them towards being 'can-do' men from 'cannot-do and will-not-do until obliged eventually by some fiendishly clever planning architect to do'. A host of out-of-town retail warehouses and parks (thought improbable in the Sixties) up to John Hall's giant Metro Centre in Gateshead bear witness to that: as do Enterprise Zones, especially London's Docklands.

As a lubricant in the planning process politicians and planners on the one side and developers on the other increasingly resorted in the Seventies and Eighties to "planning gain", a new way to describe a sort of bribe or hidden tax or payment by the developer through provision of libraries or swimming pools or statues of local worthies built for little or nothing and handed over to the local authority in return for favourable treatment for planning applications.

Unless business cycles are a thing of the past, or water runs uphill, this freer planning climate and freer market and long running boom will of course bring its own corrections with a greater or lesser degree of pain within the next few years. It is a dangerous pointer in mid-1989 that the major banks, who have a sure knack of getting things wrong when in unison, have all been lending in rising volume on commercial property and with many ingenious 'new' kinds of loan.

And if there is money to be borrowed, so the developer of the Eighties, like his counterpart of the Fifties and Sixties, will put together projects to borrow it. The jargon may be a bit different, but the commodity is the same. 'Limited resource finance' is a euphemistic buzz phrase of the Eighties meaning that the lender, not the borrower, gets into the worst trouble if the development comes unstuck. The developer of the Sixties achieved a similar effect by having a string of private companies each for one property and not dependent on one another.

Nor have the ethical conflicts of interest changed much. 'Insider Dealing' is again a new phrase to describe an old, old condition, and a sheaf of legislation and case law is piling up in an attempt to throttle it. But in the property industry, where the dividing line between agent and principal can mean the difference between a fee and great riches, these conflicts have and will lead to some unsavoury stories. One infallible prediction is that human nature will not change.

What has changed has been the public perception towards property developers and the property world, and this despite the Prince of Wales, supported by the massed ranks of the media, lamenting the low quality of post-war commercial architecture. Whereas the property developer was the hate figure symbolising capitalism, the unleashing of free enterprise in the Eighties and the softer attitudes towards capitalism have allowed the developer to fade into the general background as just another branch of business life, a lot more visible inevitably, but more respectable than before. Perhaps the new phrase "merchant developer" to label a particular class of developer is meant to have a faint overtone of "merchant prince".

OLIVER MARRIOTT

Introduction

My aim in writing this book has been to tell the story of an industry from 1945 to the present day. Commercial property has in the post-war period been an industry in the throes of one of the greatest booms in this country's history and much in the public eye, but emotion and prejudice have tended to blind many discussions of the subject. I have attempted to give an objective account of the men and their companies, the insurance companies and banks and contractors, the local authorities and architects and estate agents, and the events which contributed to the unleashing of this boom.

Some of the events are of the recent past and even the few weeks between printing and publication of the book may turn some of the facts upside down. It is always possible, for example, that retailers might have descended in a flock on some shopping centre, described here as a desolate white elephant, and turned it into a bustle of prosperity. The richest man can be struck by disaster overnight and become impoverished.

I am grateful to William Rees-Mogg, then deputy editor of the *Sunday Times*, for his encouragement before I began the book and for his help in allowing me some weeks away from the *Sunday Times* to do part of the work. I am grateful, too, to my colleague Anthony Vice and ex-colleague Peter Wilsher for their advice and exhortation. Many people in or near to the property industry have been kind enough to see me and I now thank them all collectively; it would be invidious to name only a few and a long roll call of names would be out of place. A handful of developers were not prepared to see me—an attitude which provokes rather than stifles curiosity. Harry Hyams, whom I have discussed at length in chapter 8, was one; Charles Clore was another. Mr Clore was prepared to answer questions by letter. This procedure is almost useless to the journalist wanting more than the barest detail. However, I did send some questions to Mr Clore and his reply seemed oddly revealing. I have given both letters in Appendix 2.

OLIVER MARRIOTT

CHAPTER ONE

Outlines of a Boom

THE starting gun for the most intense phase of the property boom was fired on the afternoon of 2 November 1954. Mr Nigel Birch, Minister of Works in the first post-war Conservative administration, announced to the House of Commons that building licences were to be dropped entirely: 'Licences are now issued freely in nearly all areas and neither the cost nor the inconvenience caused to architects and contractors can any longer be justified. . . .' There were cheers from the Conservative benches.

A week before this blow in favour of the freedom of the market, after fifteen years of varied controls, Gabriel Harrison, a young dealer in property in London, had clinched a deal in Grafton Street, off Piccadilly. Unable to extract a building licence from the Ministry of Works, he had sold a bomb-damaged site next door to the Medici Galleries for £59,000 to a twenty-six-year-old estate agent, Harry Hyams. Immediately he heard that licences were abolished, Harrison cursed his luck and rang up Hyams on the off chance that he might buy the site back. Hyams replied that he would sell it back for £100,000; the end of licensing had changed values somewhat.

That 70 per cent spurt in value overnight of a plot of land in Grafton Street was one abrupt reaction to the end of all restrictions on building. Mr Birch's legislation was the formal opening of the floodgates for commercial property development, one of the most profitable industrial booms ever known. This industry needed vast sums of capital, yet unlike, say, the emergence of the motor car industry, which had to be highly concentrated to achieve economies of scale and thus funnelled the great fortunes into the hands of a few men such as Henry Ford or William Morris, a relatively large number of individuals became extremely rich via property development between 1945 and 1965. I have listed in

Appendix 1 108 men and 2 women, each of whom must have made on my calculation at least £1 million in this golden period. Few of these started with any capital beyond the odd hundred pounds.

The age of the property developer was ushered in alongside a revolution in the theory and practice of the State's relationship with landowners. Planning in its modern sense was born out of a reaction in the thirties against the ribbons of ugly houses and uglier factories which advanced, with the motor car, along the roads into the countryside. Hitler's bombs forced the planners into action. When the new post of Minister of Town and Country Planning was created for Mr William Morrison in early 1943, there was almost unanimous agreement from all political quarters that far more stringent planning was needed. Fiercer powers of compulsory acquisition were imposed under the Town and Country Planning Act of 1944 (the Blitz and Blight Act), and even when the Coalition Government proposed a modified form of betterment tax on land values, based on the Uthwatt Report of 1942, there was a surprisingly wide acceptance of the principle that an increased value in land, based in part on a planning decision by a local authority, should be taxed. The political atmosphere was one in which the Beveridge Report was widely welcomed and a genuine search for social reform was flourishing.

The wartime Coalition accepted the message of the Beveridge plan and the main suggestions of the three reports, the Barlow, Scott and Uthwatt Reports, on which most subsequent planning law was based, but the Labour Government put them into effect. Lewis Silkin, a solicitor who had passionately tackled the problem of slum clearance when the LCC was won by Labour in 1934, was the Minister, working painstakingly and often sleeping in his makeshift, new Ministry in St James' Square, to introduce the New Towns Act of 1946 and the Town and Country Planning Act of 1947.

Already the values of commercial and other property had begun to rise with relief at the ending of the war. The rise probably originated a few months before the invasion of France in June 1944, when a few men, banking on a British victory, decided that it would be comfortable to be sitting on real estate when the gunfire was forgotten and the economy had to be reshaped. Some were estate agents, such as Douglas Tovey or Joe Levy and his brother, David; Harold Samuel was an ex-estate agent nursing the embryo of what was to become the City's most respected property company; Charles Clore was a general entrepreneur with a leaning towards property. Before the war his efforts had varied from developing the Prince of Wales Theatre, buying old country estates for their timber, to building the Thatcham Ordnance Depot in Berkshire and other factories. And two of the most ardent buyers were self-made tailors with an earthy respect for property, Sir Montague Burton and Sir Henry Price of the Fifty Shilling Tailors.

These men almost at once experienced a delightful sensation: the effect that soaring values had on the fortunes of the property owner, who financed his purchase by borrowing money at a fixed cost. This was the background music throughout the property boom. The sums were simple. Assume a man buys a property for £100,000. He borrows £80,000 and puts up £20,000 of his own money. Inflation and demand boost the value of the property to £160,000, 60 per cent more than it cost. The buyer has a profit on his £20,000 of £60,000, a capital appreciation of 300 per cent. He only has to offset against this relatively small interest charges.

On the immediate post-war inflationary spiral which ended in the Devaluation of 1949, many of the great property fortunes were founded. Often land was bought and sold again at a profit within a few months; sometimes vacant buildings were bought and leased; occasionally war-damaged offices were repaired. But with the straitjacket of building licences, new developments were few and far between. Morover, Silkin's Town and Country Planning Act of 1947 threatened to snuff out the function of the speculative developer.

There were two aspects of the Silkin Act. On the planning side it insisted for the first time that local authorities throughout the country must draw up development plans for approval by the Minister and stick to these plans unless there was an appeal to the Minister. A review of this system eighteen years later observed that, when introduced, it was 'the most advanced and comprehensive system of physical planning in the world. . . . it still retains much of its strength.'*

The other side of the Act was its financial provisions. These

* Report of the Planning Advisory Group on the Future of Development Plans (HMSO, 1965).

were disastrous. In the spirit of reform nurtured during the war, Lewis Silkin attempted to tax at 100 per cent the development value created when planning permission was granted. Alongside this concept was a system of compensation for those owners whose land values were bruised by planning decisions. Silkin failed on two counts: first, with a tax of 100 per cent developers lost the incentive to develop. Secondly, the ins and outs of this new law of betterment and compensation were unbearably complicated. Silkin later recalled ruefully that he was always afterwards introduced at public functions as the man who brought in an Act which nobody understood. He deserved better. The New Towns Act and the planning part of the '47 Act were more enlightened pieces of legislation than many Ministers hatch in years on the front benches.

As with most new and restrictive legislation, there were loopholes in the '47 Act. Developers who had managed to obtain a building licence escaped the development charge if they started work before the appointed day, 1 July 1948, when all development rights became subject to the authority of the Central Land Board. When Lewis Silkin did not stand at the General Election of 1950 and was transferred to the Labour benches of the House of Lords, Hugh Dalton, his successor, had to bring in an Act to stop up two loopholes caused by 'errors of drafting'. One annoyance was that a war-damaged building, even if only a few bricks were left standing, could be restored to its exact pre-war shape without any planning permission at all. In several cases this helped to thwart the local authority's new plans.

On a bandwagon of anti-austerity and anti-nationalisation the Conservatives were voted back in 1951 for their thirteen unbroken years of power. It fell to Mr Macmillan, Minister of Housing and Local Government, to untie any austerity on the property front. The use of land had been to a large extent frozen by the 100 per cent charge and some laxative was clearly needed to encourage rebuilding. In December 1952 Macmillan introduced another Town and Country Planning Bill (the 1953 Act). He had decided to drop the concept of betterment and he abolished the 100 per cent development charge entirely. His main reasons seemed to be that laws which the public found hard to understand were bad laws and that the charge was extremely difficult to administer. 'I know some people say that the development charge is all right in theory but it will not work in practice. I am sufficiently old-fashioned to believe that if there is something wrong in practice it is just possible there is something wrong with the theory. (Ministerial cheers.) . . . the people whom the Government must help are those who do things: the developers, the people who create wealth whether they are humble or exalted. . . .' Mr Dalton remarked that the abolition of the charge was a profoundly reactionary measure, and it is ironical that by the end of the Conservative reign, after the boom was over, there was again a broad, apolitical section of opinion in favour of taxing betterment.

'The people who create wealth', who were indeed mostly humble at that time, were duly grateful to Mr Macmillan and busied themselves in preparation for the end of all controls. It was already apparent in 1953 to those in the business that the demand for offices in London was strong; it was on offices and in London that the majority of developers made their fortunes. It is probable that nobody guessed even then just how strong demand was to be, although a few people, including Mr Clore,* claim to have done so. The demand was based on a variety of factors. Bombing in central London destroyed 9·5 million square feet out of a total stock of offices in 1939 of 87 million square feet. But replacement of war-damaged buildings was only a small part of the total equation, for by mid-1962 the total floorspace had risen to 115 million square feet and by 1966 to roughly 140 million square feet finished or under construction, a jump of 72 per cent over the 1939 total. There had not been a great deal of office building between the wars and Victorian offices, many obsolete, were ripe for renewal. But the big addition was due to the change in emphasis from making goods towards designing and marketing them, the tendency towards the amalgamation of industry into larger units, and the choice of London for a company's 'prestige' headquarters; many of the newer growth industries were based in the South-East. London also became more and more of an international city. Most American companies regarded London as the capital of Europe and, in their increasing penetration of European industry, located the headquarters of their subsidiaries in London.

As Mr Macmillan lifted the development charge in 1953 and Mr Birch the building controls in 1954, the pace of development hotted up enormously. The LCC granted planning permission in

* See the answer numbered 6 of his letter reproduced in Appendix 2.

1952 for 2·4 million square feet of space; in 1953 this jumped to 3 million, in 1954 to 5·7 million and in 1955 to 5·9 million.* Building itself lags behind the granting of planning permission by a year to two years, but it was from around 1955, the peak year for permissions, that property development began to make an impact on the public consciousness. The cranes and the shiny matchbox blocks were there for all to see. Occasionally some fracas hit the headlines. The St James's Theatre row in 1957 was one of the most entertaining, with Felix Fenston cast in the role of the wicked developer destroying part of the country's heritage in favour of a soulless office block and the late Vivien Leigh as the noble saviour, leading the preservationists. She interrupted a debate on the saving of the theatre in the House of Lords and was removed by Black Rod, and she held a rally of protest in Trafalgar Square. But when it came to the touch, nobody was prepared to put up sufficient money to save a white elephant. The St James's fell.

The basic economics of property development are extremely straightforward, far less complicated than the manufacture of machine tools or ladies' dresses. One of the major risks was administrative: the chance that planning permission might be refused. To return to the site in Grafton Street, which Gabriel Harrison did not buy back from Harry Hyams, a rough outline of the operation would be this: the site cost £59,000, planning permission was granted for 40,000 net square feet of offices, and the construction, including all fees, cost some £250,000, giving a total outlay of £310,000. The offices were let to a giant American corporation, Union Carbide, at 30s. a square foot, so that the building disgorged an annual income of £55,000, after deducting a ground rent of £5,000 to the freeholder, the City of London. That building was then worth about £840,000, since an investor would have been willing to buy it to give a yield of 6½ per cent. The difference between the total cost and the value was the profit, in this case £530,000. The joint owners of the project who shared this profit were Hyams and a shy solicitor named Moss Spiro. No wonder Mrs Moss Spiro hired the Dagenham Girl Pipers to parade through the building in the middle of a party when construction was finished.

Although there were endless refinements on this particular

* From a 1964 Office Survey by the GLC. More detailed figures are given in Appendix 3.

kind of operation, sums of that sort were the backbone of the property boom. Since all the money to buy the site was usually lent by the banks, all the cost of construction carried by the contractor or the bank, and the total repaid from a long term mortgage borrowed from an insurance company, the developer seldom had to find any money at all, once his credit was established. But that prelude to success was for many the most difficult hurdle.

Towards the end of the fifties the great splurge of office building, which was then spilling over into the provinces, and to a lesser extent the redevelopment of shops in High Streets all over the country, made their mark on the Stock Exchange. The fortunes of the developers were confirmed in the stock market and the property boom was taken up with wild, in due course excessive, enthusiasm.

The Stock Exchange divides up companies with a quotation into separate sections according to their various trades, such as Banks, or Shipping, or Tea and Coffee. Until 1957 property companies were considered sufficiently unimportant not to have a section to themselves. They were lumped together under Financial Trusts, Land and Property. But the statistics* from 1958 onwards show eloquently how the public rushed for property shares just as the party was nearing its end, a characteristic of most violent booms.

In 1958 there were 16,000 deals in property shares. (These figures are not definitive, as not all deals have to be recorded, but they show the trend.) In 1959 the number of deals shot up to 102,000. 1959 was the year of realisation. It was the year in which a very few property developers, and especially the rumbustious Jack Cotton, emerged as public figures. It was the year of Macmillan's Never Had It So Good general election, and investors read his victory as an omen for another prosperous decade for the developers. But it was also the year in which some of the more cautious developers were beginning to slow down or to look abroad for new projects; they were fearful of the heat of competition as new rivals jumped on to the bandwagon from other industries. Nevertheless, activity in property shares accelerated. By 1962, the peak in the stock market, the volume of bargains had reached 184,000.

* See Appendix 4.

B

The figures for the value of all these shares are more remarkable. On 31 March 1958 the total value of ordinary shares in property companies was £103 million. Four years later, within two months of the peak, the equivalent figure was exactly £800 million. Since the majority of the companies were controlled by single individuals or within a family, and since there was no capital gains tax until 1962, this extra £700 million represented an astonishing increase in personal wealth in an age which has complained as never before of the crippling effects of tax on the individual. By 1966 the market value of property companies had cooled off to £664 million.

These figures were swollen year by year by an influx of new arrivals in the stock market. In 1958 there were 111 property companies; this rose to 169 by 1962. Almost all these newcomers were companies built up from nothing since the war by one man, and some were large, like Maurice Wohl's United Real Property, valued at its debut in 1961 at £10·8 million. They came to the market partly to satisfy their backers, the insurance companies, which from about 1959 onwards, again towards the top of the boom, began to own small slices of the ordinary capital in return for providing quantities of fixed interest finance and liked to see their ordinary shares quoted in public companies. But a more important reason was the system of taxation. As private companies, controlled by one or two individuals and their families, all the profits were subject to income and surtax at rates of up to 18s. 3d. in the £ under Section 245 of the Income Tax Act, 1952. If they were floated and more than 25 per cent of the capital sold off into the hands of the public, this rule ceased to apply. At the same time, as the capital profits on buildings, as in the Grafton Street example, were mirrored in a company's balance sheet, they could be partly sold through the Stock Exchange. Maurice Wohl turned 26 per cent of United Real into £2·8 million of cash and the remaining 74 per cent was in £8 million worth of an acceptable currency, his shares, had he wished to sell them.

Property developers have often been portrayed as wizards with land and money, and men with an uncanny foresight. This is nonsense. They deserved this reputation no more and no less than any other group of proprietorial businessmen. Some operated intelligently; others crudely. But they were men who happened to be in the right business at the right time and, given the profit margins in that business, could hardly fail to make money. This is illustrated by the job in which each man started, as set out in my list of millionaires. 40 per cent of them were estate agents and another 10 per cent were solicitors. All circles of the property business revolve around estate agents and it was natural that they should see demand for certain types of property emerge and move in to take advantage of it. Solicitors are close to real estate, because they are always involved in conveyancing. They watched their clients making hefty profits and followed their example. Others hailed from trades allied to property, such as building contracting and retailing. All the developers took heavy risks, though generally it was with other people's, often the banks', money in the early stages of their careers and the ultimate penalty, bankruptcy, is not a catastrophic event for the resilient businessman in this country, as the story of Mr Pearlberg* will show. But once a developer was established, a large section of the investing public made money with him, indirectly through insurance companies or directly through shares of property companies themselves. The majority of the developers were Jews, but by no means all. It is a characteristic of the Jewish businessman to gamble on his judgment and to make for industries where the risks and the profit margins are high. The history of the cinema industry in America, or the rag trade, which tends to have the highest number of bankruptcies of any industry, or more recently the pop music business show this.

Throughout the post-war period developers have been massively abused by politicians, by journalists, by architects and by the public at large. Historically, landlords have usually been extremely unpopular. The relatively young business of estate agency—commercial estate agents only came into their own between the wars—has never had a particularly good name. One of the millionaire developers, who started as an estate agent in the thirties, told me solemnly that 'I was the first honest estate agent.' Although most public discussion of estate agents centres on unscrupulous house agents, the ethics of some big-time commercial agents leave something to be desired, as I discuss later. However unjustly, the sins of one type of property man inevitably rubbed off on the rest. Rachmanism and the activities of, say, John Gaul, who ran a public company, Sun Real Estates, owning £3 million worth of flats, offices and shops, and was fined £25,000 in 1962 on

* See page 112.

conviction for living on the earnings of prostitution in Soho, were no advertisement for genuine developers.

These were the incidents which hit the headlines and which moulded attitudes towards the property world. There has never been much sympathy for the go-betweens in business. The developer is a pure entrepreneur. The only equipment he needs is a telephone, and there were powerful developers who operated from their study at home or from a one-roomed office with a secretary. From there they wielded the talents of various professions: estate agents, solicitors, bankers, architects, quantity surveyors, consulting engineers, building contractors, accountants. The end result was a building. As the fashion for developing shops and for town centre redevelopment spread in the late fifties and the early sixties, a great deal of emotion was stirred up at a local level against the men who sat in Mayfair and enriched themselves in 'our' High Streets. The tradesmen of Heckmondwike, asked in 1963 to sell by a London estate agent, decided that if brass was to be made in Heckmondwike, it should stay there; they formed the Heckmondwike Development Company, a sort of tradesmen's co-operative. 'If there's any appreciation of property values the benefit should be retained locally, not drained off into speculators' hands,' said the chairman, an optician. Yet this turned out to be only a negative move, for by early 1967 the Heckmondwike Development Company had achieved nothing.

Speculator is a heavily emotive word, much flourished by politicians. The charge upset many of the legitimate developers, who went to great lengths to insist that they were developers, or investors, not speculators. In his statement as chairman of Town & City Properties in 1963, Barry East, a developer who had worked with Jack Cotton in his early days, assured his co-shareholders that their company was not engaged 'in any enterprise of a speculative nature'. This was absurd, as at that moment his company had a partly empty office building in a suburb of Birmingham, built on the speculation that it would find a tenant. Virtually all developers worked on this basis. And, as some of them pointed out, all private investment is speculative. But the fact that the raw material of the developer was land, and that land prices and rents rose consistently, made the developer's activities scandalous in the eyes of Labour politicians and many others.

The image of the property developer was not helped by the few who appeared frequently in the press. They tended to have colourful characteristics ideally suited to the gossip columnist. They were one-man success stories, happy to be portrayed as caricatures of the newly rich tycoon. This increased their basic unpopularity. The radical economist, Nicholas Davenport, has written:* ' . . . public opinion would not accept the creation of so many new millionaires each year as American industry proliferates. The recent crop of property millionaires was sufficient unto the day.'

The commercial developers were essentially improving working conditions for part of the population. In that sense their activities were at least as beneficial as, if not more so than, the manufacturer of soap flakes or motor cars. On another level the physical appearance of their buildings, which affected the public at large, was fiercely criticised. But what perhaps irked their critics most was the size of the developers' profit. With office buildings their profit margins were to a large extent increased as a direct result of successive Governments' policies, which restricted supply during the war and the early post-war years, unleashed it in the mid-fifties and then clamped down tighter and tighter in the sixties. As supply was held back, rents raced upwards in response to demand. George Brown's ban on more offices in London in November 1964 was the crowning gift to the developers. By then supply had caught up with demand and there appeared to be a slight surplus of office blocks. The Brown ban served gradually to fill them up and to send rents up again. The increase in rents has been as sharp since November 1964 as in any period since the war; in some places it has been much sharper.

Since the war Britain is the only country in the world to have had a property boom channelling wealth into the hands of individuals on such a large scale. This was partly a reflection of a unique system of taxation, which in retrospect seems absurdly favourable to the developers. The main profit in development lay in the difference between the total cost and the value of the finished building. Any other manufacturer was taxed on the difference between his cost and the selling price of the finished article. But the man who bought land as raw material and improved it by adding a building made his capital gain tax free, provided he kept the building at the end of the day. The man who sold his buildings regularly was taxed on his profit like a manufacturer.

* *The Split Society* (Victor Gollancz, 1964).

The justification for this big variation in the treatment of the developer/investor and the manufacturer or developer/seller was that it encouraged more investment and activity in property and that if a man did not sell, he did not make a profit. In real estate this was not true. The potential capital profit could be sold tax free through the Stock Exchange. If the difference between cost and value had been taxed whether the developer sold or not, it is possible that it would have encouraged even more activity. The developer would have been more flexible and he would have had a greater cash flow to invest in new projects.

Property was a paradise for the tax-free profit. This was modified by Mr Callaghan's Budget of 1965. But, as in the case of the Brown ban on offices of 1964; or Sir Keith Joseph's measure in 1963 to plug the most ludicrous loophole in the Planning Act of 1947, described in chapter 12; or the betterment tax on land, abolished in 1953 and reintroduced with the Land Commission of 1967, the boom was over, the horse had bolted and the Government locked the stable door.

CHAPTER TWO

Between the Wars, and Before

'PEOPLE who could pass exams would be no good to me. If any-body came along with academic qualifications I would pretend to go on with the interview, but I would never take him on. The most important thing in this business is commonsense.' Thus Dudley Samuel, a grand old man of the property business and one of the leading lights in the thirties in Maddox Street.

Maddox Street was the training ground for many of the post-war tycoons. It is a turning off Upper Regent Street, running downhill with a narrow bend past the church of the fashionable, St George's, Hanover Square, and ending at the chic of Bond Street. In the twenties and the thirties there were three main trades in Maddox Street: tailors, estate agents and prostitutes. The tailors were the traditional inhabitants, an outcrop around Savile Row near by. Hurt by the burgeoning competition from the multiple tailors, by the slump and by the shortage of skilled craftsmen, the tailors gradually gave way to the estate agents. At 11 o'clock in the morning most of the budding agents would meet in the Lyons Tea Shop in Maddox Street to swap all the property gossip.

The inter-war period saw the rise of the big commercial estate agent, and Dudley Samuel's firm, Dudley Samuel and Harrison, was among the front runners. He, like most of the property men, had started near the very bottom of the ladder. In 1918 he was sent by his father, a small property owner, to work for an estate agent in Mayfair, Samuel Walrock, at £1 a week. After a year he became head of a department and was paid £4 a week. Soon after this his father said to him, 'You're not doing any good.' 'What?' he replied, 'I started at £1 a week and now I'm earning £4 a week.' 'No,' said his father, 'first of all I had to give Samuel Walrock £1 a week for you and now I'm giving him £4.'

Disgusted with this discovery Dudley Samuel left to start up his own business.

The market in property between the wars blossomed chiefly in shops around the great expansion of the multiple shop companies. In 1920 there were estimated to be 24,713 multiples and by 1939 this had swollen to 44,487,* despite the general economic stagnation. They expanded by buying existing shops themselves or by leasing shops from developers in traditional High Streets, or in parades in the growing suburbs. At the same time investors, from private individuals to the Salvation Army, the City livery companies, Oxford and Cambridge colleges, to the Prudential, became increasingly willing to buy shops as investments, tempted by the security of the rent paid by Woolworths or Boots the Chemists or other shop companies multiplying in that period. A company is obliged to pay its rent out of its revenue before tax or dividends on its share capital; this is a basic charm of any investment in real property.

It was around this increasingly free market that the agents and the entrepreneurs of Maddox Street flourished. One of the biggest clients of Dudley Samuel was Sir John Ellerman, the shipping magnate, who died in 1933. He was a voracious buyer of all sorts of real estate between the wars. As tax on the rich individual rose steeply, Ellerman was one of the first men to apply the principle that a low yield from property and a big potential capital profit, tax free, was the ideal situation for a man with a high income. Shops were an excellent vehicle for this, because two shops next door to one another in a High Street would have a similar capital value, if the rent and the terms of the leases were identical. But assume that A and B are neighbouring shops let in different years; if A was let at a low rent with a lease running out in fifteen years' time, it will be worth less than B let at a much higher rent but with a longer lease. Known as buying reversions, it pays the heavy taxpayer to buy A with a low immediate income and value, since the rise in value, tax free, as the lease becomes shorter and shorter and finally reverts, will far outweigh the greater, but highly taxed, income from B. Dudley Samuel told me, 'I could never understand why no Chancellor of the Exchequer caught on to this sum.' James Callaghan did so, to a limited extent, in the Budget of 1965.

Dudley Samuel is now retired, a wise and handsome old man,

* James B. Jefferys, *Retail Trading in Great Britain, 1850–1950.*

full of memories of men who passed through his office, who later became household names in property: Walter Flack, Marcus Leaver, Edward Erdman, and Joe Gold, among others. They mostly joined him as boys of fourteen upwards in the early thirties. For lower- to middle-class Jewish families estate agency became a favourite halfway house between trade and professions like law and accountancy. 'If a man hadn't shown he was any good by the time he was 25, he was no good,' said Dudley Samuel. 'It's fatal for a negotiator to sit at a desk when he's got nothing to do. He must go out and look around him at properties for sale and write ten letters when he comes back.' Joe Gold remembers his old boss, in the office in Maddox Street. 'He seldom went out to look at properties. He used to smoke cigars and drink Vichy water and chew sweets.'

After the war these men who served their apprenticeship in Maddox Street were at just the right stage of experience, in their late twenties and early thirties, to make the most of the new opportunities in property. Some of them had taken courses in subjects relating to the land, but it was far from essential to later success. They mostly attended night school in Lincoln's Inn Fields at the College of Estate Management, founded in 1919 and incorporated by royal charter in 1922 on the petition of the College and two professional bodies.* That night school must have had more potential millionaires through its doors than any other before or since. Not all of them passed their exams—or were particularly keen to. Felix Fenston was usually asleep. One of Fenston's first jobs was working for Max Joseph, who soon branched out on his own in Hampstead. Fenston had to go round the East End, persuading the owners of rows of small houses, weeklies, where the tenants paid the rent weekly, to sell to Max Joseph, who would then hold an auction a month later.

The two firms which built up a dominating lead over other estate agents in the multiple shop business were Hillier, Parker, May & Rowden and Healey & Baker. Hillier, Parker came to the fore first under the direction mainly of two men, Stanley Edgson

---

* The Royal Institution of Chartered Surveyors and the Chartered Auctioneers' and Estate Agents' Institute. Enough respectability and maturity has stuck to estate agency and property that, as from October 1967, the College of Estate Management has become a new faculty of the University of Reading.

and Douglas Overall, who each managed to split their time between being agent and principal. Edgson ran a company called Central Commercial Properties, while Overall looked after Sterling Estates. Each was a big shareholder in his respective company. Like Hillier, Parker itself, these companies specialised in shops, but the success of this potentially conflicting situation between the partners as principals and the partners as agents is often cited, together with the high reputation of Hillier, Parker in property, as an example in favour of the argument that estate agents can properly fulfil the two roles; this is discussed further in the next chapter.

The bounding growth of the multiples all over the country transformed a few enterprising agents into national firms for the first time. This was the rise of the West End agent as a distinct figure and it led to some hard feelings among local agents, who were not used to competition from London. The multiples, usually operating from headquarters in London, needed to let just a few agents know what size of shop they wanted in which towns rather than deal with many different agents scattered about the country. Hillier, Parker used to advertise in *The Times* and *The Telegraph* once a year that it had done business in the following towns, and manage to run through the alphabet from A to Z, giving the name of a town beginning with each letter.

A countrywide intelligence network was vital to the West End agent in order to keep the multiples happy. Healey and Baker had photographs taken of the main shopping areas of 600 towns, so that their customers could sense the flavour of a particular shopping pitch. They also drew up street plans for all towns with a population of over 30,000, showing the exact size and name of every shop in the town centre. The Prudential, which moved into real estate more heavily than other insurance companies between the wars, at one point offered £5,000 for a complete set of street plans.

Uniformity gradually seeped into the High Streets of the country, as small local shops closed down and the blank faces of Woolworths, which jumped from 81 stores in 1919 to 768 by 1939, or Home and Colonial or Timothy Whites inexorably took their place. One company which grew up on the back of the chain stores was Second Covent Garden. This was the work of one of the great financiers of the day, Philip Hill, whose name now adorns the second largest merchant bank in the City, Hill, Samuel. In his day

Philip Hill operated from Mayfair, an address at which City men have tended to look haughtily down their noses. Hill was the son of a cattle auctioneer in Torquay, who had started work for an estate agent at the age of fourteen. Before he was twenty he was doing so well that he asked for a partnership in his firm in Cardiff, but instead he was given the sack. He considered this shock the best thing that ever happened to him, for he set up on his own and was soon on top of the estate agency business in Cardiff. He moved to London just after the First World War and turned to company promotion, setting up his own issuing house, Philip Hill and Partners. He forged a close link with Sir Edward Mountain, boss of the rapidly expanding Eagle Star Insurance; this was a source of finance for some of Philip Hill's deals.

Woolworths was one of the companies advised by Philip Hill. Whenever Woolworths moved into a new town, they tended either to buy one of the key locations in the main street, or to create the best position through their tremendous power of pulling in the customers. Inevitably the neighbouring shops became more valuable. Philip Hill suggested to Woolworths that wherever possible they should buy the next door shops both in case they needed the space for expansion and as an investment. They decided not to do this, so Philip Hill popped the neighbouring shops into the portfolio of Second Covent Garden, which flourished hand in hand with Woolworths.

In the High Streets there was thus a changeover from the local retailer to the multiple, but no redevelopment on any scale. The shop developers came into their own in promoting entirely new locations and parades of shops to serve the spawning suburbs full of semi-detacheds, the Homes Fit for Heroes. Edward Lotery was one of the specialists in suburban shops and his parades of shops can still be spotted today by his hallmark: a herring-bone pattern in bricks running horizontally along the building above the shops and below the upper parts.

Lotery was an expansive man (one of his favourite quirks was to invite people to feel the strength of his muscles) and an excellent salesman for his pioneering developments. His method was to buy or take an option on a piece of land in a new suburb. Often the land would be open field. A parade of shops would be designed by an architect—quantity surveyors were hardly ever used—and then one of the major multiples, perhaps Woolworths, would be invited to lease the finest position, where the flow of pedestrians would be most concentrated. Woolworths would be lured in with a concession, such as a very low initial rent or a five-year rent-free period or the developing company to pay for shopfitting. This was Woolworths' price for honouring the parade with its presence. Once that vital lease was agreed, all the other multiples would tend to hurry in, like bees round a honeypot. Often, in the early thirties it was possible to let many of the shops off the plan, before building began. Planning permission was easy to come by within a matter of six weeks or so, and a development of about twenty shops could be completed within around a year.

Thus Lotery and his competitors, served by the agents in Maddox Street, took shops to the new middle class of Neasden and Southgate, Queensbury, Kingsbury, Harrow Weald, Pinner or Rickmansworth, as the serried rows of semis ate into the country-side in patterns dictated by the railways and the underground lines. The developers were financed by the banks during construction, and like their post-war emulators, with mortgages from the insurance companies and other institutions. Towards the end of the thirties it became harder to let the shops. The multiples realised their power and played hard to get. Lotery used to take small retailers in his Rolls Royce, lend them £2,000 or so as capital, and set them up as minor multiples in several of his parades. Jack Cohen, chairman and founder of the now £90 million Tesco grocery chain, told me, 'Edward Lotery was responsible for Tesco's becoming a multiple. We would go out in his car in the morning around his developments and come back with six more shops. He would pay for the shop fronts and fittings; then on opening day we would give all the customers a 2 lb bag of sugar free, and bang, there was your new shopping centre.'

At one point developers became distinctly cooler about con-cessions. Traders were then being paid around £1,000 a shop for fittings. Some men approached a developer and suggested a package deal. They said that they were forming a chain of chemists' shops. Of course they wanted the £1,000 a shop conces-sion. They signed the leases for twelve shops and were paid £12,000. Then they disappeared.

The development of offices between the wars was a much more turgid and tricky business. In relative terms there was little speculative building. The Victorians had left a voluminous legacy of offices, and in the troubled economic conditions of the twenties and thirties, there was only a weak and highly unpredictable demand for new space. Except for one notable exception, speculative office building was not organised on any large scale by the Victorians. Offices were usually built either by a firm for its own occupation, or by one or two individuals or a small consortium of businessmen.

The New Court Company was an example of the small consortium. It was founded in 1872 by a special Act of Parliament, the Serle Street and Cook's Court Improvement Act. The company was promoted by a firm of solicitors, Waterhouse & Co., and its clients, to provide themselves with offices and to let out offices to other legal characters. They developed what became an island site just off Lincoln's Inn Fields, but they needed the Act of Parliament to do away with numerous alleyways all over the site, which was bounded by Carey Street, Serle Street and Portugal Street. The original cost of the land and buildings was £337,800. The architect for New Court was Alfred Waterhouse, who was the uncle of the then senior partner in Waterhouse & Co. and who had designed both the Prudential Building in Holborn and the Natural Science Museum in Cromwell Road. (In 1963 New Court was sold to Harry Hyams' company for £2½ million and a concrete and glass repository for lawyers and others is now replacing the Victorian red brick.)*

The one big exception was the City of London Real Property Company. This was founded in 1864 by two brothers, James and John Innes.† These brothers were importers of rum and owners of sugar plantations in Jamaica. They also supported the campaign for the abolition of slavery in the West Indies and the success of the campaign cut off their own noses by drastically harming their business in Jamaica. However, they salvaged what they could and decided to invest in real estate near their head office in Mincing Lane in the City. They had soon collected 1½ acres of land and floated a joint stock company with the large issued capital of £500,000. The company expanded by development and purchase of existing buildings and by 1914 the value of the properties, virtually all within the City, had grown from an original £328,957 to over £2½ million. In 1923 the properties were re-

* See page 117.
† See the City of London Real Property centenary history, 1964.

valued to give a total of £11½ million. CLRP was then by far the largest publicly quoted property company. There were in fact very few others and most were vehicles for those peculiarly Victorian phenomena, the companies which promoted Peabody-type blocks of flats for artisans, better known as Charity at 5 per cent; the founders were not only do-gooders but also astute businessmen.

The fortunes of CLRP illustrate the problems of owning or promoting office building between the wars. Their rents fell sharply. From a peak of £632,200 in 1925 there was a decline to £366,000 by 1934. Even so, despite the hazards of voids and failing tenants, some offices were built on spec. The two massive rebuilding projects of the period were the Aldwych and Regent Street. Both were conceptions of Edwardian or Victorian planners and had been rudely interrupted by the war.

The reshaping of what is now Kingsway and the Aldwych took almost 100 years from beginning to end, a forerunner perhaps of the muddle at Piccadilly Circus in the last fifteen years. It was first considered in 1836 by the Select Committee on Metropolis Improvements, the idea being both to have a wide road connecting Holborn and the Strand and to clear some exceptionally squalid slums here and there en route. There were endless delays, but finally the plans were agreed and a special Act passed in 1899. The total estimate of cost for the scheme, which involved entirely rejigging the street pattern, was put at £6,120,380, but it was thought that by the time the adjacent sites had been sold and leased off, it would pay for itself. The roads were finished in 1905, but the central site on the Aldwych island was not sold until 1918.

The developer was an American, Mr Irvine T. Bush, possibly the only American ever to have promoted a big speculative development in this country. Mr Bush was the founder of the Bush Terminal Company of New York, which developed areas of waterfront in New York at the turn of the century. An accessible businessman, who gave as his reason for promoting Bush House that he liked coming to England, Mr Bush set off a long controversy over the new skyscraper in the Aldwych; he maintained that it was not a skyscraper, indeed that they should not be built in London. This was one of the first buildings with the American open plan system for each floor. But it ran into the troubles of slow letting usual at that time—office rents were sometimes lower than rents for flats—and it was not finished until 1931.

The other huge office project between the wars was the re-building of Regent Street by a large number of small developers or owner occupiers such as department stores on lease from the Crown Commissioners (see the map facing page 82). At the north end of Regent Street, where it meets Portland Place, was the BBC's headquarters, the most celebrated development of Jackie Phillips, in many ways a prototype of some of the more flamboyant post-war tycoons. He had a large ear trumpet and, something of an actor, conveniently used his deafness to hear or not to hear when bargaining. Jackie Phillips and his brother operated from a tiny office in Oxford Street just above Tottenham Court tube station and then moved to Pall Mall in 1924. Almost every day he attended the London Auction Mart. Some dealers tended not to bid against the great Jackie Phillips and before he left the auction he would often have sold two or three of the properties which he had just bought.

Phillips took a lease on the old town house of Lord Waring at the bottom of Portland Place and let his new development of the site to the BBC off the plan. Later he sold the head lease to the BBC, making a profit of £250,000 on the deal. Realising that this building, finished in 1932, would be nowhere near big enough for the burgeoning BBC, Phillips made sure that if it wanted to expand its ownership to the neighbouring sites, he must be appoin-ted agent. He made a tremendous amount in fees in this way. In the late twenties and thirties he promoted a remarkable number of vast office blocks, but as war approached he overtraded sadly (see chapter 4).

The third and most prolific aspect of development, apart from shops and offices, was the great boom in new flats in London in the thirties. This ignores the speculative house building all over the country. Some 3 million houses were put up between 1919 and 1939. The promotion of flats was sparked off by two factors: the decline in cost of raw materials and labour after the Slump, and the demand from the rising army of white-collar middle class.

The biggest empire of flats was promoted by a partnership of two intelligent and hard-headed entrepreneurs, Anthony Somers and Reginald Toms. In only six years, between 1933 and 1939, they developed a staggering number of flats, including Park West, an ungainly giant at the Marble Arch end of the Edgware Road. The empire, known collectively as the Bell Property Trust, must have had a strong influence on the thousands of people who lived in these flats, but Somers and Toms remained almost completely unknown to the public. Toms was the seventh son of a Leicestershire farm labourer. He had a flair for engineering and served in the First War in the Royal Flying Corps. After the war he founded his fortune, in the classic manner, on a gratuity of £34 and deals in war surplus. His particular line was to buy the lorries as they came back from France, cannibalise them and rebuild a working lorry with the good parts. He also bought a huge stock of Douglas motorbicycles and sold them at a profit before he had to pay for them. After that he plunged into the operation of pirate buses, which occupied him for most of the twenties. Pirate buses used to compete, before nationalisation, with established routes, travelling to much the same timetable as their rivals, usually arriving at the bus stop just before the normal bus and always offering a slightly cut rate fare. When his pirates became profitable, Toms would sell them off to the competition.

In about 1931 Toms gave up buses and teamed up with Somers, who had been in the young and still unestablished hire purchase business. Together they were responsible for Park West, Highlands Heath, a development of flats in Putney in six separate blocks, Ealing Village, Chiswick Village, Greenhill in Hampstead, The High, Streatham and many others. Toms had capital to start with, but they borrowed largely from a joint stock bank and on mortgages from the Royal Liver and from Eagle Star; Toms and Somers were other protégés of Sir Edward Mountain's. Toms set up his own firm of architects—he was not, of course, a qualified architect—to do all the designing for the Bell developments. One of the early recruits in Toms & Partners was William Biggs, who designed Park West and reappeared after the war as senior partner in Stone, Toms & Partners, among the most active designers of office blocks.

Allowing for the fall in the value of money, Toms and Somers together made as large a fortune as most of the post-war developers. They were greatly helped by the faster pace of building before the war. Highlands Heath, a cluster of blocks with 144 flats, took only fifteen months from start to finish. Immediately after the war both Toms and Somers emigrated, Toms to live in Switzerland. He usually returns in the summer to shoot grouse on his 35,000-acre estate in Scotland.

Another promoter of flats in the thirties was the Black family. This was a family of right wing, Baptist businessmen. Robert Wilson Black and his brother John Wycliffe Black were partners in an estate agency in South Kensington, Knight & Co., before estate agency had fully emerged as a separate trade. When they joined the firm in the 1890s, Knight & Co. was a firm of estate agents, builders and undertakers. Gradually the Black brothers bought properties in Kensington on their own account. When the agency business went dead at the beginning of the First War, they moved into hotels, converting mansions in Kensington and prospering on the strength of the strong demand for hotel rooms during that war. None of the hotels, a chain known as M. F. North, serves any drink, in line with the Black principles.

After the First War Cyril Black, now Sir Cyril Black, MP and crusader against pornography, and his brother Sydney joined the business. Cyril Black specialised in buying blocks of pre-First World War flats and selling them to clients of Knight & Co., and in carving up old mansion houses into flats. He met Aynsley Bridgland shortly after his arrival from Australia and they were jointly involved in the promotion of property companies both before and after the last war.* Cyril Black's first development of flats was in the Brompton Road, a few hundred yards west of Harrods, with Woolworths on the ground floor. The economics of these developments were that the promoter had to put up about one quarter of the cost himself, borrow the rest at around 5 per cent and hope to get 8 per cent on the cost. Once the flats—and the principle was the same with offices—were let, the developer would attempt to borrow long-term finance from an insurance company or some less established lender. With the market in property much less stable and organised than after the war, operators had to scrape around to find lenders willing to produce money on mortgage. The huge block of offices on the east side of Berkeley Square was mortgaged to the Duke of Bedford, father of the present duke, for £800,000 in 1938.

* See page 77.

c

CHAPTER THREE

The System

THE developer is like an impresario. He is the catalyst, the man in the middle who creates nothing himself, maybe has a vague vision, and causes others to create things. His raw material is land, and his aim is to take land and improve it with bricks and mortar so that it becomes more useful to somebody else and thus more valuable to him.

The man who wished to develop continuously over the years needed access to fresh supplies of his raw material. The suppliers were estate agents and developers needed to be as close as possible to the estate agents who could supply unimproved sites in the greatest quantity. It is for this reason that so many estate agents themselves became developers. They saw their clients and friends, to whom they sold sites, converting those sites to great effect and thought 'why shouldn't we too?' They were strengthened in their resolve by the pre-war precedents that an agent can be both an agent and a developer, most noticeably Jackie Phillips in offices and the senior partners of Hillier, Parker, May & Rowden in shops.

The new estate agents and developers had often had a little training and experience before the war, but they were still young and flexible in their attitudes when peace returned. Not many of the agents who were also developers, or became solely developers, were highly qualified. Few had passed the examinations of the Royal Institution of Chartered Surveyors, founded in 1868. This is the biggest, oldest and most venerable of the twelve separate societies* concerned with estate agency. The eminent exception to this is Sir Harold Samuel.

---

* For an analysis of the Societies and their proliferation of identifying letters for members, see Appendix 5. The most important, apart from the RICS, are the other two chartered societies, the Auctioneers' and Estate Agents' Institute and the Land Agents' Society, and the Incorporated Society of Auctioneers and Landed Property Agents.

The chartered surveyors, who in theory knew most about land, in practice did not make the most of their knowledge through development on their own account. Sir Henry Wells, president of the RICS in 1965–66 and now chairman of the Land Commission, told me that 'chartered surveyors were by and large "reactionary" characters, in the sense that they tended to look back to existing values rather than forward to the possibilities. Because of their training before the war, when values were often static or declining, they were extremely bad at judging the future. There was also always a tradition that the chartered surveyor was not himself involved in the trade.'

These attitudes sterilised a large number of the professionals in property as far as development was concerned. Chartered surveyors were also usually Conservatives in politics and this inclined them towards a great caution in business in the early post-war years of the Labour Government. This gave the chance for the younger men with fewer political preconceptions and traditional theories about the market and values, to jump into the breach. Then, as values rose, sometimes fast, sometimes sedately, throughout the fifties and early sixties, the more traditional chartered surveyors were always trying to find their balance and adjust to the latest changes in the market.

Once an estate agent was aware of the potential in development and wondered what role he himself should play, the question of a potential conflict of interest arose between his job as an adviser or broker to clients and his personal pocket. Conversations with those on either side of the fence in the property world reveal an acute schizophrenia. There are many who object violently to practising estate agents operating a property company in which they are major shareholders, such as Joe Levy of D. E. & J. Levy with Stock Conversion, in which his family owns about £5 million worth of shares; there are others who object to estate agents sitting as advisers on the boards of companies, in which they own only a small or nominal holding, as some partners in that phenomenon of growth, Jones, Lang, Wootton, do; others again think that both these forms of participation are acceptable and inevitable, and that to try to curb either would merely lead to hypocrisy.

Given this split in the property business itself, it is hardly surprising that outsiders have fiercely criticised the ethics of estate agency. In the many instances where big commercial agents are both agents and developers, there must have been numerous occasions of possible conflict between the two roles. In the days when development was warming up, the value of sites could be transformed by developers, a transformation of which even the fairly informed public was unaware.

Abuses could arise, as this hypothetical example shows. An unsophisticated owner of urban property could approach an agent: the owner would see his site as a dull investment worth £30,000: the agent, who simultaneously controlled a development company, would realise at once a chance of development and a value for the site at auction to other aware developers of around £120,000: he would find the owner a buyer, his own company, at £60,000 without suggesting an auction: the owner would be delighted but cheated in effect of another £60,000. Few property men pretend that such things did not happen. I asked one developer, who has a vivid turn of exaggeration, why he gave up his estate agency. He replied, 'I decided to give up being a crook.' As in any industry, abuses were abuses by the minority, and today's big agencies— such as Levy's or Marcus Leaver's as agents cum developers, or Jones, Lang, Wootton or Edward Erdman as agents cum directors —are highly respected and trusted by huge insurance companies, industrial giants and development companies.

The late Lord Cohen of Brighton, that lovable and prickly pear of the property and building society world, was himself both a building society boss and an estate agent cum speculative house-builder. (His estate agency went by the memorable name of Reason and Tickle. Lewis Cohen took over the firm in 1922 after Mr Reason died on safari and Mr Tickle emigrated to Australia.) As a lifelong supporter of the Labour Party, his view might be shrugged aside by many property men. He considered that 'with the exception of one' (he meant the prestigious Knight, Frank & Rutley) 'all the main London agents are investors or developers or dealers as well as estate agents. The status and public regard of agents has become much, much worse in my lifetime. It is very bad for the profession.' However, as discussed in my final chapter, legislation and the best professional societies are gradually changing estate agency.

Whatever their ethical dilemmas, the estate agents were the fulcrum of the development world. Next most important to the developers were the architects. These men were vital intermediaries between the developers with their ideas of what might be done to a site and the planning authorities with their power of permissions to build.

The most striking fact about the architects who worked for developers is that a tiny number of firms was responsible for a hefty proportion of all the work. There were about 22,000 architects at the last count, of whom some 4,750 were in private practice. Looking just at speculative office blocks in the Greater London area, I would estimate that between half and three-quarters—there are no statistics on this subject—have been designed by a mere ten firms. They are: T. P. Bennett & Son, C. H. Elsom & Partners, Gollins, Melvin, Ward & Partners, Newman, Levinson and Partners, Fitzroy Robinson & Partners, R. Seifert & Partners, Lewis Solomon, Kaye & Partners, Stone, Toms & Partners, Trehearne & Norman, Preston & Partners and Roland Ward & Partners.

By no means all office building is promoted by developers, nor has it all taken place in London; my generalisation about the ten firms has to be seen in this perspective. It has been estimated that around half the post-war offices have been built by owner-occupiers and half by developers, and that 80 per cent of the new building has been in the London region.* Besides, office buildings represent a fairly small part of all the work done by the 4,750 architects in private practice. The strain on the construction industry imposed by the office developers has been crudely over-emphasised from time to time, mainly for political purposes. In 1962, probably the peak year for work in progress, office buildings accounted for about a mere 3 per cent of building in the country.

Even so, it is remarkable that those ten firms should have collared so much of the work. There was no ring! On the contrary, each firm was acutely competitive with the others, especially with Richard Seifert, who turned out by the middle sixties to be the king of the developers' architects. It was not that the biggest developers always went to the same architect, although there was a good deal of that. But there were many more than ten firms of developers responsible for three-quarters of the office blocks. Nor were these ten unusually gifted designers of offices.

The simple reason that so much work fell to so few is that these

* Estimates by the Pilkington Research Unit, Liverpool University Building Science Department.

firms were in every case directed by one or two men who were businessmen as well as architects. Sir Mortimer Warren, who as secretary to the Church Commissioners for England played an important direct and indirect role in the development of new offices,* thought that many offices looked as though they had been designed by chartered accountants. This was a common view, and one repeated by Professor Colin Buchanan.†

Only a minority of the developers were particularly concerned with the aesthetic design of their buildings. Since the developers were often men of little formal education, and since they were promoting their buildings for entirely commercial reasons, this is hardly surprising. I asked Mr Charles Clore, in the exchange of letters which was his substitute for an interview, which of his developments he was most proud of. His deadpan reply‡ indicated that he was fond of a massive building in the Southwark Bridge Road, 'which in fact is one of the largest office developments in London but was built in record time. . . .' The letter added gratuitously that 'He does not believe in any great architectural triumphs which end up in bankruptcy.' Douglas Tovey, one of the estate agents who organised a lot of development for Clore, said that 'he leaves it to me to find the architect. I usually have a model made. He loves a model, you see. When he sees it, he usually says "I like that". I've almost never known him say he didn't like one.'

What the developers wanted from their architects was a commercial service. They needed functional buildings designed to a certain price, usually the lowest possible, that the estimate should not be exceeded at the end of the day, and that the architect should organise the builders so that the development was finished on the specified date. This should not necessarily have precluded the architects from designing attractive buildings, though it certainly strained good design, and the blame has probably been weighted too heavily against the developers. They were just not concerned with design. But the architects could surely with ingenuity have produced fine buildings within their corset of cost. There tended to be an enormous difference between the cost of a building promoted by a developer and one commissioned by

* See chapter 7.
† In a talk to the City and North London Society of Architects on 3 March 1966.
‡ See Appendix 2, question and answer numbered 4.

a client for his own occupation. Whereas developers put up office blocks for £4 10s. 0d. to £7 a square foot in the past ten years, the owner-occupier perhaps spent £8 to £10 a square foot on average.

Some of the blame for the quality of post-war commercial architecture, and for the concentration of work into a few offices, should be borne by the profession as a whole and particularly by the Royal Institute of British Architects. Architects tend to be taught during their training that they are artists and the nasty commercial side of an architect's life is glossed over or forgotten completely. This is changing somewhat now. But an attitude of anti-developer and anti-commercial architects pervades the profession. One architect to whom I explained the purpose of my book said at once, 'Oh, that should be a sordid story.' Others say that they would refuse to work for developers; this may mean that they have not been asked to. The attitude of holier-than-thou comes through from an article, 'The Developers', written by the President of the RIBA, Lord Esher, in the *Architectural Review* of September 1965. 'Significantly, the only technical men they employed at the evaluation stage were real-estate surveyors; the architect was not hired until the decision had been taken to go ahead, and of course it often happened that by then the whole project was an architectural nonsense or a piece of vandalism. The crises of conscience facing such architects, offered such vastly profitable jobs, have gone unrecorded, but it is high time the set-up that produced such crises was exposed and put right.' Lord Esher accepted that developers would survive, but his article offered no suggestions as to how the architect should adapt to the facts of life.

Lord Esher misunderstands the mechanics of development when he says that 'the architect was not hired until the decision had been taken to go ahead'. Quite often the architect was enlisted even before a site had been bought, not 'hired' perhaps, since many architects did their initial work for developers on the basis that they were paid only if the job went ahead. This was against the rules of the RIBA. The architects were needed at that stage to perform one of their most vital functions as far as the developer was concerned: obtain town planning permission. If permission was forthcoming for a site which the developer had an option to buy, or merely had his eye on, then the development moved ahead.

At this point of contact with the local authority, the architect had to grapple with the intricacies of the law, something for which his training had not fully fitted him. The law of town planning was new, virtually all stemming from the Town & Country Planning Act, 1947, and subsequent Acts, and it was far from straightforward. What the developer wanted from the law was simple: to be allowed to build as much as possible on his site. Once he had paid X for his site, the more he was allowed to put on it, the cheaper it became in relation to the end product, so many square feet of offices: the chance of profit became greater. The developer has been attacked for his insistence on putting as much as possible on each site. This is like criticising a giraffe for having a long neck. Given that the developer was taking commercial risks, how could it possibly be otherwise?

Early on the LCC displayed a mistaken naïveté about the developer. In the first ten or so post-war years it had a team of brilliant creative minds in its planning department under Dr, now Sir, Leslie Martin. But they were essentially academics, concerned necessarily with residential redevelopment in the main, and it turned out that they often had to work against, rather than with, the commercial developers. Shortly after the war the system of control of density by plot ratio was worked out under Professor, now Lord, Holford. Plot ratio is the all-important formula for the developer. It is the relationship between the area of the site and the gross floor area of a building. Thus a plot ratio of 1:1 can be achieved by covering the entire site with a one-storey building: it can also be achieved by tipping that building on end, leaving part of the site an open space, and having a larger number of floors each with a smaller floor space (see diagram opposite).

Before plot ratio, office buildings were controlled via the London Building Acts. There were two broad techniques of control: a building could not be more than 80 feet high to the cornice with another two storeys in the roof, making a maximum of 100 feet. This was introduced in the first important London Building Act, that of 1894, because Queen Victoria objected to the 151-feet high Queen Anne's Mansions by St James' Park tube station overlooking Buckingham Palace. Secondly, the angle from the opposite pavement to a building's cornice had to be at least so many degrees, usually 56°. The idea was to ensure that a certain amount of daylight filtered on to each clerk's desk. In practice it promoted wedding-cake buildings like the one illustrated facing page 86 which edged backwards from the road layer by layer after a certain height. The same phenomenon is frequent in New York.

Plot Ratio. Plot ratio is the relationship between the area of the site and the total gross floor area of the building. This diagram illustrates some of the ways in which a building may be erected on the same site at the following plot ratios

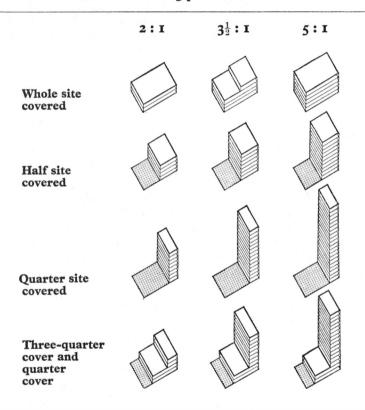

Holford's scheme of plot ratio zoning was designed as a set of theoretical limits on density of workers in given areas. Nobody dreamt that the developers would want to build as much on a site as the plot ratios allowed. As the LCC murmured plaintively in 1957 when the office boom was on top of them: 'Although plot ratios were stated to be maxima in practice they have come to be regarded as minima.'

The architect was judged by the developer largely on his ability to achieve the maxima, and to achieve them quickly. In this complicated process, the architect needed an understanding of the nuances of national and local planning regulations plus loopholes and an ability to negotiate. This was one of the secrets of Seifert's dramatic success. In 1955 his firm had about 12 employees; by 1966 it had around 200. His turnover was £30 million in 1964–65 and £20 million in 1965–66, giving profits after expenses of perhaps £300,000 and £200,000 (most firms have less than 10 employees and few can have a turnover of £1 million). It was with his ingenuity with London offices that Seifert, a quiet pipe-smoking man capable of great charm built up his practice and became something of a legend within the walls of County Hall. 'The trouble with Seifert,' a member of the LCC's Town Planning Committee told me, 'was that he knew some of the regulations far better than the LCC itself. Every now and then we had to bring in clauses to stop up the loopholes exposed by Seifert. We called them "Seifert clauses".' Planning was not administered in a series of clear cut decisions and the LCC would try to push a developer and his architect in their direction. Seifert, like the principals of the other select few firms, was prepared to fight tooth and nail for his clients' rights. Richard Edmonds, chairman of the Town Planning Committee in the vital years 1955–61, recalled with a shudder the day when Seifert exploded with rage at a session with the Committee; 'but as his practice grew more powerful, he tended to become calmer'. What is noticeable about Seifert's practice, though, for all the carping in the architectural profession, is that in later years it has produced some stimulating additions to London—there is a great difference between early Seifert and late Seifert. His most prominent building is Centre Point at St Giles' Circus and I have discussed the scourge of the town planners further in chapter 8 along with the promoter of that skyscraper and Seifert's No. 1 client, Harry Hyams.

How was it that the chosen ten pulled in such a large proportion of the work? The basic fact is that the LCC did little actively to help the architects who did not fully understand the regulations; nor was it ever clear in the Kafka-like corridors of County Hall exactly who was the best man to see about a particular problem.

If a green architect showed his plans for a building with a plot ratio of, say 4·4 : 1, and asked if that was permissible, the LCC would say yes. There would be no question of saying, 'but you are entitled, if you design the building differently, to a plot ratio of 5 : 1'. Still less, of course, would they say, 'and if you plead Schedule 3 on that development, you will be able to screw a plot ratio of 5·5 : 1 out of us'.

This policy made it a great deal easier for the business-minded, established architects to win a large proportion of developers' commissions, given the training and attitudes of the profession at large. Two of the architects who ran firms in the list of ten were not fully qualified by the RIBA: William Biggs, senior partner in Stone, Toms throughout the fifties, and David Levinson of Newman, Levinson. Biggs was a Licentiate of the RIBA, that is, someone who had been engaged as a 'principal for at least ten successive years in the practice of architecture' or for 'at least ten successive years in the practice or the study of architecture'. This was a category laid down by the RIBA in 1909 and dropped in 1956. Biggs was the designer of Park West for Reginald Toms before the war. After the war his firm designed the Empress State Building for Felix Fenston, among many other blocks. He is a practical, hard-headed gentleman, who quotes with approval the definition of an architect from a book published in 1932, Emden and Watson's *Building Contracts and Practice:* ' . . . in more recent years in addition to a knowledge of science he is required to be a man of business.'

David Levinson studied architecture for four-and-a-half years but became impatient for the real thing and never took his final examinations. His firm has produced designs just as functional and well designed, or the reverse depending on your view, as the rest. Both firms naturally employed qualified architects.

The responsibility for poor aesthetic design does not rest solely on the developer, or the architect, or the planner. It is arguable that there should be no aesthetic control. But local authorities did in reality have a great opportunity to influence design. Since the developer was seldom interested, it was open to local authorities to make suggestions, which they frequently did, though without any legal justification, in return for co-operative and efficient treatment of the application. Most developers and many architects were quite amenable to that. But it led to compromise rather than great

architecture. It must be a frustrating and negative job for an architect to work in a local authority, always vetting other architects' plans. Occasionally the local authority would refer an application to the Royal Fine Art Commission, founded in 1924. Alternatively, that pallid but prestigious body would pounce on an application and, with its architectural knights and peers and other parties from the artistic Establishment such as John Betjeman or John Piper, mull over the finer or coarser points of some proposals. Its aesthetic achievements appear limited. There is wide agreement that Castrol House in Marylebone Road or New Zealand House in the Haymarket were better before the Commission watered down the designs, or even the Shell Building before it had several storeys lopped off. Cutting off a few storeys was its favourite pastime. It is curious that before the public dismay over Jack Cotton's Monico Building, the Fine Art Commission had virtually given it the go-ahead. After the outcry, it changed its mind. Certainly the LCC came to have little appreciation for the Commission's efforts, as the story of Centre Point will show. It was not just the objections of frustrated developers that caused the Commission to blurt out defensively in its latest report:*
'We are well aware that there are some who regard the whole of our proceedings as the unwelcome addition of one more hurdle which must be surmounted before approval can finally be given and work can start.'

After a planning permission had been fixed by his architect, the next players on the developer's stage were his banker and his building contractor. The banker would probably have been on the scene before the application was through, depending to some extent on whether the developer had paid for the site or not. There was no set sequence in which the developer juggled the various professions essential to his project. Frequently he had to use them simultaneously.

But the three main sources of finance for the developer produced their critical support in a fixed order: first the banker, then the banker again and/or the building contractor, and finally the insurance company. While the development would probably only be possible with at least two of those three performers, the banker's role was usually the most important, especially in the early

* Nineteenth Report of the Royal Fine Art Commission, April 1966 (HMSO, 2s. 6d.).

post-war years when the developers were starting up on an exiguous base of their own capital.

The Big Five joint stock banks were the most voluminous providers of bridging finance, the bridge being between the purchase of a site and the arrival of a long-term mortgage, the end money, from an insurance company when a building was finished and let. The banks were taking considerable risks in lending this bridging money, for often the bridge was erected when the far side of the river was invisible. In the strictest theory of joint stock banking* the bridging money is not put up unless the borrower has a big cash stake in the project, the end money agreed in principle and the building itself largely pre-let. Seldom were all these conditions met in practice. For long periods after the war, interrupted by the habitual credit squeezes, the Big Five had more money on their hands on deposit than they could manage to lend. They were delighted to lend to property developers, for they clung to the basic and, as it turned out, sound belief that they were lending against the excellent security of real estate. Almost always the bank took a charge on the land against which they were lending, and the building too, if they were putting up the finance for construction.

The developers were men who acted on hunch. There were never any statistics to suggest that a certain rent would be paid two or three years from the date of buying a site, maybe longer sometimes. These individuals were often gambling that inflation and the pressure of demand would carry rents up over the period of development and give them a certain profit. The joint stock banks were in effect sharing this heavy risk, for if the hunch men had been wrong, if there had been a recession or a turndown in demand, the banks would have been left holding the baby: an unlet or unprofitable building. The insurance companies rarely took such risks.

It is doubtful whether the joint stock banks were universally discriminating in their advances to property developers. One of the biggest and more rational office developers told me that in his experience the banks almost never differentiated sufficiently

* See *Bank Finance for Property Development*, by E. J. W. Buckler, manager of the Piccadilly branch of the National Provincial Bank, one of three Autumn Lectures published by the Institute of Bankers in 1966 (7s. 6d.).

between a good project and a bad. Although managers of branches in central London, where much of the property lending took place, had greater authority to lend than everywhere else bar the City, the sums needed for property were too big for them and the final decision came from Head Office; but their recommendations to Head Office were of great importance. Since the decisions to lend or not to lend tended to be fairly arbitrary, the borrower could be in a strong strategic position. If refused a request, the developer could say to his manager: 'If your refusal is final, may I ask one question? Are you speaking for yourself, or for the bank? If for yourself, I'll have to see the chief general manager and explain my case. If for the bank, then I'm afraid I'll have to find another bank.' Although the manager was always in theory speaking for the bank, this technique tended to work wonders.

The relationship between a developer and his bank manager was all-important, most especially in his initial operations. There has never been any serious study of just how meticulous banks have been in their policies of lending money. The report in 1961 by Mr Neville Faulks, QC, on the Jasper affair—mainly property companies—had this to say of the breach of Section 54 of the Companies Act, 1948 (this means paying for a company with the money of the company being bought): 'It is clearly apparent from the evidence before me that this section is generally (and not merely in the transactions discussed in this report) honoured more in the breach than in the observance. The reason is not difficult to find when the fact that the maximum penalty is £100 is considered. Breaches are not only committed by companies and their directors, but also connived at by the Banks and financial institutions. I suggest that if this section is to be considered to be of any importance the following matters are worthy of consideration: 1. A steep increase in the maximum penalty. 2. A specific provision that any person or corporation aiding or abetting such infringement shall be guilty of an offence with a maximum penalty.'

All this may give a gloomy impression of the banks' role in financing the property boom, but their huge respectability has perhaps overemphasised their image as bodies of shining commercial orthodoxy. Any criticism is directed at a small minority of the total business.

The joint stock banks were not the sole sources of bridging finance. A few merchant banks were bridgers, in particular

Hambros and Ralli Brothers, since it has been partly controlled by Sir Isaac Wolfson, who became increasingly fond of lending money in his old age. The merchant banks lent at a higher rate than the Big Five, perhaps 3 to 4 per cent above Bank Rate against 1 or 2 per cent above, and on more speculative schemes. When credit squeezes reached their climax, the rates could go up to 12 to 15 per cent on the most risky propositions. The merchant banks were also liable to participate in the equity of the property company. Rothschilds, generally rather inactive in real estate, did this with the Hunnisetts' company, South Bank Estates, in which the Prudential also had a stake. The Big Five almost never forged equity links, though they might justifiably have done so if they had been a little more enterprising.

The other major source of financing was the building contractor. Historically building contractors have always been close to the actual promotion of speculative development, though often more in the residential than the commercial field. John Nash, the architect, was designer, contractor and developer. The most celebrated 19th-century contractor/developer was Thomas Cubitt, who built Cadogan Square and large chunks of Belgravia and Bloomsbury. Holland, Hannen & Cubitts are still developers to-day. Richard Costain promoted that initially dicey proposition, Dolphin Square, the largest block of flats in Europe, in the thirties. John Laing grew strong on their development of many housing estates between the wars in North London, where they kept the rows of shops and the factories as investments. They still own around 200 factories in that area.

The other way in which the contractors came into the owner-ship of real estate in the thirties was through the default of their clients, as the insurance companies did when mortgagors defaulted. The McAlpine family came to own the Dorchester Hotel in Park Lane in 1937 because of the then financial weakness of Gordon Hotels, the original operators. It is perhaps a little surprising that the contractors did not play an even greater part as promoters in the post-war era. Many were already powerful corporations early after the war and must have seen that their developer clients were making rapid headway. But for several years they were content to finance individual developments during the period of construction. This probably meant that they made a rather greater profit on the contract as the developer was in a weaker bargaining position. The money for the total cost of construction would in effect be lent throughout the period of building until the 'take out' day. The money came in many cases to the contractors from the Big Five, directly or indirectly. The 'take out' day would usually be around six to twelve months after completion, the day when the contractor took out his money and was paid, either by the developer borrowing on a mortgage or possibly from a bank if there was no tenant.

As the fifties wore on, the contractors came more and more to the conclusion that anything their clients could do, they could do as well, if not better. (They did not have the contractor's profit to add to their costs.) At the least they could share in their clients' profit when they put up the building finance. Bernard Sunley, who started life as a muckshifter with a pony and cart at the age of fourteen, jumped wholeheartedly into development, rather too wholeheartedly sometimes, as he became carried away by success towards the end of his life. The private firms of Wates and Myton, a daughter of the Taylor Woodrow group, were among the first into development, as was the ancient and prestigious Trollope & Colls in the City. In the sixties both Laing and Taylor Woodrow have made inroads into the tricky field of town centre renewal, with mixed results. But the most dazzling story was the alliance between George Wimpey, largest contractors in Europe, and Harry Hyams through the Oldham Estate Company, which is examined in detail in chapter 8.

Most developers did not personally have a great deal to do with the contractors while the job was under way. This was left to his architect as co-ordinator, with the quantity surveyor safeguarding the cost beforehand. Under the architect was the civil engineer.

The final ingredient was the financial might of the insurance companies. For ten to twelve years after the war the insurance companies, except for minor exceptions, financed property companies in much the same way as they had before the war, as described in chapter 2. The difference after the war was that the money gushed out in ever increasing volume. This was a reflection of the insurance companies' intake of funds at greater and greater speed. Finance for real estate in all its forms comes chiefly from the life insurance companies, which have long-term commitments and which need long-term assets to match. Life insurance is essentially a 20th-century phenomenon. In 1927 the total investments of the insurance companies* were £1,051 million. By 1937 they had grown 59 per cent to £1,672 million and over the next ten years by 53 per cent. But in the five years 1947 to 1953 they increased almost twice as fast: by 49 per cent from £2,561 million to £3,816 million. This absolute increase in money to invest was one reason for pouring funds into the receptive hands of the real estate market. The other was Dr Dalton. His policy of cheap money did not so much disillusion these giant investors with the credit of the Government as force them to look elsewhere, since the yields on Government and other fixed interest stocks became far too low for them.

There were two ways in which the insurance companies moved towards property.† First, they bought a lot more property directly for themselves, almost always ready made investments: blocks of offices, flats and shops. To a tiny extent a handful of the biggest life offices developed property themselves, notably the Norwich Union, the Legal & General and the Pearl. The sums invested directly in property and ground rents jumped from £149 million in 1947 to £303 million in 1953. Secondly, they lent money to developers and others as mortgages against property. The percentage of the total funds lent on mortgage, of which a large part was to house borrowers, leapt from 6·2 per cent to 10·9 per cent between 1947 and 1953, or from £158 million to £417 million. They seldom lent a developer his money before the building was up and let, so that their risk on lending on these completed buildings was minimal, especially since the loan tended to be around two-thirds of value.

The next phase in which the insurance companies made themselves even more useful to the property developers was during the severe credit squeeze of 1955–58 initiated by Mr Butler. The general clamp on borrowing was directed most fiercely at property companies, the usual form in any post-war squeeze. At this point the sale and leaseback came into its own. There are many refinements on the sale and leaseback, but its essence is that an owner or developer can realise capital by selling his property to an institution such as an insurance company and himself leasing it back again.

* See Appendix 6 for detailed figures.
† This subject is examined at greater length by Brian P. Whitehouse in *Partners in Property* (Birn, Shaw, 1964), a book commissioned by a property developer, John Bosman.

D

This is far riskier than more orthodox methods of financing, since the developer could find himself paying out more than he took in rent, if the market was to turn against him.

The sale and leaseback was quite unaffected by the credit squeeze—the Government made no effort to restrict it—and it was used in volume by the developers at a time when their commitments were expanding fast. The third phase in the relationship between the developers and the all-powerful investment managers started in 1958–59. With the end of the credit squeeze straightforward borrowing became easier again and the insurance companies decided that they would climb on to the developers' bandwagon and, in return for lending the vital finance, share in the profits. They bought lumps of ordinary shares in development companies, usually around 10 per cent of the capital.

Like the public, the insurance companies also jumped on the bandwagon too late in many cases, as the property share boom in the stock market was seething towards its peak. From 1959 onwards they made more and more equity links with the developers in return for a commitment to provide finance. This in itself added fuel to the share boom for the public became even more enthusiastic for property shares when the insurance companies were to be seen gobbling up large lines of stock. 'If the insurance companies are buying them, they must be right.' The figures show how empty that argument turned out to be.

An analysis in March 1967 of 100 cases over the past eight years in which insurance companies put up fixed interest money for property companies in return for slices of the ordinary capital revealed that in 52 cases the ordinary shares were showing a loss or the options to buy shares had been abandoned. In 15 cases the insurance companies' options were still open, though they would have been unprofitable if taken up. In 4 cases the option to buy related to a yield of $5\frac{1}{2}$ per cent and would probably be profitable. In 29 cases the investments showed a profit. Even this gives an optimistic picture since some shares were only level with the price at which they had been bought. But a ratio of success of 29 per cent is a poor rating and shows how badly timed was the insurance companies' awakening to the property boom. In short, their participation was far better for the property developers than for them. The entrepreneurs made the money and the insurance companies helped to consolidate their fortunes.

Could the insurance companies have participated more directly in development themselves, cutting out the developer ? One investment manager, who was even an opponent of the equity-linked deals, considered that it had not been practicable: the insurance companies did not have such good contacts as the developers: they could never say to a local official, 'you're a good chap, when you retire in four years' time, we'd like you to join our board': they abhor the idea of any controversy, or of having a white elephant on their hands for all the world to ridicule: mere managers would never have taken big risks for fear of the sack: nor could they pay the right man nearly enough to induce him to be an insurance man rather than a developer on his own account.

For the most part, the insurance companies were passive participants in the development world. They were merely performing a function as part of the capital market. They were seldom involved until buildings were finished. It is possible in the first year or two of private post-war redevelopment that their view of what constituted a sound investment on which money should be lent was a factor in making the more conservative developers, like Aynsley Bridgland at Bucklersbury House,* chary of modern design. But that was a momentary phase. When later they came to own slices of development companies, they rarely took any part in the management, and their own direct development was proportionately small. Criticism of the insurance companies as patrons of architecture or replanning is therefore far-fetched. The great publicity given to the Monico muddle at Piccadilly Circus, in which Jack Cotton was partnered by the Legal and General, distorted the picture. To quote Lord Esher again: ' . . . the need for ever vaster investment brought in the big life insurance offices and the pension funds, with their sharp financial appraisals and total blindness to wider considerations . . .' It would have needed a revolution in the insurance companies' attitude towards investment if they were to have taken a hand in their clients' aesthetics.

One further character in a development was the tenant. Here the estate agents were the channel for tenants looking for space. As a class industrial companies were the best customers for office space. In London they tended to be looking for headquarters to impress themselves and their clients with. But the biggest single

* See page 74.

tenant was the Government,* often referred to in the property business as the 'developer's friend'. From the early post-war period, when developers could only have a licence to build if the offices were for the Government, the Ministry of Works, which acted as the Government's estate agent for all ministries and departments, was an avid leaser of space. This was and is an extraordinarily short-sighted policy. The developer aims to receive 10 per cent on his money and on average did at least as well in post-war London. Assume that the Government is paying an average of £1 a square foot for all its 11.4 million square feet of offices in London. This, then, is an annual rent of £11,400,000. If the Government had only had the forethought to plan its needs ahead, buy land and commission its own offices, the cost would have been the cost of borrowing, perhaps 5½ per cent on average. Thus it would have saved £5,150,000 a year. It seems scandalous that no effort was apparently made to cut down sharply on rented offices.

Moreover, the cost of financing a move from rented into owner-occupied buildings could largely be raised by sub-letting offices in which the Government is placidly sitting at far below the market rent. For example, the Air Ministry uses 300,000 square feet in two early post-war blocks in Theobalds Road let at around 7s. 6d. a square foot in 1950 for sixty-three years. That space is today worth at least 47s. 6d. a square foot. The Government could therefore sub-let at a profit of £600,000 a year for forty-six years. That would pay the interest on £11 million worth of construction, enough for a baby Whitehall in itself. But the lethargy of established ways seems to be too great for the Ministry of Works to be energised out of such ridiculously improvident situations.

In one case at least Parliament's Committee of Public Accounts caught up with the general squandering of public money. This was New Scotland Yard in Victoria Street, discussed for another reason in chapter 12, for which the Police paid a developer an annual rent of £570,000 and a premium of £6 million down in 1966. For this and other extravagances in moving in, the Committee observed in mid-1967: 'Your Committee take the view that the Receiver's Department showed scant regards for the interests of the Exchequer . . .'

* For details of office space leased by the Government see Appendix 7.

CHAPTER FOUR

The War and the Beginnings, 1945–1954

THE declaration of war in 1939 set off a sudden and sweeping decline in the value of property, most acutely in London. Premonitions of war had already weakened the market since the early part of 1938. The death and bankruptcy of Jackie Phillips must have been a chilly reminder of the facts of life to all property owners. Jackie Phillips died on Christmas Day, 1939, impoverished, his banking accounts overdrawn and his credit stopped. As discussed in chapter 2, this was a man with a finger in many of the biggest pre-war developments in London. Before 1938 he had overtraded and his borrowings had risen to a high proportion of his properties, so that he was vulnerable to any decline in value of the buildings. He lived up to his reputation as a millionaire, with a fleet of cars, lavish entertainment and a huge mansion in Surrey. He also gambled heavily. While all this contributed to his downfall the immediate cause was the slump in property. At the first meeting of creditors in February 1940, the Official Receiver, a busy man during the war, said that the loss of wealth and income was due to the heavy depreciation in value of many of his properties, loss of tenants and reduced rents receivable, such losses having been apparent since 1938. The Receiver found that Phillips' estate owed £307,000 and had assets of just over £1,000.

Many other property owners and developers would have followed Phillips into bankruptcy had it not been for a moratorium on loans allowed by insurance companies, building societies and other lenders. It was a voluntary moratorium. Everybody knew that everybody else was in trouble. Where the borrower was unable to pay interest due to empties and wartime departures of tenants, the mortgagees did not foreclose or insist on the payment of interest.

They did often take the buildings into temporary receivership until times improved. Alec Colman, starting as a clerk of thirteen in an estate agent's office in his home town in Staffordshire, had graduated to building houses on spec around Birmingham in the thirties and buying small old houses. During the war he owned several hundred of these houses, all empty. 'But for the moratorium on building society loans, I would have been bust. No question of it,' he says. After the war Colman repaired the effects of seven years' emptiness and sold them for about 200 per cent more than they had cost to build in the thirties. That was the foundation for his entry into commercial property in what he calls 'those ten glorious years, 1952 to 1962.' Colman is a talkative, self-confident man, who considers that 'much of my success is due to my being deeply religious. I am an ardent Zionist and an active worker for the cause.' Colman was highly optimistic in his projections and one of those with a lot of unlet offices on his hands by the end of 1964. As to many others, the George Brown Ban came as a great help to Colman's kingdom.

Despite the precipitous fall in values at the beginning of the war, the combination of the moratorium, inflation after the war and the shortage of supply of most types of property added up to a healthy profit for many owners. During the war itself there was plenty of work for those estate agents who were not away. Douglas Tovey spent the first two years of the war looking for hideouts for Lord Kemsley's newsprint. It was too much of a risk to leave it in one warehouse where it would all catch fire at once if a bomb fell. So Tovey leased 'hundreds and hundreds of small shops which had closed down due to the war and put a small bit of newsprint in each'. Tovey had joined Healey and Baker at the end of 1939. A native of Portishead in Somerset, he had started as a rent collector on the Great Western Railway, joined Edward Lotery, the shop developer, in 1938 and a few months later found himself out of work when Lotery emigrated.

Firms and individuals who had been bombed out needed agents to find them new roofs. In London there was a big migration of small firms from the City to the West End. Another job was to deal with war-damaged property, to make surveys and record the damage and to put in war-damage claims. This could be complicated and it helps to explain the rapid success after the war of some firms which were open and active from 1939 through to 1945, for the partners had valuable experience which their rivals who were away fighting had to pick up from scratch after the war. Two examples were Healey and Baker in shops and D. E. & J. Levy in offices—both the Levy brothers, Joe and David, were busy both as air raid wardens and as agents.

There were also active buyers of real estate during the war. The philosophy of these buyers was elementary: if the Germans won the war, everyone was undone, themselves included; if the British won, prices were almost bound to recover from the extremely depressed wartime levels. As indeed they did. Two of the most eager buyers were the Harris brothers, Bob and Harry. They were two furriers in partnership with their sister in Mill Street, a short link between Conduit Street and Maddox Street, the pre-war haunt of estate agents. The Harris brothers bought heavily in and around Conduit Street and made a great fortune by sitting on their purchases through the post-war years. They lived modestly and worked enthusiastically. They always said that they had never had the time to marry. Until Harry died last year, their lunches often consisted of a brief period when they would move the furs towards the back of their shop in Mill Street, sit cross-legged on the bench and eat their sandwiches.

Joe Littman was another instinctive businessman who bought shops, several in Oxford Street, during the war. Littman was one of the major operators in property in the late thirties, forties and early fifties. He was an investor, not a developer, but he was an exponent of the technique taken up by the developers, the sale and leaseback. This he refined to such an extent that it was once known in the trade as the 'Littman cocktail'. Littman was a Russian peasant, who came to England before the First World War. In the twenties he kept a small ladies' hat and fur shop at 248 High Road, Kilburn, called Poppy's. He then bought another shop in High Road, Kilburn, sold it, took a lease back from the buyer and made his profit by sub-leasing to the retailer. Through repetition of this technique he came to own a large chunk of High Road, Kilburn. After that he branched out into other streets, especially Oxford Street, and continued to buy there vigorously while the bombs were falling, quite unperturbed by the destruction of some of his properties.

Littman was an eccentric, with a sixth sense for the value of property. He was as strong as a bull and agents who used to work for him remember especially the size of his hands. When he lifted the receiver his hand would completely enfold it and he would mumble awkwardly into the mouthpiece. He was very close about his business interests and from time to time he made enigmatic Russian remarks. On one occasion he had a business meeting with Edward Erdman, the agent, Isaac Wolfson and a banker. To pass the time of day the banker said to him, 'What do you do, Littman, do you buy on the Stock Exchange?' Littman replied, 'I once went to my physician and he said to me "I don't deal in Consols, I deal in tonsils." ' Towards the end of the forties his companies had a rent roll of £375,000 a year.

Another wartime buyer was the late Sir Henry Price. He had begun as a lad in a draper's shop in Chester and built up the Fifty-Shilling Tailor chain and his fortune between the wars. But he enlarged it greatly by buying real estate in the war. He took a psychological line. Generally he would ring an estate agent the day after a particularly heavy bombing raid. 'Take off your coat, roll up your sleeves and go out and buy,' he would say. 'Did you hear the bombs last night? There must be some bargains around this morning.'

The exact point in the war at which the commercial property market began to turn for the better is obscure, but Douglas Tovey is an advocate of the most probable theory, that the turning point was a short while before the invasion of France. 'It was amazing how the boom in values started in the last 18 months of the war once people could see that we were going to win.' Tovey should know, for towards the end of the war he began to act for Charles Clore, who was busy buying commercial sites. Clore rang him one day, saying that he had read so many of his letters that he would like to meet him. Tovey is famous for his letters which cut out the usual dry conventions of business correspondence; he had a hard-sell line, with the important words and phrases in capitals. A huge volume of business, particularly on the sale and leaseback of shops for Clore and Fraser, passed through Tovey's hands after the war.

In the immediate post-war years, 1946 to 1949, it was in theory almost impossible for the operators to do anything physically to property. Licences and controls were all-pervading. There were numerous distinctions between one type of building work and another, between essential and non-essential, between dangerous and safe war-damaged structures, between turfing a lawn and building a summer house. There were limits above which licences were needed for non-essential work: at one time the limit was £50, later it was £100. The controls sometimes led to a chronic duplication. In 1946 the borough engineer of Bridgwater was complaining that a total of thirty-seven forms had to be filled in before building work of any description could be started. But in spite of the controls a great deal of building was allowed: in the twenty months to the end of 1946 licences worth £270 million were issued, of which £176 million were for factories, shops and offices. In the calendar year 1948 the commercial and industrial total was £140 million, with £17 million allowed for war-damage repairs in the same category.

The Ministry of Works report on 1947 also revealed that there had been 454 successful prosecutions and fines totalling £152,466 for breaches of the building regulations. That report was issued the day before the Lynskey Tribunal was appointed to enquire into 'allegations of irregularities against Ministers of the Crown and public servants'. The rather pathetic story unfolded by the Tribunal of an inefficient go-between, Sidney Stanley, attempting to influence indiscreet public servants with petty gifts was not in itself hair-raising. '. . . its real significance,' as Stanley Wade Baron wrote in his book on the Tribunal, *The Contact Man,** 'was in showing that certain elements in the post-war world of commerce clearly constituted a source of corruption . . .'

Those elements were certainly present in the property business, and many of the great names, some of whom are sufficiently pompous now not to want to discuss the question at all, admit that there was corruption, 'inevitably' is usually the word. Licences for new commercial buildings were extremely rare in the first few years, but there was scope for manœuvre with war-damaged buildings. If a bombed building could be certified as a dangerous structure by the district surveyor to a local authority, then it was possible to obtain a licence from the Ministry of Works to restore it. Since the Government paid for war-damage repairs, the favours of the district surveyors were much sought after. The borderline between a dangerous and a safe structure was vague. Corruption was sometimes direct—'dropsy' was the slang for a

* Secker & Warburg, 1966. See also the Report of the Lynskey Tribunal (HMSO).

straight-forward bribe in £1 notes—and sometimes indirect. There was one particular D.S. who was apparently so showered with drink that he was seldom sober.

As the figures for the numbers of prosecutions show, there was also a considerable amount of breaking of the many controls. One unpretentious millionaire, then a small fish, told me, 'I remember going down —— Street with a pal one Sunday night and climbing into the basement with a couple of pickaxes to make damned sure the structure was dangerous by 9 o'clock the next morning.' There is no reason to suppose that there was more sharp practice in property than in any other area under the Labour Government's controls, but there may have been more scope for it. Offences were committed with innocent intentions due to the absurdity of some of the rules. A permit was needed if fitted linoleum was put down with mastic or any other heavy adhesive; if it was tacked down or laid with a light adhesive no permit was needed. A licence was needed for a dry wall bound with cow dung and bone dust, but not for one bound with earth.

*

No restrictions stopped the buying and selling of properties and a great opportunity was open to those who could see that post-war values had soared above the pre-war levels. This was by no means apparent to many owners and advisers for several years after the end of the war. The maestro at buying large blocks of offices was Harold Samuel. He was a one-time estate agent—he ceased to practise in 1935—who bought control of a tiny property company, Land Securities Investment Trust, in the spring of 1944. In the previous annual report the shareholders of LSIT had been told that 'the only real estate of the company now comprises three houses in Kensington Court, two of which, the directors regret to state, are unoccupied'. The rest of the company's assets, which totalled £19,321, was in Government securities. By March 1952 Land Securities boasted assets of £11,089,441, and by March 1967 the total was £192,716,000.

Harold Samuel's particular skill, which founded this amazing growth, was his understanding from the beginning of the effect of borrowed money on a property company. In 1944 Land Securities bought some properties at Hatch End for £15,213, with £9,477 paid by bank loan, and others at Neasden for £4,847, subject to a mortgage of £3,335. Gradually the purchases became bigger and bigger, and, as property values rose, so did the capital profits. The Defence Regulations limited borrowers to £10,000 until 1947 when the limit was raised to £50,000, but this applied to each company and one parent company could have any number of subsidiaries borrowing up to the limit. Also, if a company was bought which already had borrowings of, say, £150,000, that existing loan was not affected.

Samuel recognised, too, an important provision of the Town and Country Planning Act of 1947: that blocks of flats, which had been requisitioned as offices, could continue as offices without the payment of a development charge. He bought several former blocks of flats to take advantage of this, such as Esso House in Stratton Street, Lansdowne House in Berkeley Square or Devonshire House in Piccadilly. A thorough understanding of the laws and the loopholes affecting property could be crucial to success. Harold Samuel realised this absolutely, and it was a cornerstone of his great fortune. By no means all other owners of real estate did. Samuel bought one vast block of requisitioned flats from a powerful corporate vendor who had no idea that it could stay as offices on derequisition without a development change. He paid a correspondingly low price and made a much larger profit than might have been expected, especially at the expense of an eminent, established owner with a staff of experts.

Although his success was not built on takeovers, Harold Samuel was a skilful bidder. His earliest coup in this line was with United City Property Trust, a publicly quoted owner of office blocks in the City with an old-fashioned board of directors. Samuel bought one-third of the shares on the market. The board realised what was happening and sent out a circular advising shareholders not to sell. This woke them up to the buyer in the market and so many accepted, delighted with Samuel's price, that Land Securities soon had control.

Shot into the public eye by his attempt to take over the Savoy Group,* Harold Samuel was defeated by concerted efforts of the Establishment who were horrified at the thought of hotels turning into office blocks. With the exception of the Berkeley, which, sited in a prime pitch in Piccadilly was evidently ripe to be turned into

* See *Bid for Power* by Anthony Vice and George Bull (Elek Books, 1958).

offices, this was not the intention. But Samuel himself, who thought that, unjustly, he had come out of the Savoy fight with a worse reputation than before, a reputation as a pirate and a take-over king, decided to retire as much as he possibly could from the glare of publicity. Gradually he too became part of the Establishment. His reputation, unknown to the public, grew and grew with his company, until finally, in 1963, he became the first knighted developer. Inside the property business he has been regarded almost as a god of uprightness.

In spite of their violent protestations at the time, and the bitter fight to ensure that the Savoy Group did not fall into the hands of Land Securities, the directors of the Savoy themselves decided a few years later that it would after all be a sound move to re-develop the Berkeley. They applied for planning permission for offices, shops and flats and sold the site for £2·5 million to York-shire Insurance. A new Berkeley is being built in a less valuable site, off Knightsbridge.

Through the force of restrictions, Harold Samuel was chiefly a buyer of property in the years 1945 to 1954, though in the follow-ing ten years he was to become one of the most prominent develo-pers in London. However, it was possible to build in some circumstances before licencing was relaxed by the Conservatives in 1952–53 and removed in 1954. The easiest way to do so was via the Government 'lessor' scheme. This was the first post-war sign of the Government's masochistic policy, discussed in the pre-vious chapter, of satisfying its hunger for office space by leasing buildings from developers. On agreeing to lease the offices and then granting the developer a licence, the Ministry of Works looked cannily at the figures and screwed the developer down to the small return on his money—by later standards—of up to 8 per cent. But the profit for the developer was a certain profit, unless he made a complete nonsense of his building costs, and it also meant that with the Government as tenant on completion the developer had no trouble at all in borrowing the bridging money from his bank.

Harold Samuel built one 'lessor' block, Castlewood House in New Oxford Street. This was developed in partnership with his cousins Basil and Howard Samuel, both estate agents. Howard was an active supporter of the Labour Party, part-owner of the *New Statesman* and a contributor to *Tribune*. He died of a heart attack in 1961 while bathing in Greece. Charles Clore also developed several 'lessors'; the most noticeable is Charles House, a graceless brick affair at the western end of Kensington High Street. Another which looked much the same was Adastral House in Theobalds Road, developed by a syndicate including Stanley and Peter Edgson and Douglas Overall, all partners in Hillier, Parker, their companies, Emmanuel Curtis, another estate agent, Major Ash, an architect, James Hucker, a bank manager, Sir William Threlford, a chartered accountant, and various other estate agents. The members of the syndicate put up a total of £5,000 in November 1947 and made a total profit of some £340,000 when they sold out to Harold Samuel's company in February 1950.

The other way of obtaining a building licence for a new building was to let most of it in advance to a firm active in the export trade or which could be shown to need the offices for reasons of national importance. That was how Arthur Dollond made his killing. Today Dollond is to be found on the first floor of a small building in Moorgate in the heart of the City, a hundred yards up the road from the Government Broker's office. Dollond is a solicitor and the two rooms of his offices are dowdy and strongly reminiscent of a small professional man's lair in the provinces. Dollond, now 56, is a quiet man who does only a little general practice as a solicitor. 'I spend most of my time seeing that it doesn't get whittled away.'

'It' was about £2½ million tax free, which Arthur Dollond made out of promoting three buildings in the City. He moved into property partly as a result of a misfortune. Abraham Lazarus Dollond had qualified as a solicitor in 1934. After an involved case, and two dismissals of his appeal, Dollond was suspended from his practice as a solicitor for professional misconduct. He had been found guilty of failing to make sufficient enquiry before accepting instructions. His suspension was for two years from 3 November 1944.

While he was not allowed to practise, Arthur Dollond had to do something and after a while he took a building lease from the Church Commissioners on a bombed site in Chiswell Street just off Finsbury Square. (The Church owns many acres in that neighbourhood.) Before he took the lease Dollond made a survey to find prospective tenants. There seemed to be no demand for new office space and he knew that he would not get a licence without an exporting tenant. The Church Commissioners were fed up with Dollond's delay and threatened to find another developer; that was easier said than done at that time. But eventually he signed the lease with no licence and no tenant in sight. 'I did so with the greatest forebodings and reluctance. My father said to me "Don't be so crazy to take such a risk." I am a bachelor. If I had been a married man with a wife and children, I could not conceivably have signed that lease. I could just face the idea of standing in the dole queue by myself.'

Dollond's immediate commitment was small. He had to find £5,000 as a deposit to the Church, which he borrowed largely from his bank; he was by no means well off at the time. The lease itself cost a peppercorn for three years while building was under way—a peppercorn is the jargon for a nominal sum of £1 a year or so—and £5,000 after that fixed for ninety-nine years. He also formed a company with a paid up capital of £100. Soon after he signed the lease, he did find a tenant, a firm big in the export trade to South America. The Ministry of Works granted a licence. A contractor, F. G. Minter, was prepared to build and finance the cost, some £150,000, of the 50,000 square feet. It was let at 9s. 6d. a square foot. Dollond was home and dry. The building was worth about £250,000 more than it had cost. He decided to repeat the operation, this time taking an £8,000 a year lease from the Church on Phase 2, an adjacent site. But the lettings there went so slowly and the risk seemed so great that he sold out during construction to Fenston and Hyams. He sold both Phase 2, another 50,000 square feet, and Phase 3, a 150,000 square foot building at £17,500 a year; all three buildings became jointly known as City Wall House, and for his role in their development Arthur Dollond made a profit of around £350,000. After that he developed two more buildings, in each case with the construction financed by contractors, both of which he sold in the early sixties to Bernard Sunley. One, in Finsbury Square, cost him £350,000 and fetched £1·5 million; the other, in the shipping and insurance quarter of the City, cost £320,000 and was sold for £1·3 million.

After his three buildings Dollond stopped. That was 1955–56, when the boom was still young. He said, 'I had such trouble letting my developments, it was such a nerve-racking experience that I thought the risk was too great to continue. I did not conceive of the boom. Besides, I have interests of a more intellectual nature than

most other developers. I am a linguist and I play chess.' Arthur
Dollond added that his biggest expense was tennis balls and that
he lived with his parents in the Edgware Road in a semi-detached
house which cost £750 in the early part of the war.

*

In the early fifties, while development was in its infancy, one
operation, half in and half out of the property market, was the
devastating combination of sale and leasebacks with takeover
bids. The masters of this were Charles Clore and Isaac Wolfson,
and their campaigns and strategies have also been described in *Bid
for Power*. The essence of the operation was that most of the
companies victim to takeover had their properties in their balance
sheet at pre-war values and did not have a clear idea of their post-
war values, or indeed how to realise those values. When Clore bid
for Sears in January 1953, the directors hurried round to fight him
off and told their shareholders that at least £6 million could be
raised on the properties, which was a shock since they appeared in
the books at £2·3 million. When Clore won control he promptly
sold £4½ million worth of Freeman, Hardy and Willis shoe shops
and took back long leases; there was another £4 million of property left. The money realised from the sale and leasebacks could
then be devoted to the next takeover. The process was self-
generating. It was also greatly oiled by the eagerness with which
the insurance companies were buying real estate.

Apart from this unawareness of post-war values, the developers
were helped by an anxiety to sell on the part of some owners. The
man whose property was bombed in 1940 tended to be fairly
desperate to sell his site by 1950 and the number of buyers prepared to take the risks was limited in relation to the amount of
property available. This ensured that the sites were cheap, and it
meant that the vendors were often prepared to finance the buyer,
directly or indirectly. From 1950 to 1958 sites were often sold on a
small ground rent, with an option to buy the freehold a few years
later. Sometimes the owners were so relieved to have sold a non-
revenue-producing bomb site that they were willing not to take
payment until building took place. In this way, as in the case of
Arthur Dollond, remarkably small sums had to be found to set the
ball rolling.

The other transition caused by the war was an exodus by the

big investors from residential property in order to reinvest in commercial property. As the Milner Holland Report* said, 'the tendency . . . has been greatly accelerated by the continued existence of rent controls and the political controversy which has surrounded housing'. The 1964 Landlord Inquiry showed that only 36 per cent of all landlords were companies at all, and that only 15 per cent of privately rented flats and houses were owned by large public companies, or 6 per cent of all dwellings in Greater London. With almost all rented property controlled by the Rent Act included just after the outbreak of war, it was natural that the big companies with some mobility should sell and look to commercial property. Many of the companies, some still the descendants of Charity at 5 per cent, were surprisingly slow to do so. Their managements tended to be more entrenched than the new commercial boys. But one by one they all switched towards offices and shops in varying degrees. Extremely little new housing to rent was built due to rent control, and there was no comparison between the attraction of developing commercial property and the snags in residential.

Among the first groups to move out of residential properties were those under the control of Cyril Black and his brother Sydney. Perhaps Cyril Black's political instinct told him that the problems of owning flats and houses would be lasting. He spent the first few years after the war tidying up the empire of flats built up in the thirties by his father, himself and his brother: repairing bombed buildings with the help of the War Damage Commission and clearing up the ravages of lack of maintenance in the years of war. He then gradually sold the blocks of flats and replaced them with offices and shops.

Cyril Black was an early exponent of a financial technique known as the 'shell' operation. This is scarcely possible any longer, as the Stock Exchange has clamped down on it. But it was frequently used by property men and their City advisers, especially during the stampede to float property companies in the late fifties and early sixties. A public company was needed to overcome the surtax hazards of a private company, and it was cheaper and simpler to buy an existing company with a quotation on the stock market. An advantage which appealed to some operators was that until recent

* Report of the Committee on Housing in Greater London, 1965 (HMSO).

years it was possible to buy a quoted 'shell' and pop in private assets without giving nearly so much information to the investing public as was required on a conventional flotation. A 'shell' was essentially a company whose old business had been sold or was on the point of fading out. Malayan rubber companies whose estates were sold in the fifties were frequently material for 'shell' operations and overseas companies from all over the world, relics of imperialism, underwent the change of life. They were rechristened with far less exotic, faceless names. The New Bulawayo Syndicate was converted into Hallmark Securities, Gan Kee Rubber into Town & City, or Lady Workers Homes into Grovewood Securities. Spotting 'shells' early on in their transformation was a favourite and profitable game with investors close to the market. At one point a regular traffic developed among specialists in 'shells'.

Cyril Black, chairman of the Moral Law Society, and boss of the Temperance Permanent Building Society, bought his first 'shell' as far back as 1950. This was the Rock Investment Company, bought from a once-imprisoned financier named Martin Coles Harman. By the end of the fifties Black was running five different public property companies. This arrangement was criticised on the grounds that investors were not to know which company would be likely to make most progress at any particular time; later his stable was merged into two groups. Black also found time and energy for his work as Member of Parliament and his campaigns against pre-marital sex, easier divorce, relaxation of the drinking laws and psychiatrists.

Occasionally a 'shell' would yield an unexpected bonus. In the summer of 1955 (a summer during which he sent a cable to Attlee saying 'Please state whether it is part of the Socialist Party's case in this election to contend that a Christian cannot with consistency be a Tory') Cyril Black bought control of the Rio de Janeiro Land Company. This produced the extra of £123,750 at the expense of the taxpayer for Black and his fellow shareholders. Rio Land was formed before the First World War to promote property companies in Rio de Janeiro but this ceased to be a viable line of business after the Second War. By 1955 it was a 'shell' owning only £30,000 in cash. Black paid £40,000 for it. But it also had £300,000 in tax losses. This meant that if it continued its existing business it could offset these losses against profits and pay no tax on the

E

first £300,000 of profits. But that was not theoretically possible if it changed its business. Cyril Black wanted to change its business entirely from real estate in Rio de Janeiro to real estate in England. He was advised that he would not be likely to avoid tax against those losses. However, as he explained, 'in order not to excite the Inland Revenue too much, Rio de Janeiro made a profit of just under £1,000 in its first year under my control. This profit was set against past losses. I don't think it went to a very high level in the Revenue and the offset was allowed. After that there was a precedent and all the past losses could be claimed.' This meant that the company paid no tax on its first £300,000 of profits. If the standard rate of income tax was 8s. 3d. in the £, this would have given Rio de Janeiro a clear £123,750. A nice windfall of £123,750 off the Inland Revenue. Or not so nice, depending on whether you were a shareholder or a taxpayer.

CHAPTER FIVE

Provincial Shops, 1948-1955: Blitzed Cities and New Towns

LONDON was the centre of operations for the property men. But two men, to an unusual degree industrial pioneers, were hard at work far away from London, virtually untroubled by competitors. They were building up a long lead in prestige and skill in their speciality, the development of shops in provincial towns, a lead which was never seriously challenged throughout the property boom.

They were Louis Freedman and Frederick Maynard. Both had been groomed in that classic stable for developers, the London estate agents' office in the thirties. Freedman left school in 1932 when he was fifteen. 'It wasn't that I was stupid. I just wasn't interested.' He was the youngest of eight children and was determined not to go into the family business, a small chain of furniture shops based on West Kensington. So his father suggested that he should join his brother-in-law, who ran an estate agency in the West End, Vickers and Stanley, as a young clerk. After four years of this and two days before his nineteenth birthday in 1936, he set up on his own as a one-man firm. He called himself Newton, Smith & Co.

For three years, specialising in shops, he learnt his way around the business, buying, selling, leasing and organising the building of shops for developers in and around London. 'I was successful but I spent all I earned.'

During these three years he ran across Fred Maynard, who was working for the estate agents Healey & Baker, one of their star young men. Maynard had started work as office boy for an agent in Lisson Grove, Marylebone, and moved to the estate office of what was then an embryo chain of retailers, Bata Shoes. He joined

Healey & Baker in 1934 and as a junior was in the thick of the fray as his firm established itself as one of the dominant agents for shops in the thirties. Through their common interest in shops Freedman and Maynard met half a dozen times before the war broke out. Then Freedman was away in the army for six and a half years, Maynard for seven years.

In February 1946 Louis Freedman set up on his own again as an agent, this time trading as Mr Louis Freedman, FALPA,* rather than Newton, Smith & Co. Later that year he also started a company with the help and backing of Harold Samuel. This support was a great feather in Freedman's cap, for though Samuel, then thirty-four, was only five years older than Freedman, he was already in charge of a company with assets of £330,000 and was becoming an expert on how to finance and organise a property company. These two had met socially before the war and, perhaps recognising instinctively and respecting each other's talents as businessmen, had become firm friends.

The new company was called Ravensfield Properties, a name chosen because Louis Freedman's solicitor happened once to have been master of a masonic lodge known as Ravensfield Lodge. Ravensfield started with an ordinary capital of £2,500 and a preference, fixed interest capital of £10,000. Freedman was able to find £625 for 25 per cent of the ordinary shares but bought no preference. Samuel's company, Land Securities, put up £7,500 for half the ordinary and half the preference, and ten relations and friends of Freedman's subscribed for the remaining £4,500.

As he began to trade again, Louis Freedman came to a deliberate and crucial decision. 'I could see that those who had remained behind during the war had had it very easy. They only had to move from behind their desks across the road to pick up the business. But as more came back from the war a tough fight might develop in and around London. If I stirred myself 50 miles away I might do something worthwhile.'

For the first year and a half he operated on a small scale, buying and re-letting the odd shop for Ravensfield, and doing agents' work for others. He realised that outside the Home Counties, where most important developers of the thirties had concentrated, there would be scope for development once licensing was lifted. After ten years

* Fellow of the Incorporated Society of Auctioneers and Landed Property Agents.

of stagnation, there were High Streets all over the country which would be crying out for modernisation as rationing loosened its grip and the frustrated demands of the consumer flowed into the shops.

At this point he had to find a partner. It was physically impossible to operate all over the country as a one-man outfit. So in the spring of 1949 he lunched with Fred Maynard, who had rejoined Healey & Baker eighteen months before. They both remember a terse exchange:

'Are you committed to Healey & Baker, Fred, for the rest of your working life?'

'No.'

'Will you join me as a partner?'

'Yes.'

His initiative quickened by rapid promotion to lieutenant-colonel during the war, Maynard was restive as an employee and possible salaried partner and was eager for independence; but he had no capital and his new ally at one remove helped him to buy shares in Ravensfield. Out of that snap decision at the lunch table was formed an alliance which over the next seventeen years poured some £60 millions into new shops in over 400 developments in 150 different towns and cities in England, Wales and Scotland.

They started in Bristol. Fred Maynard heard that there was to be a competition by tender for a row of 30 shops on an estate of new council houses in the suburb of Southmead. Property development was at such an embryo stage that Ravensfield had only one other competitor, the established pre-war shop developer, Edward Lotery. No-one else—and there were many who could have afforded to compete—found the proposition inviting. Ravensfield won the tender, which was judged purely on who was prepared to pay the most.

Meanwhile they were trying to catch a second and much bigger fish. In the summer of 1949 Fred Maynard took his family on holiday to Cornwall, driving in a Wolseley 40, the Maynards' first holiday away from home after the war. On the way they stopped in Plymouth. 'I was amazed. The whole of the town centre was flat. I rang up Louis at once and said, "There are no shops here." ' In March and April of 1941 German bombers had begun the complete destruction of 140 acres in the centre of Plymouth. After three years almost all the civic buildings and 500 shops had disappeared, as well as 4,000 houses.

After his holiday Maynard visited the estates and development officer of Plymouth. The city had already laid its plans for the reconstruction. While the bombs were still falling the city engineer, J. Paton-Watson, and Sir Patrick Abercrombie, famous for the Abercrombie Plan for London, had drawn up a regional plan for an area nine times that of Plymouth itself, which was completed in 1943. Then the city began to acquire land compulsorily for the re-building. In the centre the old, narrow streets of shops were forgotten. Wide, straight and parallel was the new pattern. Maynard enquired if Ravensfield might lease some of this land to build shops. The estates officer was cool. He had never heard of Maynard, or of Freedman, or of their company. They seemed very young. In any event the city had already agreed with the Pearl Assurance that it should build a major block and was in the process of negotiating with the Norwich Union Insurance for another block. But Maynard wrote to the estates officer, rubbing home that Ravensfield was interested if there should be any change of mind.

Some months later the Norwich Union changed its mind. It decided that it was more interested in financing development than in instigating it. So the estates officer suggested that the Norwich Union's surveyor should go and talk with two young fellows who had been pestering him; it might like to let them have a look in. Freedman and Maynard were delighted to see the Norwich Union's man in their small, dowdy two-room office in Duke Street, St James', looking a little surprised to find himself there. Then he asked if they would be prepared to take on half the development which the Norwich Union had originally been discus-sing. Ravenseft (its name was changed from Ravensfield in 1949) soon agreed the terms of a ground lease with Plymouth. Why did Plymouth take on such an unknown quantity? First, no-one else then wanted to do the scheme. Secondly, the city had little to lose. If Ravenseft had not paid their rent, another tenant to take over the lease could possibly have been found. Finally, the reputation of Harold Samuel and Land Securities helped in the background. In all Ravenseft built forty-one shops in Plymouth in the early post-war years.

By this time Freedman and Maynard were on the way to a snow-balling success. After only a year together in business the chief probable drawback to rapid progress had vanished. They were now visibly acceptable in a way which would appeal to local authorities. No other developers, except the insurance companies like the Pearl or the Norwich Union, which were not interested in operating on a big scale, had experience of rebuilding shops in bombed cities. And many people in the property business, deeply cautious in the tough economic climate immediately after the war, thought at the time that the ground rents being paid by Freedman and Maynard for their first few schemes were stupidly high, and that the young fellows would soon go broke. As it turned out they were the only ones in step.

Exeter followed Plymouth. 'We had a story to tell Exeter.' The story was that they had been accepted as developers by the landlords, the local authorities, in Bristol and Plymouth. Those projects were in the middle of being built. The wise men of Exeter were not able to see if Freedman and Maynard's judgment was correct, if the shops let. But their credentials as accepted developers were enough. Leafing through the Municipal Year Book, they wrote letters out of the blue to the officials of all towns with a population of over 50,000, offering their services as promoters of new shops. Following up these letters, Fred Maynard, a small, neat extrovert, dashed around the country displaying their good intentions to the councils. He was away from London most of the year. Soon deals were in train with Hull and Swansea, Sheffield, Sunderland and Coventry. Louis Freedman, less of a salesman than his partner, stayed in London mostly, arranging finance for the developments.

After the council estate in Bristol, all their early developments were in blitzed towns. This was from necessity, not choice. Building licences were only granted for replacing bombed shops or for shops on new housing estates. Each local authority was given permission by the Ministry of Housing for a certain amount to be spent in its area, and if the allocation was not taken up by the year-end, it lapsed. This spurred the local authorities to busy on with re-developments and quickened the flow of work into Ravenseft's eager hands between 1950 and 1955. In these crucial years Freedman and Maynard had virtually no oppositon. One reason was that they were opening up a type of redevelopment which had previously been almost unknown. This was large-scale co-operation between municipal authorities and private enterprise. Having once taken the decision to launch out into provincial shops in 1949, this was the only way Ravenseft could operate because of the building restrictions. Before the war the promotion of new shops in provincial towns was generally done by the shopkeepers themselves or by local businessmen putting up three or four shops at a time. But the acres destroyed by bombs changed the scale of rebuilding and changed the ownership of land as local authorities used their powers of compulsory acquisition. To build thirty-four shops in Coventry, or forty-six in Hull, was beyond the scope of the pre-war type of local operator, and the countrywide developer, apart from the occasional insurance company, had not yet emerged. At the same time, in the latter years of the first post-war Labour Government, most of those in the real estate business, deeply conservative by profession, did not know quite what to make of the new deal between a local authority as landlord and a developer as middleman.

By the time competitors did appear Ravenseft were at a great advantage, for they could always point out the successful results of their early developments. Their judgment had turned out correct and the shops had filled up with tenants. Their rivals did not have projects anything like so impressive to boast of. The grapevine of local officials also helped Freedman and Maynard; at their annual conferences the town clerks or the surveyors or the borough architects would discuss the developers, which for a few years meant a word of mouth advertisement for Ravenseft. Freedman and Maynard were acutely aware that the slightest ethical lapse on their part would spread like wildfire round the town clerks' coffee tables. In Sunderland they agreed to develop shops on a site which, they were assured by the Council, was stable and would not be affected by mining. Just before the legalities of the lease were complete, they discovered that the Coal Board was to increase extraction from the area and that subsidence would add 45 per cent to their total costs. Ravenseft could legally have backed out of their original agreement, but they decided to carry on and make no money on the deal. They didn't want the town clerk of Sunderland telling his opposite numbers that Freedman and Maynard were a tricky pair to deal with. And usually they built more than one scheme in a town.

Sometimes a project would take several years to mature, but Ravenseft, unruffled by the lack of competition, took their time. In Coventry they started to negotiate in 1949. They heard of the scheme through Edward Erdman. 'I was generally punting it around at that stage,' says Erdman. He sent them the details which he had learnt from Coventry: ' . . . the site is to be let on a ground rent for 99 years . . . no development charge . . . 2,640 square yard site . . . fully licenced hotel of 200 bedrooms . . . first refusal to rent the shops is to be given to those who lost their shops during the war . . .' Erdman recalls, 'This last clause was a token because they couldn't afford to take up the leases at full market rent.'

Nothing came of the early talks. Each side had different ideas of what the ground rent should be. In November 1950 the site was advertised in the national press, and developers were invited to make offers. In February 1951 Edward Erdman was writing to Coventry again for Ravenseft, protesting that his clients were already dealing with sites for Bristol, Exeter, Plymouth and Hull, and that they were negotiating with Swansea, Sheffield, Yarmouth and Sunderland. Later that month he wrote again to say that 'the figures did not work out after vigorous investigation. Our clients have not had time to work out a plan with hoteliers . . .' (This was the big snag in the scheme, since at that time hotel companies were not keen to open any new hotels.) ' . . . we think that the other offer of £8,500 a year may not materialise . . .' This remark was pouring cold water on Coventry's negotiations with another developer, Jack Cotton, who was more sanguine about the chances of finding a hotel keeper.

In early 1952 Erdman wrote once more to Coventry: ' . . . you will note that after 18 months there is no binding contract . . . appreciate that the letting market has weakened . . . Ravenseft are interested only if Coventry were not to negotiate elsewhere . . .' By June 1952 another letter enquired: ' . . . we shall be glad to learn that our clients can be given the sole right to negotiate . . .' Eventually the lease was signed in May 1953, four years after Coventry had started to look for a developer. Freedman and Maynard decided to build the hotel on the speculation that it would find a tenant and almost as soon as the builders started Ind Coope leased it. This is now the Leofric.

As patrons of architecture, Freedman and Maynard had little choice in the design of these hundreds of shops which they planted all over the country. 'Aesthetically we had virtually no control. The local authorities always dictated. But we were adamant about the functional part; on aesthetics we didn't really care, provided we didn't feel the building to be offensive. The local authorities always took the credit when the buildings were praised and the developers were blamed if the design was attacked.' The parentage of some of their architecture was fairly involved, though the developers of a building are generally credited or discredited with the physical result. The President of the Royal Institute of British Architects in 1965 to 1967, sometimes known as Lionel Brett, sometimes as Lord Esher, has written:* 'Taking the rough with the smooth, you could say that the developers' architecture stayed pretty well in the mainstream of its time. Louis Freedman's post-war shopping blocks in provincial cities like Plymouth, Coventry, Swansea, Southampton and Portsmouth were just about what Abercrombie's and Sharp's perspectives led us to expect.' In practice commercial impatience led to some strange compromise. 'In one city we got so fed up about the details of the architecture being messed about by officials that we said to our architect: "Go down to —— with a blank sheet of paper and ask that damned City Architect to draw on it exactly what he wants." He did more or less. Then, when the architecture was criticised, the City Architect said, "Ah well, it was a privately promoted scheme." '

Towards the end of 1953 Freedman and Maynard saw that before long they would be running out of blitzed cities. They began to look at the New Towns, which were then on the drawing board. In 1954 they signed building leases in Harlow, Aycliffe and Peterlee. In retrospect the building of those shops seems to have been easy money. At the time it was less simple. The New Towns were only on the planners' table when they signed the leases; no houses had been built and it was unknown whether anybody would be prepared to dump themselves down in an anonymous town in the depths of the countryside; a change of Government or of Minister could easily alter the plans; and once the newcomers set up home in the New Towns, they might well have decided to make the journey to the more friendly atmosphere of some established shopping centre. As it was, the multiple shops flocked in to the New Towns' centres—and so did the New Townspeople.

In late 1954 they moved to Scotland, to develop the shops in Glasgow's new satellite town of East Kilbride. There they stumbled on a new formula in this local authority/developer partner-

* In an article, 'The Developers', discussed earlier on page 29.

ship, a formula which was to become standard practice a few years later. East Kilbride's housing was being built over a much longer period than was normal. In the first phase about one-third of the town was built; after ten to fifteen years the remaining two-thirds would be finished. Normally Ravenseft would sign a lease, agreeing to pay a fixed ground rent for ninety-nine years, and would themselves grant leases to the shopkeepers for twenty-one years, though they did not then expect the rents to have risen much by year 21, for inflation was not an accepted fact of life in the early fifties. But in East Kilbride it was clearly tough on Ravenseft to pay at once the full ground rent geared to the eventual population; equally, East Kilbride would be the loser if Ravenseft paid a ground rent appropriate for the initial, one third, population. From year 15 to year 99 66 per cent more people would be able to use Ravenseft's shops, and the shopkeepers would be able to pay 66 per cent more in rent. So it was agreed that the ground rent should be revised upwards after twenty-one years. This was one of the first 'rent revision clauses'.

In 1955 Harold Samuel's Land Securities bought out Freedman and Maynard and friends and took its holding in Ravenseft from 50 per cent to 100 per cent. This deal valued Ravenseft at £2,100,000. In this 1955 consolidation of his empire Harold Samuel's personal holding was worth £3¼ million. The two shop developers kept their shares in Land Securities, exchanged for Ravenseft shares in the takeover, and continued to run in harness with Harold Samuel. The two main companies, one in provincial shops, the other in London offices, were independent but complementary and each created the most solid, not the most sparkling or adventurous, reputation in its sphere. In due course the stock market was to catch on to the great professionalism of Samuel and Freedman and Maynard, and in its zeal for their talents, greatly to exaggerate the value of Land Securities. Yet by the summer of 1967, after the property share boom had cooled, Harold Samuel's holding in Land Securities was worth £12,400,000, Louis Freedman's £1,850,000 and Fred Maynard's £845,000. The entire company, including the much bigger stake of the public and the insurance companies, was valued by the stock market at £62,000,000.

CHAPTER SIX

The City of London

MORE criticism has been fired at the City fathers for the quality of the early redevelopment of the City of London after the war than at any other local authority. As H. Anthony Mealand, chief architect and planning officer for the Corporation of London from 1948 to 1961, confessed in an article in 1960,* it 'has often been unfavourably compared with the rebuilding that followed the Great Fire of 1666'.

The Great Fire destroyed 437 acres, or three-quarters of the City at that time, while the bombs of the Second World War destroyed 225 acres, or one-third of the City. In both cases the logical redevelopment of the City to take advantage of the destruction and to adapt its physique to the times was severely hampered by the speed with which private enterprisers reacted. But in both cases something of value was gained out of the initial muddle of replanning.

The new shape of the City after the Great Fire was settled within days. The fire broke out on the evening of 1 September. It stopped on 6 September, but soon started again to smoulder intermittently for months. Christopher Wren was then a young Surveyor of His Majesty's Works, who had taken up architecture only four years before, and he was extremely quick off the mark with his plan for the City, knowing that his must be the first. He presented it to the King on 10 September. It was an idealistic plan, largely of rectangular city blocks and wide avenues pivoted on the Stock Exchange and St Paul's, and a grandiose octagon on the site of Fleet Street and the Temple. It ignored entirely the previous boundaries of individual properties and this was its undoing, for by the time Wren handed his drawing to the King, owners had begun to rebuild on their original sites. Moreover, the machinery

* The *Investors' Chronicle*, 12 February 1960.

for reorganising the ownership of the land was non-existent. Charles II, however, appears to have liked Wren's plan. On the same day that he received it one of his secretaries wrote to the Lord Mayor: 'My Lord—his Matie being informed that some persons are already about to erect houses againe in the Citty of London upon their old foundations, hath commanded mee to signify his pleasure unto your Lordship that you inhibit and straightly forbid them. . . . your Lordship may assure them (as undoubtedly it will come to passe) that whatever they raise in such manner will be demolished and levelled again.—I am, Your lordship's most humble servant, Will Morice.'

It did not come to pass. The merchants continued to build, the City's politicians clearly told the King that his plan was impractical and unacceptable, and only three days after sending that letter the King issued a proclamation effectively abandoning Wren's plan. But the proclamation was full of commonsense, and it laid down plans for widening streets and constructing new sewers, and above all for buildings to have walls of brick or stone so as to prevent another fire of wooden houses.

The main rebuilding after the Great Fire took about five years. The rebuilding after the blitz is not yet finished, but the problems of bureaucracy have been more intractable. Given the newfangled machinery for planning, though, it is arguable from their early post-war results that the City's bosses in the 20th century have shown themselves to be less farsighted than their predecessors of the 17th century.

The replanning of the City was started during the war. The first plan, presented in 1944, was rejected. A second plan by C. H. Holden and W. G. Holford (Lord Holford) was presented in 1947, but was almost at once overtaken by the obligation, under the Town and Country Planning Act, 1947, to prepare a Statutory Development Plan and to co-operate, to the City's disgust, with the LCC. This was a source of much friction in the years to come between the two kingdoms on either side of the Thames. The Statutory Plan, which incorporated a greatly modified version of the Holden/Holford suggestions, was shown to the Minister and approved in 1951.

Already, before the Plan was finally approved, rebuilding by developers and owners had begun to a limited extent and, on a much greater scale, planning permissions had been given for new buildings which did not necessarily conform to the Plan. Rudolph Palumbo's coup was under way between St Swithin's Lane and Walbrook before the middle of 1948. He rushed the excavators on to the site before the development charge came into force on 1 July and promoted a huge Portland Stone building of crude design. Palumbo—his family came originally from Naples, where his uncle was a Bishop—was an obscure operator who had pre-war links with Bridgland. He first appeared in the small print of a prospectus of 1934, selling St Regis House in King William Street for £25,000 to a company being promoted by Bridgland. He was partly financed by a Middlesbrough shipping family named Constantine and, in one way or another, had his finger in many pre-war office deals. Apart from St Swithin's House, Palumbo promoted several office developments after the war, all in private companies and virtually unknown to the public. But he was no small fry. An examination of his companies—and in particular his master company, Rugarth Investment Trust—suggests that Rudolph Palumbo must have made some £8 million from property development. He operates from a tiny mock Georgian house with the air of a vicarage tucked away at the back of St Stephen's Walbrook in the City between Rothschilds and his own giant office block of 1948 vintage.

Rudolph Palumbo is 66. There is no name on the house in Walbrook and his name is not to be found in telephone directories. An associate of his said that 'he will go to any lengths to avoid publicity. He doesn't even like his right hand to know what his left hand is doing. Sometimes, even on a normal business matter, he flicks a switch on his intercom and says tersely to me, "you take this, I don't want my name to appear".' Even now he is working on a grandiose project which may be a landmark for the daytime population of the City to gaze at. This is on a triangular island site next door to the Bank of England and the Mansion House. It is bounded by Queen Victoria Street, Poultry and Bucklersbury. Palumbo's companies have been quietly amassing this block bit by bit over the years and now have control. He plans to destroy the existing building and promote a thin tower block on one corner of the site, with an underground shopping concourse and an open square for pedestrians. The self-effacing Mr Palumbo is dreaming that before he dies this monument to Mr Rudolph Palumbo will be built and christened, not Palumbo Plaza, but Mansion House Square.

Before 1951 planning permission was granted in the City for a massive 4·8 million square feet of offices, compared with a total of 6 million square feet destroyed in the war; another 21 million square feet of warehouses and other buildings were bombed.

At the same time the City was busy acquiring large tracts of land under its new powers of compulsory purchase. So far since the war it has bought up 115 acres at a total cost of some £31 million, and has become one of the biggest new urban ground landlords in the country since the war. It already owned around 50 acres through legacies and Victorian schemes of improvement, including the markets.

Its first efforts at disposing of its new acquisitions were unimpressive. The area around Fetter Lane, between Holborn Circus and Fleet Street, is an example. Here the old street patterns were largely reinstated. The sites were leased off to individual developers, who seem to have been allowed a more or less free hand in their designs. Whatever may be thought of the individual buildings, they do not look like part of a cohesive plan.

The other area which has been violently criticised by town planners and architects lies immediately to the east and south-east of St Paul's. Cheapside has been rebuilt in a variation on pre-war Portland Stone Solid, the new Bank of England outpost is a Neo-Georgian barrack, the *Financial Times* Building is the *Financial Times* Building, surrounded by four normal examples of Developer Curtain Wall. Again, these buildings appear to have no relationship with one another.

Almost dwarfing the regrets is the City's one great achievement: the resurrection of the Barbican. This northern area of the City was the centre of the rag trade in London and was razed by bombing on the nights of 26 and 27 December 1940. The surviving firms departed, chiefly to the West End, north of Oxford Street, never to return. Around 40 acres were flattened at the Barbican and this was one of the comprehensive development areas bought by the Corporation. Before anything actually happened to this lake of rubble and annual flowering of Old Man's Beard, there was a long period of proposals and counter-proposals. It was a planner's dream to have such an acreage lying fallow so close to the heart of a city and a local politician's dream to promote a civic pride on the ruins. One plan was rejected partly because its buildings grew so high and their foundations so low that the water table below ground might have been interrupted and made St Paul's shaky. It was at least one virtue of the private developer that the less a local authority was involved, the quicker the work was done.

Eventually a scheme designed by two teams of architects, one working at County Hall under Sir Leslie Martin, the other at the Guildhall under Mr Mealand, was accepted and pushed slowly forward. The Barbican was divided into two parts: a commercial zone of 28 acres, now largely finished, and a residential area for over 6,000 people, designed by Chamberlin, Powell & Bon. This will more than double the population of the City, which has steadily ebbed away from 113,000 in 1861 to around 5,000 today, as the rising value of the land for commercial uses has pushed out the inhabitants. The residential zone should be completed in 1969, provided bitter strikes among the contractors' workmen, which have greatly increased costs, do not still further cripple the work. With its 44-storey blocks of flats, Guildhall School of Music and new concert hall for the London Symphony Orchestra, the Barbican is one of the biggest comprehensive schemes in Western Europe, and one of the most progressive. It promises a new dimension for the City, and is one answer to the critics who say that the City is run by conservative clubmen.

Five 18-storey office blocks (there is to be a sixth) provide the guts of the commercial zone. They line Route 11, one of the more absurd stretches of urban planning. This is a six-lane highway which appears to go from nowhere to nowhere for just over a quarter of a mile. It does in fact make a fairly unimportant link between Moorgate and Aldersgate. It was originally planned in the early post-war days as part of a northern by-pass to the City and was opened in 1959. But today not even a start has been made on most of the remainder of the northern by-pass, so that the money spent on Route 11 has been largely unproductive. Responsibility for this would be hard to pin down, but it probably lies somewhere between the Ministry of Transport, the Treasury and the old system of planning public investment.

The Corporation paid £4 million for the land in the commercial area. Having approved a very specific design for the towers, and put the developers' architects into a straitjacket, it then proceeded to offer the sites to tender to the highest bidder. In the early stages there was great scepticism about the idea of building offices on a site peopled before the war by rag trade merchants and their warehouses. Moor House and Lee House today stand on the first two sites to be put out to tender, Moor in June 1957 and Lee in October 1957. Twelve developers tendered for Moor and the winner was Charles Clore. He paid the Corporation £33,250 a year fixed to 2070, or 5s. 9d. for each square foot of lettable floor space. Four months later the property world was gloomier about the prospects for Route 11; only three developers wanted to take the chance to bid for Lee House. Everyone was doubtful whether Route 11 was not 100 yards too far for a stockbroker to sprint from Throgmorton Street. Joe Gold carried off the dubious prize with a lower bid than Clore's on Moor. Gold tended to be a highly optimistic character and that he decided to sub-lease the entire project shows just how nervous the developers were of the risk. (His company also needed extra finance at the time, and in order to float off some shares to the public, it was better to have a secure, let investment rather than a speculative, unlet maze of scaffolding.)

Between 1957 and 1960 rents in London had moved up from around 25s. to 35s. and Joe Gold was able to sub-let for £67,538 more a year than he was paying the Corporation, which gave him a capital profit of roughly £1 million for no outlay at all. He leased it to a syndicate of Felix Fenston, the Rose brothers and Prince Radziwill,* and it was Radziwill's wife, Lee, sister-in-law of President Kennedy, who topped out the block and gave it her name. This syndicate had made a profit of some £1·8 million by the time the building was let.

Between Moor and Lee is St Alphage House, the one tower which was not put out to tender. This was due to the fruitful negotiations of Maurice Wingate, who came to this country from Poland in 1931 'with a £5 note in my pocket'. In 1957 he and his friends bought control of a Victorian textile warehouse company, the Fore Street Warehouse Company, whose most valuable asset was the ownership of a heap of rubble, once the Fore Street Warehouse, just north of Route 11. The company was paid £250,000 in compensation for this 1-acre site by the Corporation, higher than the average for the zone, and was also granted a lease across the road in order to rebuild its warehouses. Maurice Wingate was not in the least interested in rebuilding the warehouses for their own sake. He was attracted by the tower of offices above the warehouse space which accompanied the permission.

* See chapter 8.

The upshot was that Fore Street Warehouse took a lease on the ground for £31,000 a year, which it in turn sub-let for £64,000 to St Alphage House Ltd, thus netting a profit of some £500,000. St Alphage House was owned 25 per cent by Wingate Investments (controlled by Maurice Wingate), and 25 per cent by Neil Westbrook, largely in return for persuading Sir Robert McAlpine & Sons to provide the building finance; 40 per cent was owned by private companies of the McAlpines and 10 per cent by Gerald Glover. On one view, by the highest standards of City ethics this 50 per cent might well have been put into a public company with public shareholders, Edger Investments, owned partly by the McAlpines and partly by Mr Gerald Glover. On another, held by McAlpines and Mr Glover, this is not a valid criticism because agreement to put the St Alphage development into a private company had been reached by January 1959 and Edger did not go public until April 1959. (The private company, St Alphage Investment Company Ltd, was incorporated in May of that year.)

The two towers on the south side of Route 11 were put out to tender as the spiral in rents was gathering pace. The site of Royex House was leased by Oldham Estate, the Hyams/Wimpey company,* in 1959 at 11s. 6d. a square foot and 40 Basinghall Street by Wates and the Phoenix Assurance in 1960 at 15s. a square foot. Even though these prices were well above those for the first three, they were probably rather more profitable than the

THE FIVE BIG BLOCKS ON ROUTE 11

	Rents paid to Corporation per lettable sq. ft.	Developers	Office rents received by developers	Capital profits inc. on profit rentals
Moor House	5s. 9d.	Charles Clore	32s. 6d.	£1·4 million
St Alphage House	4s. 6d.	Wingate/Westbrook/ Glover/McAlpine	31s. 6d.	£2·5 million
Lee House	3s. 10½d.	Gold/Fenston/ Roses/Radziwill	35s.	£2·6 million
Royex House	11s. 6d.	Hyams/Wimpey	60s.	£2·9 million
40 Basinghall Street	15s.	Wates/Phoenix	65s.	£2·7 million

* See chapter 8.

blocks on the north side. Wates leased their floor space to IBM at 65s. a square foot, roughly double the rents paid in Moor House.

Nestling under Route 11 and slightly to the south is another office block, fitting with a more squat design into the Barbican pattern. The ownership of this block, which was completed in 1965, is somewhat different from that of the other five, although the land here also belongs to the Corporation.

This is Gillett House, named after and partly owned by Sir Harold Gillett, a chartered accountant who was Lord Mayor of London in 1958–59. Negotiations to lease the site began in 1960.

The unusual aspect of this development is that the site was never put out to tender by the City Corporation, unlike the other five sites, with the exception of St Alphage House. The City Corporation has never publicly explained why it was not put out to tender, but was instead disposed of by private negotiation. There was almost every reason in favour of a tender. By the time the Gillett House site was dealt with—the agreement to lease was signed in July 1962—the other tenders were being eagerly competed for by developers. With an office block and where there are restrictions on the developer's design, as at the Barbican, there is nothing to be lost by a tender to the highest bidder. Moreover, the public can see that their local authority is pulling in the best possible price for the land.

There was one important restriction on the developers of Gillett House, which holds 64,000 square feet of offices and 14,000 square feet of shops. The offices had to be let in not less than seventeen separate tenancies. The purpose of this clause was apparently to help some of the smaller firms in the City who might find it hard to lease space in new buildings. Developers prefer, whenever possible, to let a building to one tenant; management is easier and the security of the rent paid by one first class tenant is more valuable than rent from a cluster. However, there seems to be no strong reason why this restrictive clause could not have been written in to a competition by tender. It would not have been a barrier for most developers.

I am not suggesting that Sir Harold Gillett and his friends did not pay a fair market price for that slice of the City's land. At £66,000 a year, again fixed to 2070, it was significantly higher per square foot than the offer made by Wates for the site of 40 Basinghall Street in February 1960. However, there is no way of telling that another more optimistic developer than Sir Harold Gillett's consortium might not have paid several thousand more to the City.

The agreement with the City in July 1962 was that a lease should be granted to the Prudential, which was providing the finance and which would then sub-lease to Gillett House Ltd when the building was finished and the cost of construction could be met by a mortgage. The shareholders in Gillett House Ltd were mainly Sir Harold Gillett and his partners in Dixon, Wilson, Tubbs and Gillett, chartered accountants, Messrs Tubbs, Hardie and Gaston. But officials of the City Corporation were astonished to find an advertisement in the *Estates Gazette*, as Gillett House neared completion, inviting applications from tenants, and announcing the building as 'a Town and City development'. It was no part of the original agreement that Gillett and friends should almost at once sell off their shares in Gillett House. However, it turned out that Town and City only owned 57½ per cent of the capital.

Sir Harold Gillett and his partners did nicely out of their development. The building can hardly have cost more than £600,000. It was complete and largely let by the end of 1966. At £3 a square foot for its 64,000 square feet, ignoring 14,000 square feet of shops and a restaurant, the value will be around £1,780,000 after ground rent is deducted. Gillett House Ltd will then have made a profit of some £1,180,000, or £120,000 for Sir Harold Gillett, £329,000 for Mr Tubbs and Mr Hardie, who owned some shares jointly, and £31,800 for Mr Gaston. This ignores any profit which they may have made on selling 57½ per cent to Barry East's powerful Town and City Properties.

Apart from the blocks along Route 11, where regimentation was successfully forced on the developers by the City, few of the developments in the Square Mile have attempted to break away from the accepted speculative norm. Two exceptions, late arrivals on the scene, are Seifert's skyscraper for Hyams in Drapers' Gardens, a stone's throw from the Stock Exchange, and the group of buildings near the Tower of London by George, Trew, Dunn for the City of London Real Property.

One of the largest post-war developments in the City was the Bucklersbury House and Temple Court project. This was promoted by Sir Aynsley Bridgland and his associates in conjunction with the Legal and General. It is the first building discussed by

Ian Nairn in his paperback for London Transport, *Modern Buildings in London*. He says of it: 'This mass of building has a lot of storeys, a lot of windows, freedom from pointlessly applied period detail, freedom from obvious gracelessness, freedom from obvious megalomania. It has no virtues and no vices: it is the null point of architecture, the base line for the judgments in the rest of the book . . .'

The history of this development has several aspects, aesthetic, financial and political. Its design was not of Sir Aynsley Bridgland's choosing. Sir Aynsley, who died in 1966, was one of those self-made men who was fiercely conservative in every sense of the word. He objected to modern architecture both on the grounds that he did not like the look of it and that, being new and untried, it was less likely to be readily acceptable to the institutions which lent money on security of the buildings. He started to buy bits and pieces of the 5-acre site bounded by Queen Victoria Street, Walbrook, Cannon Street and Queen Street in the late 1940s. Bucklersbury House was designed in the early 1950s, before the rise of curtain walled modernism. Bridgland plumped for a massive Portland Stone affair, at which the planners of the LCC gibbed, although the City rather liked it. After a long four-cornered tussle between Bridgland, his architect, the LCC and the Royal Fine Arts Commission—'Bridgland could be a very foul mouthed man,' said one of the participants—the building was transformed into an entirely different shape from the original plan, which was to have marched around the edge of the site with a courtyard in the middle, and new materials were summoned up. This became the first of London's glass boxes, the guinea-pig for its successors. Bridgland grumbled heartily all through the period of building but at the end he was quite pleased since he reaped the glory as the promoter of the first glass box.

Once the design of Bucklersbury House was settled, a drama arose at its foundations. As the excavators gouged out the site for Bucklersbury House in 1954, Professor Grimes, now director of the University of London Institute of Archaeology, dug about on the bed of an old stream, the Walbrook. The bombs had opened up an unexpected opportunity for archaeologists to delve into the early history of the City. To Grimes fell the thankless task of making the most of this rare chance. His operations—from 1947 to 1962—were supported by a grant of £2,500 a year from the

Ministry of Works and small private contributions. Naturally he had a minimum of staff and equipment. The City itself gave two incredibly mean grants: one of £250 and another, after it had received some magnificent and free trophies from the Temple of Mithras, of £300. Nothing was done by the City to clear the rubble in order to help excavation in the early post-war years before rebuilding started.

Grimes was continually faced with a race against time to excavate between preliminary clearing of a site by contractors and the start of construction. So it was on the Bucklersbury House site. Without much evidence it was thought to be an important Roman site. Nothing exciting was discovered until the last Friday of the work. The last cutting was made, one of the diggers found a vaguely promising featureless stone at the bottom and asked Professor Grimes for advice. Grimes replied that the stone should be left on one side and that tomorrow, extending the excavations by one day, they would slightly widen the trench. The next morning, after it had been moved, an inquisitive visitor picked up the stone and called out, 'Look what I've found'. It was the head of Mithras. A press photographer appeared and the public ballyhoo about the Temple of Mithras began to snowball. Long queues of visitors, Ministerial statements in the House of Commons and pleas to Bridgland to delay his office block. At first unwilling, he did delay. But not long afterwards he was paid back with the CBE and, a few years later, a knighthood. The fate of the Temple of Mithras itself, though, was less august. It was to be dismantled and reconstructed as near to its original site as the huge office block permitted. For several years the pieces mouldered in a builders' yard in Surrey. Then, prodded by private criticism and some lobbying that the Temple was decaying, the Legal and General, occupiers of the offices, prepared plans for reconstruction. Professor Grimes was consulted. Then he was invited to a press conference to inspect the reincarnated temple. He recalled that he was horrified by what he saw. 'A building of that sort has certain characteristics. The reconstruction bore little relation to them. The levels were all wrong. The well in one corner was ridiculous. Above all there was that extraordinarily stupid business of putting down crazy paving.' However, the rebuilt Temple of Mithras stands above the pavement, next to Bucklersbury House, happily visited by tourists. But it has a somewhat flat and meaningless look to it, a sad outcome to a dramatic and significant excavation.

What has never been excavated in any depth is the precise ownership of the two companies, Legenland and Cantling, which developed Bucklersbury House itself and its neighbour Temple Court, the head office of the Legal and General. The two buildings sit side by side on the same island site. Both companies were owned 50 per cent by Legal and General and both were private companies, so that there has never been any special reason to look at the owners of the other 50 per cent. However, the shareholders' register does throw up some interesting reflections for the 87,000 shareholders of Lloyds Bank.

Legenland Property was registered on 1 September 1949. By 21 October the first properties on the site had been bought and a mortgage was registered in favour of Lloyds Bank, Lombard Street, for a loan of up to £130,000. On 9 November the shares in Legenland were allotted at a price of £1 apiece: 25,000 to the Legal and General, 15,498 to two companies connected with Aynsley Bridgland, 1,500 to Cyril Black and his wife, others to associates of Bridgland and of Black. Towards the bottom of the list was a small parcel of 500 shares, allotted to Ernest Whitley-Jones (address given as Lombard Street and occupation as banker), who happened at that time to be a chief general manager of Lloyds Bank. Mr Whitley-Jones was a Welsh ball of fire, who had worked his way from clerk in 1907 in the Union Bank of Manchester via the Bank of West Africa in Egypt, where he was assistant manager in Alexandria, and then up the Lloyds Bank tree to the pinnacle of chief general manager in 1946.

Legenland prospered with the help of Lloyds Bank, and as it bought more and more of the island site, Lloyds provided virtually all the bridging finance. By the end of August 1956 the site was finally bought and construction was well under way. All seemed rosy. So it was. On 15 January 1957 all the other shareholders were bought out by the Legal and General at £30 a share, a profit of 3,000 per cent, or a total of £1·5 million on the building. Mr Whitley-Jones, for his part, had a profit of £14,500 tax free.

Meanwhile, another project promoted by Aynsley Bridgland was moving ahead opposite Knightsbridge Barracks. The company here, Malkay Investments, was also to develop an office block which, isolated at that time from any near-by offices—Bowater

House was not yet built—was thought by Bridgland to be a particularly wild speculation. Malkay started with ten shareholders each chipping in £1,000. One of these was Mr Roy Matthews, a non-executive director of Lloyds. Once again Lloyds lent the bridging finance and again Whitley-Jones was in the deal as a shareholder with 500 shares. By then he had retired as chief general manager, but had joined the board. However, another chief general manager, Arthur Hinton Ensor, subscribed for 1,000 shares at the same time as Whitley-Jones, in January 1954. In October 1957 the Malkay shares were bought at £5 each by a public company with Bridgland as chairman. Whitley-Jones made £2,000 tax free; Ensor made £4,000 and Matthews £4,000. Ensor justified this participation to me by pointing out that, although he was still chief general manager when he subscribed for the shares in Malkay, he had been promised by Bridgland that he would be a director of the company once he retired in July 1954; and that Lloyds did not lend any bridging money to Malkay until after his retirement from the executive.

Cantling Property Company was set up in 1955 for the second stage of the Bucklersbury site. Ensor too had been elected to the board and is still a director. Mr Whitley-Jones died in 1965. With Cantling the pattern was much the same as with the other two companies. Lloyds lent the bridging money, both Ensor and Matthews were shareholders, and in January 1957 Legal and General bought out Bridgland and friends, who included many distinguished medical gentlemen. (Bridgland was an active patron, in his autocratic way, of the London Clinic.) The profit on the Cantling shares was 1,460 per cent.

These cases raise important points of principle. For the directors of a joint stock bank to own shares in a private company, which relies on finance from that bank, seems a pity. However, the non-executive directors of a bank are often there partly in order to bring in new business and perhaps they need some reward for that. Besides, they seldom take decisions on whether to lend or not to a particular company. But, by the strictest standards and to escape any possible criticism, it looks a weak principle.

For a chief general manager, on the other hand, who has overall responsibility for day-to-day lending of big sums, it might be thought undesirable to participate in this way in his borrower's company. With Legenland and Malkay these were big sums—up to £2,800,000 to Legenland. The profits for each man were not spectacular, but they were handsome in relation to the probable savings of a career banker. It takes a good many years for a man even on a high salary to save the equivalent of £14,500 tax free. Could the judgment of Whitley-Jones have been completely detached and impartial when he was in effect lending money for a scheme in which he had a share, albeit a small one?

Ensor's case was somewhat different; he had ceased to have executive powers when the first loan to Malkay was made. But it raises the question of bank managers joining the boards of property companies on retirement. Mr Ensor told me that he took up the shares in Malkay while still in office because he knew from Bridgland that he was to join the company's board when he retired.

In the last fifteen years or so several ex-West End or City branch managers have joined the boards of property companies. It is, of course, not uncommon for professional men to join the boards of companies on retiring from or leaving their jobs. But a retired bank manager is not an obvious choice for the board of a property company. It would be interesting to know whether any of these gentlemen knew that they would be asked to join particular boards when they left their banks. For an executive banker to be a shareholder in a private company to which his bank lends money or to know that he will be a director of such a company on retiring seems altogether undesirable.

Were Lloyds Bank an American company and the watchdog Securities and Exchange Commission in operation, it is highly likely that it would have used sanctions against the company on behalf of Lloyds' 87,000 shareholders.

CHAPTER SEVEN

The Old Estates, the Church and the Railways

THE City of London, Birmingham and other local authorities all over the country were the new ground landlords of the post-war era. Bit by bit, from about the time of the Reform Bill onwards local authorities had been extending their ownership, under powers of road building, slum clearance and other improvement schemes, on which the Victorians congratulated themselves so warmly. But since the war the growth in that ownership has been explosive. In Birmingham, one of the most acquisitive cities, and controlled by Labour politicians for most of the period, as many as 4,795 acres of land have been bought since 1945.

While the new landlords of the people were rapidly adding to their possessions, the old ground landlords, the great aristocratic and institutional estates, were holding their ground against rising taxation with uncanny resilience. The idea that these ancient estates have been broken up and scattered by taxation is largely a myth. Some, caught on the wrong foot by death duty, have been weakened. But many have remained static, or, managed by astute delegates of the beneficiaries, have adjusted to the changes in the property market and emerged richer than ever. In London one major newcomer, Ellerman, has in this century taken his place alongside the Grosvenors and the Cadogans, the Russells and the Howard de Waldens, the Portmans, Rugby School and Eton College, the City Livery companies, and, not least, the Church Commissioners for England. The Livery companies owned about a fifth of the building land in the City in 1939. They probably own a similar proportion today.

The transformation of the Church from a static, rather passive landowner into a live wire in the property business was the most dramatic revitalisation of a great landlord. In the process it has in London sold 300 acres of houses and flats and land to local authorities, an area about half the size of the City of London, and plunged with skill into the arms and the profits of property developers. The assets of the Church Commissioners, £336 million in 1966, exist primarily to pay clergymen their salaries and the Commissioners have quite reasonably inferred that it is their duty to earn as high a commercial return as any normal, safety-first trust and to make this income grow. When this policy has meant building high-class flats they have been attacked, sometimes by their parsons, for not providing homes for the needy.

The needy tended to be the C. of E. clergymen. In 1948, when the Church Commissioners was formed by the merger of the £70 million of the Queen Anne's Bounty with the £140 million of the Ecclesiastical Commissioners, Archbishop Fisher was aiming at a minimum gross salary for every clergyman of £500 a year; by 1966, after eighteen years of financial revolution, the average was a net salary of £1,189. Before the merger, which had been recommended for over half a century before, the two bodies existed for almost identical and sometimes overlapping purposes. But Queen Anne's Bounty was an unwieldy giant. It had 700 governors. The Measure of the Church Assembly which set up the Church Commissioners laid down the important rule that, besides the traditional gilt-edged stocks and land, the assets could be invested in industrial ordinary shares.

One of the acquisitions to the new body was Mortimer Warren, a chartered accountant who had joined Queen Anne's Bounty in 1927 and was appointed financial secretary to the Church Commissioners. Soon after the merger Warren produced a decisive document, suggesting that the Church should sell large amounts of gilt-edged and re-invest in ordinary shares; similarly, that it should sell many of its properties yielding a fixed rent for 99 or 999 years and invest in properties let direct to tenants at or near the market rent. The Archbishop of Canterbury, Archbishop Fisher, persuaded the Commissioners forcefully of the change of policy. The Commissioners did not all take strongly to the change at once. Some did not understand it; some were worried; some understood and accepted. For about three years there were doubts but then the new investments began to be seen to be swelling the Commissioners' coffers and acceptance was general. If the equities had fallen, Mortimer Warren would have been in grave trouble.

As it was, he was knighted ten years later for making the temporal life of the parsonage more tolerable.

The turning point for the Church's property portfolio came in the mid-fifties. In 1954 Sir Malcolm Trustram Eve, later Lord Silsoe, a shrewd lawyer who had been chairman of the War Damage Commission and of the Central Land Board, became First Church Estates Commissioner. Had the Church Commissioners been a private investment trust, which in effect it was on a huge scale, the hierarchy would have been the Archbishop of Canterbury, president, Trustram Eve, chairman, and Warren, managing director. Like Warren, Trustram Eve was a keen advocate of moving as fast as possible out of fixed interest investments. The policy of selling acres of houses held on ground rents was speeded up.

In 1955 the Church put up for auction one of the biggest acreages it ever sold, 65 acres of its troublesome Paddington Estate. At the end of the war it owned about one-third of the Borough of Paddington, or 500 acres, most of which had belonged to the Bishops of London since the Middle Ages. Part of the estate had degenerated into slum and it held pockets of prostitution, but since the land was mostly let on long, loosely worded building leases in the last century, the Church was often powerless to combat the problems. Attacks from its critics that its rents were 'tainted money from slums' or suggestions that the Church was in some way allied with brothelkeepers were not in line with its aspirations. Quite apart from much of the estate being unsuitable purely as investment, it became politic to sell to owner-occupiers, or to the local authority for slum clearance and redevelopment, or to private investors.

In November 1955 the Church Commissioners made an historic deal in Eastbourne Terrace, alongside Paddington Station, with Max Rayne. Since the war the Church had lent money on mortgage to several of the new developers, to Harold Samuel and to his cousins, Basil and Howard, to Arnold Silverstone, to Dudley Witting, and to Max Rayne himself. But it was Rayne, who was then thirty-seven and had been in property for only eight years, who took this august body to the site and made them taste the profit in actually being the developer themselves.

It seems appropriate that Max Rayne was the man, more than any other, who tapped the natural resources of the great estates

THE GREAT ESTATES OF CENTRAL LONDON

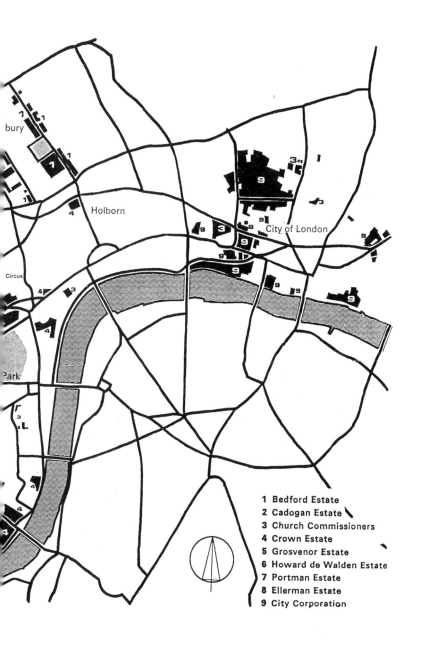

bury

7

Holborn

Circus

City of London

Park

.L

1 Bedford Estate
2 Cadogan Estate
3 Church Commissioners
4 Crown Estate
5 Grosvenor Estate
6 Howard de Walden Estate
7 Portman Estate
8 Ellerman Estate
9 City Corporation

and helped them to help themselves. Apart from the Church, he formed associations with Lord Portman on the Portman Estate north of Oxford Street, with Eton College in Swiss Cottage, and with a Scottish laird, Colonel William Stirling, on a 5,000-acre estate just outside Glasgow. He was also called in as director and adviser and saviour by the New River Company (the oldest company quoted on the Stock Exchange) which had been roused to action by takeover raiders. The New River Company was begun in 1619 by Sir Hugh Myddleton and 'his company of co-adventurers' to dig the canal and bring water from Hertfordshire to London; at the opening ceremony King James I fell in. From 1904 onwards the company only owned the land on either side of the New River.

The grandchildren of the developers will no doubt be the aristocrats of the next century, in fact if not in name, but Max Rayne seems to have started as one, quite apart from having married Lady Jane Vane-Tempest-Stewart. His manner and appearance are as far from the brash as could be. He is soft-spoken and elegant to a degree, but extremely businesslike and tidy-minded, with an immaculate eye for detail. He works from an office off Wigmore Street, furnished in flawless good taste and unusually small, 'every square foot of our own building is carefully costed'. One wall is entirely covered by a huge map of London. He is the son of a Polish immigrant in the rag trade and worked for his father before and after his spell as a corporal in the RAF during the war. He moved into property in 1947 after sub-letting and mortgaging an office in Wigmore Street hired by his father and himself for their tiny textile business.

Max Rayne is a man who realised as much as anybody the value of contacts in property development, and he was more able than most to inspire confidence in the Establishment of that disestablished world. An early piece of luck was his relationship with Sir Edward Gillett, a chartered surveyor who ran Daniel Smith, Oakley and Garrard, one of the old firms of estate agents and surveyors which advised the traditional landowners of London. Not long after his first deal in Wigmore Street Max Rayne formed British Commercial Property, a company owned one-third by him, one-third by a relation, Arnold Lee, and one-third by Rayne's father. Arnold Lee was a solicitor with a special liking for conveyancing, who graduated naturally to property. Starting with 103 Mount Street, the property British Commercial was specifically formed to buy, Lee and Rayne worked together on half a dozen of their earliest projects. They drifted apart as each became more powerful and Rayne's master company, London Merchant Securities, bought out Arnold Lee's share in British Commercial in 1958. Lee then built up his own company, Imry, and floated it in 1962 with a market value of £2 million. That first joint deal, 103 Mount Street, was financed by the Norwich Union, which took the advice of Edward Gillett on the property.

This contact with Gillett in 1948 bore rich fruit in due course. The Norwich Union put up millions for the developments of both Max Rayne and Arnold Lee. But Gillett was also surveyor to the Portman family, which until shortly after the seventh Lord Portman died in 1948 had owned 258 acres of London, most of it since 1533. After two big auction sales in the early fifties to contribute towards £7·5 million of death duties, the Portmans were left with 108 acres (see the map facing page 82) including four squares, Portman, Bryanston, Montagu and Manchester, and a slice of the most valuable land in the country: that stretch of Oxford Street from Selfridges to Marble Arch which houses a Marks & Spencer, thought to be the busiest store in the world. Gillett's confidence in Rayne gave the entrée to a highly strategic stock of raw material and Rayne developed several more profitable buildings around Baker Street.

Lord Portman was the original owner of Rayne's first big deal, a £2 million office development in Wigmore Street which was almost a disaster. The ground landlord was then Selfridges, which had been bought in 1951 by Lewis' Investment Trust. At the back of Selfridges was an island block which Lewis' offered to developers by tender in 1952. Gillett was also the surveyor to Selfridges and Max Rayne was nominated the chosen developer. Rayne had lined up Marks & Spencer as prospective tenant for the offices and this secured him finance from the Norwich Union. At the last moment Marks & Spencer decided on a different building in Baker Street so that Rayne's plans were on the point of collapse. However, he eventually persuaded an established property group to take up 37½ per cent of the project and supply the finance. He was saved. His company came out of the deal with a profit of £850,000, a turning point in his career. When Charles Clore was in the throes of his £62 million takeover bid for Lewis'

Investment Trust in 1965, he remarked gruffly that the best thing Sir Rex Cohen ever did with Selfridges—the Cohens were effectively the controlling shareholders in Lewis'—was to make Max Rayne a millionaire.

The deal with the Church in Eastbourne Terrace was also lubricated by Max Rayne's contact with Sir Edward Gillett. The site was to have been sold in January 1956 by Daniel Smith, Oakley and Garrard as part of the reorganisation of the Paddington Estate. Max Rayne suggested to the Church Commissioners that they should keep the site and redevelop it in partnership with him. Sir Edward Gillett sang the praises of Max Rayne to Mortimer Warren and the deal was clinched. The net effect of this alliance was startling. First, the group of office buildings designed by C. H. Elsom was praised by the architectural press,* which was a rare event for a developer's building. Secondly, the cost of the buildings was £1¾ million and the profit to the joint company was £5·8 million by 1966. The Church financed the entire cost. Max Rayne had put up a mere £1,000 as his share of the joint company and his company, London Merchant Securities, made half the profit, £2·9 million. What had Max Rayne done to achieve this profit? In essence he had produced an idea. From the joint company, of which they admittedly owned half, the Church received an income via ground rent on the value of the site had they sold it. But had it not been for Rayne's idea and judgment, they would not have made a far higher income from the joint company and a potential profit of £2·9 million. Such was the value of a developer.

But this was not all that the Church Commissioners gained from Eastbourne Terrace. It opened their eyes to the possibilities of active co-operation with developers, not only on land they already owned, but in new pastures. Between 1958, when it was apparent that Eastbourne Terrace would be a cracking success, and 1962, the property development company specially formed by the Commissioners, the Church Estates Development and Improvement Company, had taken shares in another twenty-five joint companies with a variety of developers. By 1966 the total cost of developments in the CEDIC companies was £38·1 million, of which £20·4 million was completed. Much the biggest office project was the £9 million Paternoster group by St Paul's, delayed for several years by planning wrangles over its design, in which

* See the *Architects' Journal* of 16 April 1959.

the Church took three contractors, Laing, Wimpey and Trollope & Colls as partners.

Through the late fifties, as the Church moved deeper into commercial property, it was all the while selling large areas of small houses around London, in Southwark and Camberwell, Hammersmith, Ealing and Notting Hill. Even so it had 20,000 houses left in 1966, and 160,000 acres of farmland. It sold the freehold of Paddington Station, which was leased for £2,500 a year for 2,000 years, for £43,000 in 1958. The original lease from the Church to the Great Western Railway Company had stipulated that 'engines shall consume their own smoke'. In 1959 it sold the freehold of Millionaires' Avenue, The Bishop's Avenue, Finchley—presumably to the millionaire householders.

By 1958 there was a second daughter of CEDIC in existence, also jointly with Max Rayne. Here the Church was stepping out of its old boundaries and was using the second main formula for its developments. In this case, as well as the skill, Max Rayne found the land. The Church again put up all the money and the company's capital was shared 40/60 in favour of Rayne. The land was the 5½-acre Cartwright Estate, the bulk of four city blocks in the gridiron of streets touching and just to the west of the Tottenham Court Road. This was a case of the end of a family estate, sold to pay death duty when a tree fell on the car of Mr Cartwright and his son, killing them both.

This estate was to be auctioned, but Max Rayne, like many other developers, approached the selling agents before the auction. Rayne bought it for £320,000. After spending £275,000 on buying neighbouring bits and pieces, another £200,000 on buying out leaseholders, and rather over £3 million on new buildings, a total cost of £4 million, the value had jumped to £11 million by 1966. The Church, by trusting the relatively untried Rayne in Eastbourne Terrace, had let themselves in for a deal showing a capital gain of £2·8 million in the Tottenham Court Road. And, more important to them than the capital appreciation, a very high income.

One single office block on the Cartwright Estate rubs in the mathematics of the era. This was a building of 60,000 square feet, which Max Rayne estimated would let at 12s. 6d. a square foot soon after he bought Cartwright. Had it been let at 12s. 6d., its value would have then been around £640,000 against a cost of £300,000, a profit of £340,000. As it was costs rose to £500,000.

But rents rose too. By the time it was finished, the floor space was let at 60s. a square foot, giving a value of £2·7 million and a profit of £2·2 million instead of £340,000. That amazing spiral in rents was a combination of four factors: inflation, demand shooting up ahead of supply, Government restrictions on offices and the developer's peculiar skill of making such an impact on a locality that he improves its values at a greater speed than the market as a whole.

The most daring enterprise of the Commissioners, the re-development of the entire 90-acre slice of London in the triangle bordered by Bayswater Road, Edgware Road and Sussex Gardens, was based on the same developer's principle of elevating an area by the very momentum and scale of the development itself.* The Hyde Park Estate, once considered the wrong side of the Park, was one of the bits left after the Paddington Estate had been tailored to fit the modern needs and public image of the Church. It was a faded residential area, first built over in the 1830s, and with the leases falling in the Commissioners decided to bring in an architect, Anthony Minoprio, to draw up a general plan for the whole area and rebuild en bloc. They enlisted three partners—Cotton and Clore's City Centre fell out because of liquidity problems at the time—in order to add a finer appreciation of the market; the three were Wates, Max Rayne's London Merchant Securities and Great Portland Estates, the Basil and Howard Samuel company. Relatively little private residential development has been attempted inside London since the war for fear of politics and the high cost of building, so that the provision of £12 million worth of 763 flats and 112 houses involved a big risk. But in one corner the Commissioners launched out on their own and developed their first 100 per cent controlled project at a cost of £4 million: the Water Gardens. Finished in the spring of 1966, 228 of the 238 flats in this pleasant development were let by the spring of the following year, a remarkably high rate of success.

One side effect of the pruning and trading up of the old estates was that the fall out presented a magnificent opportunity to the property dealer, that is, where they were not sold to the local authorities. When an estate was spread over a wide area and was split into hundreds of individual properties, there were few buyers

* See also Joe Levy and the Euston Centre, page 157, and Bill Zeckendorf and the United Nations, page 199.

around with the know-how to value such mixed bags or the inclin-
ation to manage them. This is where the incomparable dealer of
the period, Max Joseph, came in. Of many deals, perhaps his
most breathtaking was his purchase of a 25-acre chunk of the
Church's old Paddington Estate, known as the Hyde Park North
Estate, or occasionally Sin Triangle. It stretched from Paddington
Station to Lancaster Gate and took in 680 properties, mainly large
Victorian houses split up into flats.

Joseph bought Hyde Park North for £500,001 in October 1958.
The sequence of events was that the Church sold its 65-acre
parcel specifically to a buyer who it thought might keep the
estate intact, to the Royal Liver. But the Royal Liver passed on a
lease of 25 of the acres to a certain Lucaston Share and Property
Trading Company. Having paid £500,001, Joseph then popped it
into a 'shell' controlled by himself and one of his lawyers, Leonard
Tobin, who was a shareholder in Lucaston. The 'shell' was Lintang
Investments, which was the following year to be the lynch-pin of
the biggest post-war financial scandal, the State Building Society
Affair, though Joseph and Tobin both had clean hands throughout.
However, at the end of 1958 it was their unobtrusive 'shell', own-
ing Hyde Park North. The next step was to have the Estate re-
valued in order to float Lintang. Bourner's Goddard & Smith did
so and came up with the impressive figure of £1·2 million in
February 1959, with the result that Max Joseph had bought the
Estate at well under half its true value five months later. A second
property was then inserted into Lintang, the celebrated Dolphin
Square, the mammoth block of flats in Victoria. Joseph had
bought this from its pre-war builders, Richard Costain, in November 1958 for £2·375 million and that too was valued by Goddard &
Smith the following February—at £3·1 million.

Now came the pay-off. Lintang was floated in March 1959 in
one of the most exciting scenes ever seen on the Stock Exchange.
This was triggered off by the dual magic of a new property issue
and the name of Max Joseph. By that time Joseph had impressed
the inmates of the Stock Exchange as an operator of great financial
finesse, which he was. He ran a one-man office; at his headquarters
in a house in Mayfair there was himself and a secretary. The rest
of his empire was delegated elsewhere. Later he was to be better
known to the public for the large number of hotels which he had
gathered into his Grand Metropolitan Hotels group. Their success

rested to a large extent on his managing director, the brilliant hotelier Fred Kobler.

The commotion caused by the arrival of Lintang was said to be even greater than the sensational rush for Morris Motors nearly thirty years before. When the house opened at 9 o'clock, half an hour earlier than usual to cope with the rush, the queue of 400 brokers eager to buy Lintang, some waiting from the early hours, stretched most of the length of Throgmorton Street. The shares had been offered at 11s. 6d. each. They started off at 16s. and within minutes shot up to 22s. In effect investors at large were deciding that a company, valued by experts in the offer at £3·6 million, was immediately worth £7 million.

This hullabaloo over Lintang had all the ingredients of a shanty town gold rush. It is fantastic in retrospect that a share with net assets, recently valued, of 10s. apiece should have been lapped up at once at over double that. But this ignores the heady glamour of property shares bubbling up in 1959, and the unquestioning faith in the heroes of the property world. Max Joseph, though, always cool-headed and a master at understanding the stock market, was calm in the face of the investing public's hysteria. He and Tobin sold their shares steadily through the summer of 1959, so that by July they controlled only 54 per cent of the capital, against 70 per cent in March.

It was in July that Lintang was unwittingly sucked into quite another orbit, the world of the State Building Society, a scandal outside the scope of this book. In essence what happened to Lintang was that Mr Grunwald, sentenced to prison for five years, approached Tobin in order to buy the shares of Lintang at 24s. each, largely with money to be provided by the State Building Society, whose managing director, Mr Murray, was sentenced for five years too. This attempted takeover of Lintang failed since Grunwald could not find enough money to pay for all the shares, and that in turn led to the exposure of the Murray group of companies. The flavour of that hugely intricate affair can be savoured from the otherwise dry but gripping report by Neville Faulks, QC,* now Mr Justice Faulks.

The end result for those investors who had put their faith in

---

* Investigation into the Affairs of H. Jasper & Company Limited (HMSO, 1961). This report is as good as a detective story for students of company affairs.

Max Joseph in March 1959 and rushed for Lintang at 22*s*. apiece
was far from disastrous. Lintang was salvaged and they were
bailed out by the buoyancy of the property market. Hyde Park
North and Dolphin Square were sold in 1963 for well above what
Joseph had paid for them and in liquidation the shareholders were
paid over 20*s*. The liquidation was not without its complexities;
the report to the Inland Revenue on tax alone took a week to type.

Max Joseph bought another cast-off of an ancient estate, the St
George's Estate, a 42-acre swathe of Pimlico, which was once part
of the richest estate of all, the Grosvenor Estate. The St George's
Estate was bought and sold at rising prices for thirteen years. It
was sold by the Grosvenor Estate in 1952 for much the same reasons as prompted the Church to evacuate most of Paddington.
Troops had been billeted there during the First World War and
afterwards the area had gone to seed. Again, the properties were
let by the Grosvenor Estate on long leases with little control over
the end use. Max Joseph bought it in 1959 for £630,000. He in
turn sold it on to Kennedy Leigh for £970,000 three years later.

Any visitor to the offices of the Grosvenor Estate, known as the
Grosvenor Office, can see at once why its trustees would feel un-
comfortable at the mere suspicion that it owned slum property. A
few doors along from Claridges, it is a large house blending discreetly into the calm of Mayfair. Inside is an atmosphere of mature
country house, panelling and stone floors and well-used antique
furniture; a young man with a labrador, plus fours and twelve-
bore gun might appear in the hall at any moment. In fact this is
just the steward's house of the Duke of Westminster, the steward
in this case being a staff of thirty-five, surveyors and valuers,
accountants, experts on tax, rent collectors, structural engineers,
quantity surveyors and so on. Upstairs in a large, high ceilinged
room adorned with carving by Grinling Gibbons sits Geoffrey
Singer, Surveyor to the Grosvenor Estates, administrator of half
Mayfair and the whole of Belgravia, which is the Duke of Westminster's present-day London parish. Inside that house and that
office it would be hard to think of a farther remove from the world
of, say, Bernard Sunley, with his invitations to champagne and
oyster parties on any one of three consecutive nights. But Westminster and Sunley were in one and the same market, dealing with
the same raw material.

Mayfair and Westminster and other choice pieces of London

were acquired through marriage by Sir Thomas Grosvenor in 1677. The heiress was Mary Davies, aged twelve, who was available only because Lord Berkeley (a Berkeley Square Berkeley) had not been able to find £5,000, the price of marrying Mary with his ten-year-old son. Thomas Grosvenor was at the time far richer than Mary Davies, whose land was then a modest collection of meadows. It had passed to her father from a notorious lawyer and money-lender of the 17th century, Hugh Awdeley. There is a dispute over his character. Soon after his death in 1662 a pamphlet appeared called *The Way to be Rich, According to the Practice of The Great Audley, Who begun with two hundred Pound, in the Year 1605, and dyed worth four hundred thousand Pound.*

Relentless usurer or wise old lawyer, Awdeley's estates did the Grosvenor family a power of good as the years went by. Grosvenor Square was first built over in 1725 and Belgrave Square in 1826. Cubitt and Cundy were the two great builders in Belgravia, and their speculations were on the mark. The rich and the fashionable flooded in to be close to the rebuilt Buckingham Palace. In Belgrave Square in 1860 lived three dukes and thirteen peers, a clutch of baronets, and thirteen MPs. The Duke of Westminster's income grew and grew.

The two wars forced a great change on Mayfair, and to a lesser extent on Belgravia. While the billeting of troops in Pimlico led to the sale of the St George's Estate, the gradual commercialisation of Mayfair and bits of Belgravia made the core of the Grosvenor Estate increasingly valuable. Grosvenor House, the old town house of the Dukes, was sold in the mid-twenties, one of the very few pockets—Claridges is another—where the freehold has been given up. Faceless blocks of flats started to replace other private houses in Park Lane, and Grosvenor Square began its descent into mock Georgian. At the end of the thirties and during the war the residents of Mayfair gradually emigrated, and the Government and other businesses moved in.† This intrusion is supposed to be temporary but the latest extension for office use was until 1990. Hugh, 2nd Duke of Westminster, initiated one of the first chunks of

---

* See also Merryweather's *Lives and Anecdotes of Misers, the Dictionary of National Biography* and Charles T. Gatty's *Mary Davies and the Manor of Ebury.*

† See *Mayfair, A Town Within London,* Reginald Colby (Country Life, 1966).

private redevelopment after the war, 108 flats in four blocks built in 1950–52 in Ebury Street and Cundy Street, let at first at £200 to £250 a year. The other early post-war operation was the lateral conversion of much of Eaton Square (the gardens in Belgravia are looked after by eight Grosvenor gardeners) out of the private house era into luxury flats.

In 1953 the Duke died and an epic of taxpaying began. The exact sum netted by the Revenue from this death has never been disclosed, but the Grosvenor Office is at least prepared to say that it was somewhere between £15 million and £20 million. But even so the domain of 180 acres of Belgravia and 90 acres of Mayfair stayed intact. Instead 50,000 acres of agricultural land was sold, and the estates, which had been spread around eleven counties when the 2nd Duke died in 1953, were made more compact.

Though the Grosvenor Estate is now split up among several beneficiaries as well as the present, 5th Duke, it is still administered as one estate, more like a free enterprise corporation with a board of trustees in place of a board of directors. The senior trustee, George Ridley, began life as a trainee forester sweeping up leaves on the main estate of the Grosvenors at Eaton outside Chester. He graduated slowly to the equivalent job to managing director, a man of sound bourgeois principles of the sort which have saved other aristocratic fortunes from decline. He takes the long view of the assets which he looks after, 'Our ability is to look far, far ahead. Fifty years is nothing to us and 100 years is normal.' The huge Victorian pile, Eaton Hall, ceased to be the Westminsters' country seat before the war and, after a spell as a training college for budding army officers, was demolished. This gives George Ridley quiet satisfaction. He says 'Mansions have been the millstones round many an estate's neck. I believe that families should live in the smallest houses possible.' He can hardly have approved of some of the 2nd Duke's habits: he used to hire an entire train for his hunting expeditions in France.

In this century there has been relatively little new building on the ducal acres of Mayfair and Belgravia. There might well have been much more redevelopment if the land had been in multiple ownership and open to the probing commercialism of the developer. An already hugely wealthy landowner was less interested in raising profitability. Also, the fabric of the 19th century buildings did not need renewal. The increase in value as offices took over in Mayfair and Belgravia was merely a quirk of the passive law that the rich get richer. The spread of embassies was also a helpful support for land values. By 1966 there were twenty-eight embassies on the Grosvenor Estate, including Eero Saarinen's eagle-topped American embassy dominating one side of Grosvenor Square. The Grosvenor Office is proud to tell you that this is the only American embassy in the world whose freehold is not owned by the Government of the United States.

Apart from approximately 150,000 acres of agricultural land remaining with the family, the other urban stronghold of the Grosvenors is Chester. Land in and around Chester belonged to the Grosvenors before they were fortunate enough to be linked to Miss Davies' London dowry. Here the estate has moved decisively into the sphere of the commercial developer. Through a joint company, Grosvenor-Laing, combining the modern skills of the contractor/developer with the land of the ancient estate, sixty-eight shops have been added to the centre of Chester. The Grosvenor Centre is among the best of the modern shopping centres in the country. It is ingeniously fitted in to complete the square of land behind the most famous and bustling of Chester's Rows, Eastgate Street and Bridge Street; it becomes an easy extension of mediaeval and Georgian buildings on the street fronts. The Grosvenor Estate already owned the land, thus avoiding the problem of a developer paying too much and then overloading the site.

Grosvenor-Laing has made pioneering incursions into Canada, mentioned in chapter 13, and has followed up its success in Chester, which happens to be the city or town with the highest rate of spending per head in England, with two major schemes in Liverpool. Although it has missed out as an active participant in the property boom, the Grosvenor Estate may become more and more a developer in its own right both on land which it owns and on land which it does not. Its policymakers take a dim view of future political attitudes towards landowners. Leasehold enfranchisement in theory threatens all private urban estates, but not the variety proposed by the Labour Government in February 1966 and, after the interruption of the March 1966 General Election, again in 1967. That Bill gave the opportunity of enfranchisement up to an arbitrary level of value for each property of £400 rateable value. The idea was that leaseholders in low value property were in much greater need of enfranchisement than those in high value property; the leaseholders in the back doubles of Cardiff and Birmingham, at whom enfranchisement was largely aimed, had to be given some liberating protection from their ground landlords and thus the right by law to buy their freehold on a given formula. The Government was not interested in the leaseholders of Belgravia.

The effect of the £400 rateable limit is to exempt most of the central London estates from the fear of enfranchisement, certainly the Grosvenor Estate and the other estates shown on the map facing page 82. But Geoffrey Singer is pessimistic: 'It only needs a stroke of the pen to raise the limit to £800 or £1,000.' And worse, 'land is now in the same position as steel, and no end can be seen except total nationalisation'. With that ultimate prospect, since the Grosvenor Estate believes that it has a fundamental knowledge of land and wishes to continue to invest in it, it is building up a team so that it can play the active role of developer. In the very long run the Grosvenor Estate may consist only of self-developed properties held on lease from the Crown or from local authorities, while its traditional estates will have been diminished by enfranchisement or compulsory purchase.

The guardians of the great estates, men who talk about their squares as a farmer talks about his fields, tend to be wary, for though some of the most powerful estates are largely intact and certainly more valuable, there are a few notable cases of shrinkage or even total dissolution. Mr Leonard Ayling is Steward of the London Estate of the Bedford Settled Estates, or in other words, the present Duke of Bedford's man in London. His domain in Bloomsbury has been considerably eaten away since the war. The decline began, in fact, just before the First World War, when the Duke of Bedford's grandfather, unusually inept as a man of affairs, sold Covent Garden and invested most of the proceeds, some £2 million, in Tsarist bonds.* 'London University came to us in the late forties and showed us their plans for the next 100 years. We agreed to sell them Gordon Square and Tavistock Square and a few streets adjoining them. Then, after the 12th Duke died in 1953 a large area south of Great Russell Street had to be sold to pay death duties. It makes one mournful to see the estate whittled away,' said Ayling.

* See *A Silver-Plated Spoon*, by John, Duke of Bedford (Cassell, 1959).

Even so, Bedford still makes a lucrative impression on the map of London. One of the few cases of complete break-up was the sale just after the First World War by Lord Berkeley of much of Berkeley Square and land near by to Lord Bearsted, heir to the millions passed on from the Marcus Samuel who helped to found the Shell oil empire in the late 19th century. The Bearsted control over those 14 acres first weakened when it was from 1961 owned jointly by two publicly quoted property companies, the Cotton-Clore City Centre Properties and Samuel Properties, and then disappeared; it sold to City Centre. In turn City Centre sold to the B.P. Pension Fund for £6 million in 1967.

In 1925 the other private new landlord, Sir John Ellerman, made his biggest buy, almost all Great Portland Street and a worthwhile chunk of Oxford Street. The seller was Lord Howard de Walden, who was trimming some of his huge and well-regulated fiefdom of doctors and dentists centred on Harley Street and Wimpole Street. Sir John Ellerman, like his son after him, energetically shunned publicity. But, as the shop purchases described by Dudley Samuel suggest, see page 14, Great Portland Street was only one large aspect of the Ellerman estates. He certainly owned the freehold of the Drury Lane Theatre after the Duke of Bedford. The old Sir John was also a great dealer. He bought a 78-acre estate in Earl's Court in 1930, sold it in 1933. Similarly he sold a 14-acre estate in Hans Place shortly after he had bought it, in 1929, from Lord Cadogan.

Since the war Lord Cadogan has trimmed his sails to the modern winds rather more than most big landowners. His awareness of the financial delights of development stems to a large extent from his association with the solicitor/developer Gerald Glover, who in turn had close links with the contractors McAlpine, see page 72. Glover, Cadogan and McAlpine were ardent followers of horse-racing. Glover's companies leased land from Lord Cadogan for commercial development, notably the Carlton Tower Hotel, and this led to joint companies both with Lord Cadogan and his son, appropriately named Lord Chelsea. A third stage was that the estate drew up an elaborate plan for the gradual development of the whole estate on much more active lines than was normal for a big ground landlord. For part of Pont Street a twenty-six storey residential project was designed by the Japanese architect Yamasaki. These plans were slowed down by the 1965–67 credit and building squeezes, and the uncertainties of the Leasehold Reform Bill.

For those rich families who cared to make the necessary provision of handing property on to a younger generation at the right moment, death duty could be a largely voluntary tax. But a series of unexpected deaths could still upset the best laid plans. Mr Tim Abel-Smith inherited a fortune in one line of the powerful Smith family,* who are descendants of the banker Thomas Smith of Nottingham, 1631 to 1699. One part of his inheritance was a rectangle of freehold property bounded by Park Lane, Hertford Street and Shepherd Street. Exactly how his family had come by this property was uncertain, but it was thought to have arrived in payment of a bad debt in 1815. Tim Abel-Smith was saddled with a gloomy bill for death duty, as there had been two male deaths in his family within seven years. His reasons for wanting to sell the most valuable slice of his London property, the frontage to Park Lane, typify the change of ownership of the old type of landowner to the new. There was a mortgage of £230,000 on it, 'and I was keen to pay off the horrible mortgages'. The developers on the contrary were keen to borrow as much as possible.

Mr Clore bought the Park Lane end of the Abel-Smith property for £550,000 in 1956 and in due course built the Hilton there at a cost of another £5 million. Tim Abel-Smith regretted that he never met Charles Clore; the deal was done discreetly by his agent. Clore knew that the land was for sale and approached the agent at lunch in a restaurant. With the shrewdness of the banking Smiths in his blood, Abel-Smith re-invested the proceeds in two large Scottish estates, which multiplied in value five and a half times over the next ten years. In relative terms he probably did better than Mr Clore, whose total cost was £5½ million and whose hotel was worth £7 million.

The State is a landowner in many different guises, and since nationalisation of the railways in 1947 British Rail has owned strategic and potentially valuable chunks of land, 280,000 acres in all. But to a large extent the potential was ignored. By the time it was realised the boom was over and it was impossible to unlock a vast amount of wasted assets.

The idea that railway land might be used for other than the purposes strictly of carrying passengers was not new. The famous

* See the *Economist* of 28 March, 1959.

façade above St Pancras and the other Victorian terminal hotels show that the private railway companies were fully aware of the possibilities. The very names of Metropolitan Railway Country Estates or Metropolitan Railway Surplus Lands speak those companies' histories. But for a long while after the war the newly incumbent bureaucrats did not participate even indirectly in the spate of rebuilding which should have been evident all around them. The scope was almost unlimited for the imaginative railwayman. In London alone, leaving aside an historic building like St Pancras, all the other main termini were in need of rebuilding. Had they been rebuilt with massive quantities of offices above the booking hall areas and extending down the platforms, the operation would not only have paid for modern stations but also have brought in a handsome profit to counter slightly the railways' continual deficits. Virtually nothing at all was done.

The objection to this indictment is that it is drawn up with hindsight. Yet British Rail does not have the excuse that the potential is only obvious after the event, for the suggestion was made to them long before it was too late by several private developers. British Rail was not allowed to promote speculative developments singlehanded on its own sites. It may have been too much to expect it to lobby the Government vigorously to be allowed to do so. That demands a sense of enterprise and perhaps a willingness to take risks which is not generally expected of bureaucratic institutions, though Signor Mattei took a thrusting, imaginative spirit to state-run industry in Italy with signal success. But at least to have granted building leases to developers of the air rights over important stations would have been far better than to have done nothing. The LCC continually fought what ambitions the railways had for commercial development, but it is doubtful that the railways counter-attacked with nearly enough bite. Hammersons once advanced so far through the jungle of red tape that it was able to hold a press conference in 1956 to tell the world of its plans for Victoria Station, but that scheme was bogged down and the building is the same as ever today.

Railway stations were and are plum sites for office buildings and sometimes shops, but it was not until the fabulous fifties were over and the increasingly restrictive climate of the sixties was under way that the landowner with sheaves of these sites under its arm woke up. In October of 1961 Railway Sites Limited was set up as an offshoot of the British Transport Commission 'with the object of securing that the development potential of railway land is fully exploited'. By December 1962, seven months after the stock market had signalled the top of the property boom, the BTC was ready to announce the names of the private property companies which were to collaborate in joint developments with Railway Sites on railway land. The companies were split up into eight consortia, each concentrating on a different region.

Even though the railways were late in attempting to exploit the development potential, progress was still slow after the consortia were set up. One main trouble was that the standard financial terms suggested by the nationalised industry were so tight, in the fear of giving away too much profit, that there was little incentive for the companies to push ahead. Membership of a consortium was a commitment to nothing, it was merely useful to be on the ticket in case something juicy was offered. Some developers did not bother to join the consortia on the grounds that it was difficult enough to do business with the railways alone, but that in a consortium it would be impossible. After a slow start in 1963 to mixed enterprise on the railways, some projects got off the ground, but just as the pace was warming up Government restrictions on property development firmly put the brake on almost everything in the pipeline. The Brown Ban halted forty-three developments in which British Rail was involved.

The *Economist* once discussed the railways' property doings under the heading Dragsville. That British Rail made such a feeble showing on the real estate side was ultimately the responsibility of the top management. Though technically superb in its knowledge of the ins and outs of property, it tended to try to squeeze the last ounce out of any deal for the railway side. In theory that was excellent, but in practice it meant that many projects were stillborn. Four minor stations in London were redeveloped: Cannon Street, Holborn Viaduct and the periphery of Waterloo. (Moorgate, which is still under way, is a London Transport baby.) Various promoters were involved in the early stages but these four were all carried out by Barry East's Town & City Properties. Discussions on Holborn Viaduct started as early as 1955, so that the possibilities of the far bigger main line stations should have been clear to British Rail long before the LCC and then the Government were fully able to hinder its plans. Skyscrapers over Charing Cross, Waterloo, Marylebone, Euston, King's Cross and Victoria, perhaps the finest site in Western Europe, would have made the taxpayer many millions. When Euston's plans to rebuild were finally approved in April 1966 the chairman of the London Midland Region said, 'It is a great disappointment to me that our original scheme, which included a considerable part of commercial development over Euston Station, was not allowed to go forward. If it had been allowed to do so it would have paid for most of the new Euston.' The new Euston cost £5·5 million.

In relation to the number and potential of the sites which it owned, London Transport achieved much more than British Rail. The properties used by the underground and the buses were looked after by a cheerful chartered surveyor named Ian McGillvray, a realist who appreciated that some developers tended to be fly—'you had to be on your guard to see through some of the stories'—but at the same time saw that to push development ahead the deals should not be too tough.

After the Beeching axe and the Transport Act of 1962, a great inventory of the railways' non-operational property was drawn up. It was found to have a total value of £72·5 million, and slices were sold off in rising volume: £2 million in 1963, £4·5 million in 1964 and £12 million in 1965. These sales were a logical shedding of surplus assets, but they should not divert attention from a first priority when next the squeeze on property development is relaxed: the proper exploitation of the properties which are operational but have other highly profitable and desirable uses. If, for instance, more offices are ever to be allowed again in London, surely office developments over the main line stations should be allowed through before any other? It would be unneccessarily self-punishing to let private developers start operations again at random without first making the best use of the State's own prime sites, which are now lying idle.

CHAPTER EIGHT

The Fenston Group; Harry Hyams; and Centre Point

JOE FENSTON was an impresario of the theatre. His son Felix became an impresario of the property world, among the most fertile developers of the period and surrounded by a coterie of accomplished individuals, one of whom, Harry Hyams, graduated from the Fenston fireside into the most prodigious developer of all.

Fenston Senior, Joseph Fenston, was of Swiss-Jewish extraction and Felix's mother was Irish, an O'Donovan. Joe Fenston was a man of parts.* He managed Mark Hambourg and Benno Moiseiwitsch on their tours of South America. He toured Europe with Irving Berlin. In 1940 he revived *Chu Chin Chow* at the Palace Theatre in London. But he was also a flexible businessman as he moved around the world. He traded in pearls in China, Havana cigars in Cuba and oranges in Brazil and Greece.

Joe Fenston wanted his son to be a concert pianist, and although Felix was and is a talented player, he was not up to concert standard. Instead he drifted around in the thirties from one estate agent to another. During the war, not long after his father had successfully revived *Chu Chin Chow* in London, Corporal Felix Fenston collided on a motor bicycle with a car clocking 60 miles an hour and received a tin leg from the accident. The tin leg did not later stop him from shooting or playing squash or diving underwater for fish. But it did end his war and he moved back towards commercial property in 1944, as the market was warming up.

He saw early on that offices were likely to be the best side of the market; he remembers writing a memo for his father in 1945 suggesting that as large a fund as possible should be collected

* See his autobiography, *Never Say Die* (Alexander Moring).

together to invest in offices. The secret of Fenston's later success was his appreciation that, in order to turn the handle of development fairly often, he needed to be close to estate agents. 'A developer can't be prolific unless he has friends who are estate agents,' he said. His friends included Dudley Witting, who worked for Jones, Lang, Wootton and retired to Nassau in 1955 in his early forties having made his £2 million, and, more important than Witting, the Rose brothers, who ran their own estate agency, and Harry Hyams, who was with Hamptons. In order to make absolutely certain that they remained his friends in business, Fenston would invite these agents to put up a part of the equity capital and share in the profits—not an uncommon formula—in return for having initiated the development. He also formed an alliance soon after the war with Prince Stanislas Radziwill, an emigré Polish aristocrat married, at the time, to the daughter of a rich Yugoslav shipowner. Radziwill from time to time provided some of the finance for Fenston's deals and he too shared in the equity in return. The net result of these and other informal human links was that Fenston didn't make so much on each scheme, but he made it much more often.

Even in this industry of individualists, Felix Fenston stands out. Unlike most other developers, he was not obsessed with his work and dedicated to business. He appears more like an Edwardian dilettante, born to a cultivated life of pleasure, playing with a shrewd talent for property as a sideline. Fenston's headquarters from 1952 onwards was his home in London in Hill Street off Berkeley Square, a house which he bought from the late Duke of Devonshire. It is manifestly not tarted up. A stuffed tiger, victim of one of Fenston's spells away from property development, stands in the hall. His first floor study is reached by an inconspicuous lift to accommodate the tin leg. This is a highly civilised room. The walls are lined with old books. The only thing to suggest that its occupant might be a man of business rather than a rich don is a small battery of telephones by a well-used armchair. There are no ordnance survey maps of London, no deceitful architect's drawings of Fenston's buildings. On a table sits a fine edition of Squire Osbaldeston's Autobiography. From this room were planned the Empress State Building in Earl's Court, the huge BP Building in the Barbican, and the Royal Garden Hotel in Kensington. (In fact something rather different was planned for the Royal Garden site but a combination of Royal objection to eyes intruding into Kensington Palace and Kensington preservationists stymied an enormous office block.) It clearly pains Fenston that people meeting him for the first time should say, 'Oh, you were the man who pulled down the St James' Theatre.'

Fenston's basic staff for his work from Hill Street has never been more than a secretary and an assistant looking after the accounting side. He is frank about the advantages of being a developer: 'It is congenial if you don't want to be involved with the troubles of personnel and the management of labour.' It is also possible to cease operations, far more easy than for a normal industrialist, and then to start up again. Fenston was an extremely active developer in the fifties; by 1959 he was involved in three separately quoted property companies: Eron, Barranquilla and Alquife. By that time he had made a fortune of probably £4 million. Then he gave up completely for a couple of years. He read a great deal, travelled in Kenya, Tanganyika and Mexico, shot big game, played the piano a lot. He was forty-four and bored with the idea of developing property for the rest of his life. 'It was a sort of repetitious formula', buying the site, getting planning permission, having the building put up, letting it and financing it, with each development taking five years or so from start to finish.

But then he began again. This time he formed rather more of an organisation, so that he did not have to play so large a part in the day-to-day management. The market in offices continued to be so strong that by 1963, when Metropolitan and Provincial, his new company, was floated, it was worth £3¾ million. Fenston still kept up his many other interests. One might well find him on the telephone to his bailiff from his estate in Wiltshire, discussing some trouble with the partridges.

Partridges are not Jack Rose's idea of fun. His game is property. Jack Rose was the dedicated professional in the Fenston circle, one of the few most knowledgeable experts in the office development business. He and his younger brother, Philip, were a formidable pair, both as estate agents and as developers. They were the sons of a publican, who kept the Black Horse in the Tottenham Court Road, next door to Woolworths: 'we were even born in a good trading position,' says Philip. Felix Fenston and Jack Rose were at school together. They shared a desk at the age of eleven in the Regent Street Polytechnic.

Jack Rose was the author of a work which first appeared in 1949, *Leasehold Valuation Tables*, more commonly known as the Valuer's Bible. He has an orderly mind and a remarkable filing system in his office with details of almost every property of any consequence which has come on the market in London since the war. The Rose brothers have not concerned themselves with any of the pretensions that sometimes come with sudden riches—in their case about £3 million each. Someone once said as much to Jack. 'No,' he replied, 'I'll leave all that to my sons.' He loves to talk at length and in detail about the past. He told me about some deal on which he and his brother had lost £70. 'And that meant a lot to us in those days. Or no, were we away by then? Yes. We were away. It didn't matter much.'

The Fenston formula suited the Roses admirably. They were extremely cautious in their business and careful with their money, unwilling to take on some of the big risks of the early fifties. 'Jackie Rose never put his toes into the water until it was warm,' said a rival. He was quite prepared to find sites for Fenston, do all the work of organisation and take a share of 30 per cent or so in the profit. He had to find none of the finance and took none of the risk. In return he worked furiously. He knew all the deals floating around Hill Street and Fenston would ask him for figures at any hour of the day or night.

The Roses gave up their estate agency in 1957 in deference to the conflict between agency and development. They probably initiated a greater volume of new office building than Fenston, but it was not all for themselves. At the end of the fifties, buttressed by their many minority interests, they built up their own company, Land Investors. The minority interests were not just in companies with Fenston and Hyams; there were others with Jack Cotton, Charles Clore, Moss Spiro, Jacob Lottenberg and Joe Littman. The two Rose brothers saw that developers were to a large extent impotent without an efficient estate agent and they made the most of it; here were two brothers who made fortunes while taking hardly any risk at all.

Jack Rose insists that the greater part of property development is just good housekeeping. He pays fanatically close attention to detail. After the hectic working hours of the fifties, he now follows a singular routine: in bed until 10.30, busy with telephone calls, then out visiting the sites on which building is in progress. He is

H

the rare developer who cares sufficiently about detail and cost to check such things as whether the right kind of bricks are being used. These details and the feeling of a deal itself, rather than the money made at the end, are of such importance to the Roses that they will be a continuing force in development, even in the worst conditions, long after many competitors have departed for Cap d'Antibes or Barbados. Equally, in his home Jack Rose is just as keen to impress on you the economics of his plastic flowers as to show the merits of his Rubens and his Rembrandt.

Among the most profitable developments promoted by the adherents of Fenston was Woolworth House, a plain building in the Marylebone Road. This site, parts of which had housed the headquarters of Robert Maxwell, the publisher, in his struggling days, was hit upon by Jack Rose and Harry Hyams almost simultaneously. It was exceptionally cheap to build and was rare for a modern building in that the structure was supported with no cement or steel frames. It was built entirely on load-bearing brick, partly because bricklayers were plentiful at the time. It cost £800,000 to build in 1955, but was not let until 1959, after the much heralded arrival of Castrol in Hammerson's block just down the road turned Marylebone into a fashionable office area. After Woolworth had signed their lease, the value shot up to over £2 million and a mortgage of £1·5 million was raised from an insurance company. In 1966 the Roses' company bought all the shares of Woolworth House. They had originally been shared between Hyams, Fenston and his father, the Roses, Moss Spiro, Prince Radziwill and a stockbroker friend of Hyams.

Not long before Felix Fenston decided to take off for a while from the repetitions of property development, he and Harry Hyams had a shattering row, varying versions of which have passed into the lore of the property world. It led to the unravelling of most of their alliances, and each went his separate way. Hyams took over a 'shell' in 1959—he was then aged thirty-one—and at a time when many other developers were slowing down for fear of increasing competition and lack of sites built it up in one of the most sensational expansions ever seen from a company with net assets of £25,000 into one worth around £60 million. Harry Hyams' share of this is £24 million. In spite of running this huge enterprise and promoting several of the most dramatic skyscrapers in London, Hyams manages studiously to avoid any publicity for himself or his company. Yet he has become the daddy of all developers.

The career of Harry John Hyams spanned the golden age of the developer. He was seventeen in 1945 when he went to work for Joe Levy's estate agency. Their fathers were both bookmakers and great friends. He only stayed there about nine months. 'We disagreed on a few points,' said Levy; 'he was a very go-ahead lad, even then.' Then he moved to the general office of Hamptons as a junior negotiator. Hamptons was one of the older estate agencies with a strong line in country houses and then run in a rather gentlemanly way by Peter Hampton, who was interested in old Bugattis as well as his family estate agency. (Hamptons was sold in 1965 to Gerald Leigh and resold since.) Hyams worked in a small but active commercial department. After a few years he moved to another agency, Dudley Samuel & Harrison. On his first day of work he astonished and delighted his colleagues by taking the entire negotiating staff, bar partners and typists, out to lunch at the Bagatelle, a lush West End restaurant. He was much younger than most of them. But he did not see eye to eye with Mr Harrison and after six months he returned to Hamptons.

Harry Hyams was an enigma to some of the staff at Hamptons. Leslie Brown, who became one of the leading developers of factories at an early age, started in the accounts department at the age of sixteen. One of his jobs was to hand out the wages. He used to have to run around looking for people if they didn't collect their wages. Hyams was an ordinary negotiator on a weekly wage, but he was the one man whom Leslie Brown could seldom find. 'Sometimes he was as much as four months behind with his wages. He never seemed to need them.' That was one of the special things about Hyams' work at Hamptons; he was seldom there. He finally left in 1956, and in his last few years the advice would often be 'try Felix Fenston's house in Hill Street'.

Hyams spent much of his time chez Fenston. He operated on the same principle as the others in that circle, taking a cut in the equity of the projects found by him. His time at Hamptons must certainly have helped in the finding. Of the various operators who were in and out of Hill Street, it is probable that Fenston felt closest to Hyams. In some ways they were alike. Hyams, too, was not interested exclusively in property. He was a rather tall, extremely elegant figure with a black Spaniard's beard, neatly trimmed. In a quiet way, Hyams was a living legend in the property world. There was a great fund of admiration for his unobtrusive achievements and his gentlemanly, diplomatic manners. One developer referred to him as 'the modern Rothschild'. Young estate agents would discuss him in hushed tones at cocktail parties as the hero of their orbit. Hyams himself was a highly unpredictable man, even to his intimates. No one quite knew when he would turn up where, or what attitude he would take on any particular issue. His only predictable line was his policy of silence about his or his company's affairs towards the world at large. Some of his contacts found Hyams formidable. But almost all found him charming. Among other talents he was a fine mimic.

Their similarities in character may have intensified the split between Fenston and Hyams. The split may also have spurred Harry Hyams to thrust forward his own company, the Oldham Estate Company. Hyams first heard of Oldham in January of 1959, standing at the bar of the Mirabelle restaurant. A freelance agent, Harford Ellis-Jones, rushed in and told him that he had heard of a suitable 'shell', a tiny property company in Oldham, Lancashire. Would he like it? Ellis-Jones did not have time for a drink, and Hyams displayed one of his characteristics as a businessman: decisiveness. He committed himself firmly within two minutes. Yes. A fortnight later Ellis-Jones and Hyams drove up to Oldham in the snow in Rolls Royce number HJH 1 to look at the Victorian cottages and cotton mills, which stood in the company's balance sheet at £20,611.

Hyams and his associates bought up virtually all the share capital of Oldham at a cost of around £50,000. Some deals were done through the Oldham Stock Exchange in order to keep the quotation for the shares alive. But none of the new shareholders was willing to sell. Two enterprising stockbrokers in London, Victor Sandelson and Roger Whipp, were among the first to get wind of the dynamic change which had overtaken Oldham. In 1960 the shares had at one time a nominal quotation of 50s. to 60s. Sandelson made a wild guess that with Hyams at the helm the shares might be worth not 55s. each, but perhaps £200 each. He rang up a broker in Oldham and asked if he could buy just a few. The answer was that none could be bought, but the broker suggested to Sandelson that he should offer above the nominal quotation, say 62s. 6d., to tempt a seller. 'No', replied Sandelson,

'I'll tell you what, I'll offer 80s. a share.' The Oldham broker was wide-eyed at such recklessness. 'No, lad, don't be daft,' he said. But still no shares could be bought. Today they are worth perhaps £7,550 each in that old form. In 1961, because there was no market in the shares, the Oldham Stock Exchange suspended the quote.

Between March 1959, when Harry Hyams took control, and March 1966 the figure for properties owned by Oldham Estate altered as follows:

1959	£22,328
1960	£152,163
1961	£6,482,579
1962	£7,571,645
1963	£11,829,602
1964	£23,364,503
1965	£31,597,748
1966	£38,978,403

A mere £300,000 of new capital was subscribed by the ordinary shareholders in this period. The rest of the expansion was financed on borrowed money. For all the meteoric metropolitan expansion of the company, its official headquarters remain rooted firmly in a crumbling two-storey building in its home town of Oldham, though the effective operating centre was tucked away discreetly in an old office building close to St James's Palace.

One secret of the explosive growth was that Hyams took the contractor/developer link to its logical conclusion. He formed an alliance with George Wimpey, the biggest contractors in Europe, who bought 40¼ per cent of Oldham, an identical share to Hyams'. Wimpey was the ideal partner for Hyams, since its policy was to pay out in dividends to its shareholders a small proportion of its profits so that it had a large flow of cash to use for financing buildings being constructed. In return it was sure of the contracts for most of Oldham's office blocks, one of the most profitable types of work for a contractor, and it was likely to receive in due course from its shareholding a solid income based on rents as a buffer against the ups and downs of contracting. Wimpey was also temperamentally suited to Hyams. It was quite happy to give its public shareholders a minimum of information about Oldham.

The other two sources of finance for Oldham have been the Westminster Bank and the Co-operative Insurance Society. The latter, which owns 10 per cent of Oldham's equity, has been a particularly canny investor in property, but this is a paradoxical link between an extreme manifestation of capitalism and an arm of the workers' movement.

Although there are fortunate public shareholders involved via Wimpey, Harry Hyams has himself publicly disclosed minimal detail about Oldham, of which he is chairman and managing director. However, as Roger Whipp discovered, it is possible with some research to build up a fairly accurate picture of the company. It is common in property development to finance each project separately and to form a subsidiary company for each. Certain details of all companies have to be filed at Companies House by law. For the analyst of a property company the crucial details are the directors, the balance sheet, the shareholders and the register of charges. As a development is financed on borrowed money, the lenders tend to take a charge or mortgage on the property as security and this charge has to be registered at Companies House. In this way the properties being developed can be identified. Any director of a company is legally obliged to file all his other director-ships, so that all the companies graced by Hyams or his co-directors can be traced, and those companies in which Oldham has a shareholding can be found. (It is true that an investigation on these lines could easily be thwarted under existing company law by a lavish use of nominee directorships and nominee shareholdings.)

Having identified the properties, planning authorities will tell the curious, sometimes reluctantly, what permission has been granted. From the balance sheet a vague idea of the cost of the properties can be gleaned and it is not difficult to estimate roughly what an office block will cost to construct. Given the total cost, the net value to a company of a development can be guessed by a crude estimate of its value once let. Any pair of eyes can interpret whether the building is under way, finished, falling down, let or unlet.

So that no-one can accuse me of overestimating the wealth or achievements of the Howard Hughes of British business, I have set out in Appendix 9 my analysis along these lines of Oldham Estate and a handful of other projects in which Harry Hyams is involved. From that I deduce that Hyams has made a fortune of around £27 million from property development, the great bulk of it in the last eight years. It may be that some of the offices owned by Oldham will not be let, but this seems improbable. And if they

£ s. d.	LIABILITIES.	£ s. d.	£ s. d.
	NOMINAL CAPITAL—		
	£100,000 divided into 40,000 Shares of £2 10s. 0d. each		
	ISSUED CAPITAL—		
19,840 0 0	7,936 Shares, £2 10s. 0d. each fully paid		19,840 0 0
	SURPLUS AND RESERVE—		
	Future Taxation	350 19 9	
2,500 0 0	Reserve Fund	2,500 0 0	
2,906 8 0	Profit and Loss Account	2,955 6 10	
			5,806 6 7
	CURRENT LIABILITIES AND PROVISIONS—		
	Taxation to date of		
44 1 0	Balance Sheet....................	164 7 2	
	Midland Bank Ltd.—		
34 13 4	Share Division Account ...	34 13 4	
56 10 5	Undrawn Dividends..............	52 5 11	
570 9 7	Proposed Dividends..............	570 9 7	
82 6 3	General Accounts.................	318 12 1	
			1,140 8 1
£26,043 8 7			£26,786 14 8

THE OLDHAM ESTATE COMPANY LIMITED
and Subsidiary Companies

CONSOLIDATED BALANCE SHEET as at 31st March, 1966

1965 £		£	£
	SHARE CAPITAL:		
	Authorised:		
£10,000,000	20,000,000 shares of 10/- each	£10,000,000	
	Issued and Fully Paid:		
8,000,000	16,000,000 shares of 10/- each		8,000,000
	CAPITAL RESERVES:		
979,162	See note (1)		992,855
6,681	PROFIT AND LOSS ACCOUNT (Adverse balance)		(8,935)
8,985,843			8,983,920
409,964	INTEREST OF MINORITY SHAREHOLDERS		409,764
	SECURED LIABILITIES:		
4,888,000	Mortgage Loans	7,743,000	
4,310,656	Bank Loans and Overdrafts	4,416,989	
12,159,057	Other Advances	15,912,045	
21,357,713			28,072,034
	CURRENT LIABILITIES:		
1,165,343	Sundry Creditors and Accrued Charges...	1,461,065	
94,473	Taxation	51,620	
1,259,816			1,512,685
£32,013,336			£38,978,403

ASSETS.	£ s. d.	£ s. d.	£ s. d.
FIXED ASSETS—			
Chief Rents, Land and Property			
less Sales and amount written off............	17,250 10 11		20,611 17 5
CURRENT ASSETS—			
Mortgages	6,565 13 5		4,308 8 4
Chief Rents...........................	648 7 4		629 4 7
Cottage Rents	8 4 0		4 10 10
Midland Bank Ltd.	2,279 5 8		376 6 11
Midland Bank Ltd.—			
Share Division A/c	34 13 4		34 13 4
		9,536 3 9	

PERCIVAL E. LEES, ⎱ Directors.
JOHN H. RITSON, ⎰

R. T. CHEETHAM, Secretary.

	£26,786 14 8	£26,034 8 7

1965				
£	FIXED ASSETS:	£	£	£
	Freehold, Leasehold and other Interests in Properties:			
16,158,369	At cost	23,196,847		
14,794,630	As valued by the Directors (see note (5)) ...	14,794,630		
30,952,999			37,991,477	
4,731	less: Amortisation		19,114	
30,948,268			37,972,363	
	Investments in Associated Companies:			
	Shares:			
50	At cost	100		
608,036	As valued by the Directors (see note (5)) ...	518,036		
608,086		518,136		
39,403	Advances	41,823		
647,489			559,959	
1,991	Motor Vehicle and Office Equipment, at cost, less Depreciation (£5,370)		4,842	
31,597,748				38,537,164
	CURRENT ASSETS:			
297,085	Sundry Debtors, Deposits and Prepayments	367,577		
118,503	Cash at Bank and in hand	73,662		
415,588				441,239
£32,013,336				£38,978,403

are unlet for some while they are more likely to increase in value the longer they are empty.

Harry Hyams is a past master at the art of keeping buildings empty. This is not the crazy tactic it sounds. In a market where rents are rising it can pay hand over fist to leave a building empty almost deliberately. Hyams once bought a small shop and office building in Oxford Street, occupied by Treasure Cot before he bought it and by Hepworths afterwards. He paid a price which assumed that it would produce a rent of £12,500. His estate agents thought that with luck it might bring in £13,000 to £14,000 a year. Hyams instructed them to let it at £20,000 a year, and the agents thought for a while that he was joking since £20,000 was far above the going rent. But he wasn't joking and the building stayed empty for month after month. It was unoccupied in all for about three years, a drab blank in the neon of Oxford Street. Finally it was let—Hyams relented slightly—at £18,500 a year. The level of rents had risen sharply. Producing £18,500 a year that building was worth some £270,000, whereas producing, say, £13,500 it would have been worth £200,000, a difference of £70,000 tax-free. That capital gain would have far outweighed the loss of interest on borrowed money, which could be offset against tax, and the loss of rent, which is worth less than it appears to a high taxpayer. Moreover, no rates had to be paid on empties.

Harry Hyams and Felix Fenston and Prince Radziwill jointly own a large Victorian building at the bottom of St James' Street, the old Bath Club, which they bought in December 1957. In December 1966, nine years later, it was still unoccupied. This was not because no-one was willing to rent it, merely that the rent asked, £185,000 a year, may have been unrealistic in relation to offices elsewhere in the West End. White Elephants are not all that they seem to be. The old Bath Club was growing more valuable year by year. As Felix Fenston observed succinctly, 'Keeping a building empty is just a question of how much money you've got'; interest has to be paid on the borrowed money. There is of course a certain risk in leaving buildings empty by asking more than the market rent. But since the war office rents have moved in one direction only. With a development in Paddington, Telstar House, empty for several years, Hyams has been periodically raising the asking rent.

Another cornerstone in the Hyams formula was that he

surrounded himself with some of the finest talent available to a property developer. Richard Seifert was his architect. As his number two in Oldham he had William Allen, a solicitors' clerk recognised to have one of the best brains in London on the conveyancing of property; the giant Oldham was run by a full-time staff of two men and three girls. His accountants were Silver, Altman, wizards on tax in relation to property. He had several shrewd estate agents working for him on various projects: two of the partners in Jones, Lang, Wootton, the brothers Eric and Noel Taylor, and two less known agents, William Grainger of Hamptons and James Gray of Waite and Waite. His lawyer was Arnold Goodman of Derrick, Goodman, another mystery man until elevated to public posts and the peerage by the Labour Party, which he supported. Arnold Goodman suddenly shot into the limelight as the 'Mr X' who solved the television technicians' strike of July 1964. All these men were extremely loyal to Harry Hyams and almost all of them had a handsome reward, apart from their fees or salaries, through being on the inside and being able to buy shares in Oldham. As Seifert said with throw-away calmness, 'Harry told me that it might be "a good thing" to buy a few.' Seifert's shares can only have cost him £400 or so and must now be worth some £106,000, a reasonable nest-egg even for the most successful commercial architect in the country. There is no trace on the shareholders' register of Lord Goodman's owning any shares in Oldham but he and others might do so through some of the nominee holdings.

On rereading the references to Lord Goodman, I find they might carry a meaning I did not intend, particularly as he has never owned a single share in any of Mr Hyams' enterprises—or for that matter ever been personally engaged in any property transaction—and his firm was one of several solicitors employed by Mr Hyams and never in the capacity of financial or business advisers—nor did they act until the company was already a firmly established entity. I should emphasise that the phrase 'mystery man' did not intend to convey that there was any mystery about his professional or other activities but only that—like all reputable lawyers—he avoided the limelight until he was reluctantly dragged into it by the television strike.

Hyams' extreme aversion to publicity has paid big dividends in terms of his business. Had he spilt the beans, it is doubtful whether

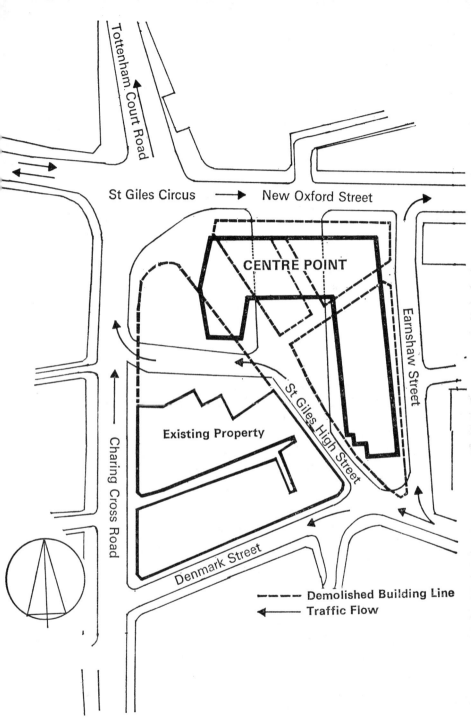

THE PLAN OF ST GILES' CIRCUS AND CENTRE POINT. THE ROAD RUN-NING UNDER CENTRE POINT FROM NEW OXFORD STREET TO ST GILES' HIGH STREET IS UNUSED; THAT ROAD, PROSPECTIVELY PART OF A ROUNDABOUT, WAS THE RATIONALE OF THE DEVELOPMENT FOR THE LCC

Centre Point, the thirty-two-storey skyscraper at St Giles' Circus, would ever have been built. For Londoners this was one of the more mysterious new landmarks suddenly to emerge from the ground. The planning of Centre Point was indeed a curious and ironical affair had anybody known about it, but had anybody known, the building almost certainly would not have got off the ground. As it was, this will probably be in absolute terms the most profitable single building ever promoted in this country. It is also that rarity, an admired piece of speculative architecture.

The saga of St Giles' Circus began on 17 July 1956, the day the LCC approved a plan to reorientate the road pattern at this vital intersection of Oxford Street, Tottenham Court Road, New Oxford Street, St Giles' High Street and Charing Cross Road. The plan was to buy up the properties around the circus and squeeze in a roundabout. It was not so simple as that. The LCC had not allowed for an encounter with an extremely resourceful property dealer, Mrs Beatrice Pearlberg, as the key owner at St Giles' Circus, and her husband Henry Hyman Pearlberg.

Henry Pearlberg was a bankrupt in 1956. He was a property dealer and mill owner from Lancashire, and he and his wife had a tendency to be caught up in litigation.* He was declared a bankrupt in 1943 and only ceased to be in Carey Street nineteen years later, in December 1962. However, his wife Beatrice was a shareholder in a variety of private property companies after 1943, in later years with the Pearlbergs' sons, Henry and Paul Pelham. Mrs Pearlberg did a lucrative deal early after the last war with a derequisitioned building in Bloomsbury Street, which she let to British Insulated Callenders Cables.

The Pearlberg flag was hoisted at St Giles' Circus in 1949. In January of that year the Ve-ri-best Manufacturing Company, a property rather than manufacturing company belonging to Mrs Pearlberg, bought 15–19 Lawrence Place and in June it took over a lease from the Crown of the frontage on to New Oxford Street, Nos 93–109. By the time the LCC plumped for a roundabout at St Giles' the Pearlberg and Pelham companies controlled the heart of the site. The LCC did not set a lengthy compulsory purchase order in train. It invoked the Metropolitan Paving Act

* See, for example, Pearlberg *v.* Refuge Assurance, 1938; Pearlberg *v.* Public Trustee, 1940; Pearlberg *v.* May, 1950; Pearlberg *v.* Commissioners of Inland Revenue, 1953; Pearlberg *v.* Penfold, 1955.

of 1817, known after its originator as the Michael Angelo Taylor Act; this let the LCC negotiate to buy land needed for road widening. After normal negotiations proved abortive, the LCC served a Notice to Treat under the Michael Angelo Taylor in early 1958. By then the LCC had bought several other pockets of land at St Giles' and in April it was announced that the Ministry of Transport had issued a grant of £627,000 towards the road improvement; work was due to start towards the end of 1958.

The Notice to Treat did not have much effect. The LCC was only entitled to offer compensation on pre-war values, which merely appeared ludicrous to the Pearlberg side. It also made the mistake of serving two Notices to Treat: one on part of the relevant Pearlberg buildings and the other on all of them. The next stage was that the case went to the Lands Tribunal. The affair moved no faster. Discussions at the Tribunal just centred on which Notice to Treat was valid, and because that could not be resolved the Tribunal was adjourned in October 1958. The LCC's hopes of starting work during 1958 were crushed and it was clear that the wrangle with the Ve-ri-best Manufacturing and its sister companies might continue for months or years.

Shortly after the Tribunal adjourned, an unexpected solution to the LCC's tangle with the Pearlbergs presented itself. Richard Edmonds, chairman of the LCC's Town Planning Committee, was telephoned by his lawyer Arnold Goodman and asked to pay a visit to the offices of Goodman Derrick. Edmonds remembers the meeting in the autumn of 1958 as the turning point at St Giles': 'When I arrived a reddish-faced young man with a beard was already with Arnold Goodman. "This is Mr Hyams," said Goodman, "he thinks he may be able to help you on St Giles' Circus." Hyams said to me, "You're in trouble with St Giles' Circus," and I replied "Yes, we certainly are." ' Harry Hyams then produced his solution, which was that his company should buy out the Pearlberg stronghold at St Giles' at a price which the LCC could neither afford nor were allowed to offer under the rules of the Michael Angelo Taylor Act. Hyams would also buy up the rest of the site not already controlled by the LCC and make an unwritten 'Land for Planning Permission' deal with the LCC, so that the LCC could end up with land for its road and Hyams with his planning permission.

The description of an introduction effected by Lord Goodman to Mr Edmonds, when the matter was already under way, should have made it clear that Lord Goodman played no part in any financial negotiations connected with the transaction.

This was a well-known formula of the LCC's for solving its poverty, a formula used with the road under Bowater House in Knightsbridge, at the Stag Brewery development opposite Victoria Station and at the Euston Centre (see chapter 11). It avoided any breach of the laws against selling planning permissions but was a method of giving the developer of adjacent land the privilege of paying for the land cost of the public road. Thus at St Giles' Hyams bought much of the land on which the road now runs, gave it to the LCC, and was in return allowed to transfer the plot ratio from that land to the rest of the site. The smaller site with a denser plot ratio was just as valuable as the bigger site with a smaller ratio. These deals fell into great disfavour inside the LCC in the fierce anti-offices years of the early sixties, as they produced a far higher density than the ordained plot ratio on the land. The plot ratio at St Giles', taking just the area actually built over, is 10 : 1, which is exactly double the normal permitted maximum for that area.

Richard Edmonds and the officials of the LCC were delighted with the idea of Hyams' solution. Negotiations were joined with the Pearlberg camp and eventually a deal was struck at around £500,000 for land which the LCC had at one point been able to offer only £55,000 for and which must have cost the Pearlberg companies well under £100,000. By July 1959 Richard Seifert wrote to the LCC to say that his clients had a contract to buy from the Pearlberg interests and in August 1959 he sent in the planning application, pointing out helpfully that 'we shall be glad to discuss any amendments'; he need hardly have added, 'but it is most important that the bulk of the building should not be reduced'.

The actual date on which the application was presented, August 12, 1959, was no coincidence. On 16 August the Town and Country Planning Act, 1959, came into force. One major provision of this Act was that people who applied for planning permission for a particular property had either to own the property or certify that the owner knew of the application. Before this Act it was possible for a developer to receive planning permission for a piece of land, thus often increasing its value hugely, and then buy the land from the owner, who might well not know at all that planning permission had either been applied for or granted. Under this ridiculous law many developers bought properties far cheaper than they should have done, had the owners been aware of what was likely to happen to their land, or, indeed, what their local authority had agreed might happen to it. Admittedly, naïvety and ignorance of the law are no excuse; a man could discover any plans from the local authority if he took the initiative.

Many of the old buildings at St Giles' Circus were bought after permission to redevelop had been given. And some of those sellers had not the faintest idea that a 385-foot-high skyscraper of offices would replace their properties.

The L.C.C.'s Planning Committee were strongly recommended to pass the application that autumn 'as it is the key to the road scheme'. Permission was granted in November. Over the following year various modifications were made to Seifert's original plan and at the same time Hyams' agents were furiously buying up the freeholds or the leases of properties down Earnshaw Street, up and down St Giles' High Street, into Lawrence Place and even at the top of Charing Cross Road.

By March 1962 a subsidiary of Oldham Estate named Sovmots had given all its properties at St Giles' to the LCC and signed a lease with the new freeholder of the entire area. Under this lease Oldham was to pay the LCC £18,500 a year for a fixed period of 150 years with no provision for revising this upwards during the 150 years. By the time Centre Point was finished, the rent of £18,500 seemed absurdly low, even though Oldham had given £1·5 million worth of properties to the LCC. It may have seemed about right at the time. But the LCC was not and its successor the GLC is not under any obligation to explain to the ratepayers the basis of this sort of deal, regarded as a private negotiation between two parties. It does, however, seem scandalously unbusinesslike that the rent should have been fixed for 150 years. By the time planning permission was granted, November 1959, it was common for the landlord to insist on rent revision clauses. By March 1962, when the lease was signed, such clauses were all but obligatory. The LCC included rent revisions in the lease which followed the Elephant & Castle public tender, first announced in September 1959. Why not at Centre Point too? The loss through such bad business is colossal. A revision at year 21 must have given a rent of at least £120,000 a year, so that crudely piling one lost chance of £100,000 on another, the local authority has lost out on a mammoth £12·9 million.

Demolition was in train when the lease was signed, but the problems of construction of a 385-foot skyscraper on a tiny traffic island were daunting and it was not until the end of 1963 that the thin oval tower, to be labelled by architect Ernö Goldfinger as 'London's first pop-art skyscraper', began to emerge. It was a surprise not only to the public but also to that arbiter of public taste, the Royal Fine Art Commission. This body was supposed to approve the plans for all buildings of particular importance, either in height or location. Centre Point must have qualified. It was at the time the second highest building of any kind in London. It was undoubtedly a landmark. Richard Seifert took the view that the Fine Art Commission would delay, if not obstruct for years. But the onus, only voluntary, of referring the plan to the Commission was on the LCC, and the Planning Committee shared Seifert's view. 'You could say that there was a distinct lack of rapport between the Town Planning Committee and the Fine Art Commission', said Edmonds. Had the Commission objected to Seifert's soaring landmark, the delay to the LCC's roundabout, started by the impasse with Mrs Pearlberg's Ve-ri-best Manufacturing, might have dragged on year after year. As it turned out, Mr Marples, Minister of Transport, had changed the road system by the time Centre Point was finished; Tottenham Court Road and Charing Cross Road became one way and the roundabout lay useless and unused.

The Fine Art Commission was not the only one whose nose was put out of joint by the secrecy at St Giles'. Other developers knew that the LCC was planning roadworks there and had expressed their interest. One discussed it with the LCC in 1958 and was assured that nothing would happen until the end of 1960 and that he would then be given an opportunity to tender for the scheme in a competition. He was furious when he discovered that Oldham had walked away with the project in a private deal.

If Harry Hyams, like Jack Cotton, had been well known to the press; if his fine collections of pop records and of Georgian silver, his Maserati and Rolls Royce and Mini-Minor and Bugatti, his yacht and his beard had all been food for the gossip columns, then his property developments would almost certainly have been public knowledge too. Centre Point, like Cotton's Monico project, could have been delayed *ad nauseam* by public debate and official enquiries. No sensible developer could afford that. Whereas Cotton's motto appeared to be 'it's gotta be big', Hyams' might well have been 'it's gotta be quiet'. The sums on Centre Point were phenomenal. The land which Hyams handed over to the LCC cost some £1·5 million. Construction and interest charges might have added £3·5 million, a total of £5 million. I doubt whether the total rent on the whole building will be less than £1,160,000 a year, giving a value to Centre Point of around £16·7 million and a profit of £11·7 million on a single building.

Centre Point would not be the only building on which Oldham Estate pulled in a rent of over £1 million. The other was Drapers' Gardens, another major coup. This was a site a stone's throw from the Stock Exchange and the Bank of England owned by the Drapers' Company. It could hardly have been in more of a plum pitch. The Drapers very wisely offered the site by competition to the highest bidder when the leases on the Victorian buildings fell in. Hyams won with a rent, some £270,000 a year, which left most of the competitors gasping that this time the great Harry must have over-reached himself. Far from it. The basis of the undiluted triumph which followed was once again Seifert's skill with plot ratio and the Government's artificial restriction on offices. The all-important figure for plot ratio laid down in the invitation to tender by the Drapers' Company was 4:4. By scrapping the plans of the architect Milton Cashmore, who had won a conditional planning consent for the Drapers, Seifert managed to raise the plot ratio to the limit of 5:5, adding another 40,000 square feet of floor space. He achieved this by use of an absurd loophole in planning law known as the Third Schedule, explained at length in chapter 12. Seifert also put all the space into one highly impressive twenty-eight-storey tower, instead of four dull blocks of varying height.

The new Drapers' Gardens building was finished shortly after George Brown brought in his ban on more office building. One victim was a massive project of the National Provincial Bank's to create a headquarters for itself just across Old Broad Street from the Stock Exchange. The bank seemed to have a plausible case for exemption from the Brown ban, but the Board of Trade was firm. It had to find somewhere else and the alternatives were very few.

Harry Hyams personally bargained with the chairman of the National Provincial and let him Drapers' Gardens at the highest rent ever seen in the City, over £5 a square foot, a rent which turned white the hair of the stockbrokers gossiping in its shadow; they were fast being forced out of business anyway. Oldham's profit on this 'rash' operation, even after deducting £270,000 to be paid to the Drapers', was of the order of £7·3 million.

Seifert's encounters with the planning authorities were not always smooth. After Hyams had bought New Court in Carey Street for £2½ million (see page 19), Seifert tried to have the existing planning permission changed. This was granted and it meant another 28,000 square feet. But one crafty condition was tagged on to the permission after some discreet lobbying by lawyers worried about the rent. The condition was that the building must only be used by lawyers. The snag with that was that the lawyers could with little difficulty have formed a solid front on the level of rent they considered appropriate. Seifert appealed to the Minister of Housing against this straitjacket. The Minister's inspector recommended that the condition should be discharged, but the Minister, Richard Crossman at the time, decided that 75 per cent of the space must be let to lawyers. This was still too risky for Hyams and the building was put up on the original permission, which had no condition. Carey Street is just behind the Law Courts and in the thick of the legal quarter. But the rents in new New Court may be such that the lawyers will have to look elsewhere.

Harry Hyams is a developer with a style all his own. Even inside the property business, where almost everybody knows everybody else, only a handful know Hyams well. When he turned up at Jack Cotton's memorial service in an aeroplane he went to great lengths to explain that it was not his in order not to appear ostentatious. The names of some of his buildings are more imaginative than the usual run: Astronaut House, Space House, Orbit House, Planet House (that was changed by the occupants to Kellogg House), Telstar House and Early Bird House. Therese House was named after his wife and Anneuel House after his mother, Anne, and father, Uel. Mohican House was named after the Last of the Mohicans, as he thought it would be his last before the clamp on offices. When he bought himself a new house in 1965, it was no ordinary mansion in Millionaires' Avenue. It was Ramsbury Manor in Wiltshire, the most perfect example of Charles II architecture not on show to the public. Once the house of the earls of Pembroke and Wilton, Ramsbury has in recent years mirrored economic changes; Harry Hyams, the property king, bought it from the late Lord Rootes, the motor car king. With its parkland and contents it is reputed to have cost a few thousand either side of £600,000. It may be some years before it is open to the public.

With the ban on offices in London, where Oldham has almost exclusively concentrated so far, Hyams must expand elsewhere or stagnate for probably a decade or so. Aged thirty-nine he can afford to. He is already the richest of all the self-made men who started from scratch after the war. But there are signs that he is moving to new pastures. He is redeveloping the town centre of Oldham itself, at a cost of £5 million, a bonus for the 'local' company; the notepaper of the Oldham Estate Company has an embossed coat of arms with 'Established 1874' underneath, though its pre-1959 history is almost totally irrelevant.

In 1966 Harry Hyams was preparing to descend on Liverpool with a mammoth complex of offices on a 55-acre slice of dockland. Planning consent in principle for 10 million square feet of offices, more than in the whole of Birmingham's central area, was given in April 1966. The theory behind this apparent overdose of offices for Liverpool was that the Government and other office users would be driven towards the North by restriction in the South. The scheme would be built bit by bit, 1 million square feet a year over a decade. A spoke was thrown into the wheels in mid-1966 when it was realised that a splendid example of industrial architecture was to be demolished, the Albert Dock. At the beginning of an anguished outcry about this a Liverpool architect, Herbert Thearle, wrote to the *Sunday Times* after an article by John Barry, 'People of Liverpool will be grateful for your article giving information which, hitherto, we had received only sparsely. It seems curious that consent in principle has been given to the developers for an office complex which would mean the destruction of the Albert Dock Buildings . . . But perhaps it's already a case of "Here's Harry" . . .'

I

CHAPTER NINE

Provincial Shops, 1955–1961: Sam Chippindale and Walter Flack

WITH the exception of Harry Hyams, office developers in London produced their most concentrated burst of building in the years 1955 to 1960. Though it continued at a rapid pace from 1960 through to 1965, the heat was off. Measured by the total volume of work, developers were operating on London offices to a much greater degree than on any other type of development through the fifties, but by the end of the decade the pressure of competition became apparent. From about 1960 there was suddenly a switch of emphasis towards shops and the centres of provincial towns.

In contrast to the activity in London, the period 1955–60 was relatively quiet for the shop developers in the High Streets. The main reason was that the raw material, land, was hard to come by in any quantity. Developers tended to be interested only in the main shopping streets, where they could let shops to the multiple companies or shopkeepers who were strong enough financially to afford the high rents of the central area. (The rents from such companies were the most acceptable as security when it came to mortgaging the finished product.) By about 1956 the bombed sites in provincial cities, in which Louis Freedman and Fred Maynard had specialised, were largely rebuilt. Looking for new opportunities, their company, Ravenseft, started up an offshoot in Canada in 1956.

The supply of land in existing shopping pitches was slowed down by the policy of some of the biggest retailers, notably Marks & Spencer, Hepworths and Montagu Burton, of owning their own freehold wherever possible and acting as their own developers; they became increasingly keen on this policy as they watched inflation carrying rents upwards and developers shortening the initial period of a lease against the shopkeeper to take care of future inflation. With some of the multiples in the most active stretch of shopping as owners of their own freeholds and determined to stay put, it was difficult for the developer to find the land for more than a few shops here and a few there. The shoppers stuck to their traditional preferences of where to shop and so did the retailers, especially those with a vested interest through their freehold in ensuring that the land around them remained as valuable as possible. The prime shopping pitch, known in the trade as the 100 per cent position, has not moved in some towns for centuries. The 100 per cent positions in Colchester or Gloucester or Chester —by the crossroads in the centre—have remained unchanged since the Romans built the cities.

The importance of position in relation to other shops is the big difference between the development of shops and of offices. In theory the office developer should be influenced just as much by position, but in practice, in post-war conditions, almost any position proved adequate. There are other subtleties with shop development which make it a more sophisticated operation than office promotion: the routes followed by pedestrians, the level of rents which varying types of retailer can pay, and what sort of shops flourish next door to one another, are a few of the factors which the office developer did not need to bother his head about.

In the early fifties Ravenseft was the only big shop developer operating all over the country. By the middle sixties a host of other developers had climbed on to the bandwagon, and some had already climbed off again. But there were six important companies, the Big Six, which looked as though they would be a continuing force: Ravenseft, Arndale, Hammersons, Laing, Murrayfield and Town & City.

Arndale was the first of those companies, after Ravenseft, to specialise in shops. Arndale was a peculiarity. It was one of the very few property companies of any size not run from London. Two others were Scottish Metropolitan, run by a shrewd Glaswegian named Issy Walton, and North British, run by John Bell from Newcastle. John Bell was a small builder made good who has owned a large slice of Le Touquet in recent years. Arndale was based on Bradford and was founded in 1950 by two Yorkshiremen, Arnold Hagenbach and Sam Chippindale. Hagenbach was a third generation Swiss baker from Wakefield. During the war some misguided inhabitants of Wakefield painted slogans on the walls and windows of many German sounding businesses. After the war Hagenbach sold his chain of bakers' shops, which still flourish in the North under his name, to the Canadian multi-miller and baker Garfield Weston.

Arndale began by developing small parades of shops in Yorkshire. Its first big operation was Jarrow, arranged in 1958. This was also one of the earliest and best examples of the type of development which was to bring a rush of developers' money from London to provincial towns and a simultaneous attack of *folie de grandeur* among a great many local councils. It was a comprehensive development in co-operation with the local authority. This was not a new formula. It was used in the blitzed cities, where the local authorities bought up the land and let it to developers to conform with their master plan. Jarrow needed this treatment almost as much as those hit by bombs. After its famous hunger march days of the thirties and the neglect of the war, it was in a thoroughly depressed state. Its councillors and officials made valiant efforts to pull the town up by its bootstraps; it was one of the most enterprising towns in attracting new industry.

The facelift to the town centre was part of the process of revitalisation. The council compulsorily acquired a site of seven acres for some £85,000 as the new focus for shopping in Jarrow. Its plan was to shut down completely the old main shopping street 100 yards away and use it as part of a site for blocks of flats; it is quite possible to ignore the traditional shopping pattern if it is killed entirely. Then in 1958 the council interviewed a bunch of developers to whom they might lease the land for the shopping centre. They chose Sam Chippindale from among his rivals from London. Chippindale's base in Bradford and his birth in Otley, home of Chippendale the carpenter, was one of his assets. North Country councillors were sometimes suspicious in their encounters with developers and estate agents from London. The borough treasurer of Jarrow spoke admiringly of Chippindale. 'He was a bit blunt and outspoken and he impressed some of my councillors who were more than a little difficult to impress. You see, he spoke a language we understood.'

Over the next seven years Arndale built ninety-three shops in a T-shaped precinct with wide avenues free of traffic. Arndale paid Jarrow £9,000 a year for its land at the start, rising to £14,000 by the twenty-first year, after which the rent was fixed at £14,000 for another 178 years. By later standards of town centre development that agreement was absurdly unfavourable to Jarrow, as Arndale will probably receive a higher and higher income on its original investment as its fourteen or twenty-one-year leases to retailers are renewed, while Jarrow will pull in the same rent for almost 200 years. The council's only regret now is the financial part of the deal with Chippindale, but the formula then used was the official advice of the Ministry of Housing and Local Government. The shops themselves, built in stages, readily found tenants and the liveliness of this modern mart in the heart of Jarrow boosted the low morale of the town. The centre claimed the busiest pie shop in the North-east.

It is typical of Sam Chippindale that he should have delighted the dignitaries of Jarrow with the new shopping centre and at the same time pulled off such a fine financial deal for his company. As Arndale flourished, Chippindale kept his feet firmly on the ground. He was a tough negotiator, but his strong Yorkshire accent and no-nonsense approach were a welcome relief to some of the local councils which regarded the world of property development as slick and dangerous. Chippindale had patience and was a specialist in buying up backland for his developments over a period of years. If he could buy the land at the back of a shopping street and integrate it into the street as a new retail pitch, he could dramatically jack up its value.

An example of this is Arndale's shopping centre at Crossgates, on the northern outskirts of Leeds. There the traditional rows of shops form an L-shape along two roads at right angles. Behind the shops Chippindale bought a disused goods depot from the railways, a nursery garden and land from the Gas Board; he is building another L-shaped street of shops, for pedestrians only, to complete the square. Shoppers will find themselves naturally drawn into the mouths of Arndale's precinct from the old streets. The price of the backland was relatively cheap for use as shops, but a high one for the railways or the gardener or the Gas Board. To average out into the total cost Chippindale had to buy other pieces of backland and two slices of the expensive frontage on to the streets at either end of the precinct: one was an old Victorian house and the other a shop.

One inspired use of backland and among the neatest developments in the country was the St George's Centre at Preston,
which was initiated by Walter Flack and his lusty baby, the Murrayfield Real Estate Company. Flack was a strong contrast to Sam
Chippindale. A highly emotional man, instinctive in business, his
dramatic career was often in the news: his sudden rise to fortune,
his merger with Cotton and Clore, his quarrel with them and his
tragic death soon after, in 1963, at the age of forty-six. Walter
Flack was the son of a tailor, like Charles Clore and several other
developers. His parents had wanted him to become a solicitor, but
he failed five times to matriculate and drifted into estate agency.*
During the war he rose to sergeant in the Eighth Army and
afterwards returned to his pre-war employers, Dudley Samuel
and Harrison. As a negotiator in the general office he insisted on
smoking a long, curly pipe and Samuel, who thought this out
of place in an estate agency, sacked him when he refused to give it
up. He worked for Marcus Leaver and in 1949 formed his own
agency with two partners.

It was not until 1958, when the boom was far advanced, that
Walter Flack started his own development company. Murrayfield
was the 'shell' of a company which once owned a few properties
at Murrayfield, near Edinburgh, and its only worthwhile asset,
for which Flack paid £11,000, was its quotation on the Edinburgh
Stock Exchange. Into Murrayfield Flack dropped a few developments which he had begun over the previous two years. And for
the next four years, which coincided neatly with the rush for
property shares on the stock market, Murrayfield expanded at
a breathtaking pace. Walter Flack did not find it easy to raise all
the capital needed to cope with the speed at which he took on new
projects. He was a bearded man with an engagingly open, buccaneering manner and people tended either to like and trust him at
once or to be suspicious of his charm. A panel of executives of one
of the Big Five interviewed Flack at one point to consider his
request to borrow money from the bank. They turned him down,
telling him disapprovingly that he was a 'merchant adventurer'. An
early development was a cluster of shops in the middle of Basildon.
Flack leased the land from the New Town Corporation also when
he was short of finance. At an interview with the officials and

* Part of Walter Flack's story is told by Michael Pearson in *Millionaire
Mentality* (Secker & Warburg, 1961).

councillors of Basildon, Flack was asked to give a guarantee that he would pay the ground rent. Normally a bank or another company would provide guarantees. Flack walked up and down the Council Chamber, thinking. Then he said, 'Gentlemen, I will give you my personal guarantee.' Basildon accepted it.

Flack operated from a pretty, white painted house in St James's Street. He was less of a one-man band than many developers. As non-executive chairman of Murrayfield he enlisted his old boss from his days in the desert, Field-Marshal Sir Claude Auchinleck. Flack's right-hand man, and successor as managing director at the age of thirty-two, was Alan Wright; the estate agency became Walter Flack, Wright & Partners. Alan Wright looks like the dark, handsome stranger from a film and one of his favourite phrases, 'Kiss Goodnight Sweetheart', which means that the deal is off, fits him perfectly. He is the only property developer to play rugger every Saturday afternoon of the season. Both Flack and Wright were always full of little jokes, and they were talented at putting people at their ease, a vital accomplishment in endless negotiations with local officials. A hobby of Flack's was to serve behind the bar in his local pub in Westminster on Sundays.

The third leading player in the Murrayfield cast was a practising Socialist, Alderman, later Sir Frank Price. Price was an aggressive, controversial local politician, leader of the Birmingham Labour Party and a Lord Mayor of Birmingham. He was working on hire purchase accounts in the Birmingham Co-op when he first met Flack through a local architect, Seymour Harris, whom Murrayfield used for many buildings. Flack and Price liked one another at once. They mutually admired each other's outspoken approach. Frank Price recalled that Walter Flack always spoke in straight lines. 'In negotiations always give it 'em straight' he used to say, 'the only trouble is that they often won't believe the truth.'

These two soon saw how useful they could be to one another. Price had been chairman of Birmingham's powerful Public Works Committee through the main period of rebuilding after the war. He had sat in on many deals with developers and had come to know the essentials of the property business. To be a director of Murrayfield was a far more interesting and better paid job for Price than being in the Birmingham Co-op for the rest of his working life. Many of his Labour colleagues thought that he had sold the pass when he joined Murrayfield. As shop developers had

to rely more and more on their relationships with local authorities
the experience of a forceful local politician who had fought his
way to the top of Birmingham was invaluable to Flack. As Price
himself explained, 'You can sell a project because you understand
the system from the inside.' Price took over from Wright as
managing director in early 1967 and, in the spirit of his tutor
Walter Flack, became an independent.

It was an extra asset that Price was a Labour politician. It was
no coincidence that by far the majority of the ambitious town
centre schemes, where the local authority bought the land compulsorily and then leased it to a developer, took place in Labour
controlled areas. The existing retailers, especially the small
shopkeepers who had great influence with the local Conservatives
and the Chamber of Commerce, were seldom in favour of redevelopment. It could drastically alter the pattern of trade and put
the weaker shops out of business. In crude economic terms this
may have been a progressive process, but it cut little ice with the
backbone of Conservative support on a local scale. The Labour
Councils were much more occupied with the glory of their towns,
keen to embark on grandiose projects, and impervious to the squeals
of small shopkeepers.

In his elegant office Walter Flack kept his 'English Bible'; it
became English in 1960 when Murrayfield bought a mansion on
the Avenue Foch in Paris in order to pull it down and build 88
luxury flats, and Flack opened a 'French Bible'. The 'Bibles'
listed the vital statistics of each development and through 1958 and
1959 the list grew longer and longer. Flack mostly used the sale
and leaseback method of finance. This involved the least amount
of capital and allowed the fastest possible physical expansion. But
to overcome his difficulties in raising enough permanent finance,
Flack made an unconventional deal with Jack Cotton at the end
of 1959. Murrayfield issued 375,000 shares to Cotton's City Centre
and City Centre issued 375,000 shares to Murrayfield. At the same
time Cotton agreed to lend Flack money for his buildings.

Two years later, after Cotton had merged with Clore, the enlarged City Centre bought up the rest of Murrayfield's shares.
This is discussed in the next chapter. Although there had been a
strong link for two years, that second deal was given much more
publicity than the first. At the time Murrayfield was in the middle
of negotiating a property deal with Huddersfield Corporation.

Frank Price was surprised to have a letter from the Huddersfield officials asking him and Walter Flack to visit Huddersfield and explain to the planning committee exactly what was the meaning of the takeover of Murrayfield's shares. The burghers of Huddersfield wished to be reassured about Mr Cotton and Mr Clore. At first Walter Flack refused to go. He thought it childish of Huddersfield to object to a deal which would not in fact change the relationship between Murrayfield and the Corporation. But eventually Frank Price, with his insight into local councillors, persuaded Flack that it was important to soothe any worries by appearing in person.

When Flack and Price arrived in Huddersfield they found 'Cotton and Clore Go Home' painted on the old theatre which Murrayfield had bought as part of its embryo shopping centre. The planning committee gathered solemnly to listen to the two developers. 'Well, Mr Flack,' said the chairman, 'can you explain to us this business about a takeover of your company by Mr Cotton and Mr Clore?' At once Flack replied, 'I know what those other two C's did, but I don't know what these two have done yet.' There was a puzzled silence among the committee and the chairman observed tetchily that he did not understand. Flack said: 'I know all about those two C's, Crippen and Christie' (the murderers), 'but I've not learnt much yet about these other two.' After a pause of astonishment, the committee burst out laughing and the meeting subsided smoothly into accepting that the Murrayfield-City Centre merger was harmless for Huddersfield.

Flack's temperament burst upon the public in February 1960 when he made a takeover bid of £1 million for Whitehall Court, a great grey block of flats in Whitehall inhabited by some distinguished tenants. His offer was treated very coolly at first by the old-established directors of the company. Flack liked the possibility of redeveloping the block in the long run and in the short run reckoned that the rents were too low. Flack pressed on with his bid in spite of the cold reception, explaining openly: 'If any tenant is there at a rent below the market he is living on the backs of the shareholders. It's as plain as the nose on your face, boy! The shareholders should be sacred. I should be surprised if many tenants stay after we have reorganised the property.' He won the day, but his bark was worse than his bite. Most tenants stayed.

Walter Flack did not live to see Murrayfield's masterpiece, the

St George's Shopping Centre, completed and clattering with the heels of Proud Preston's shoppers. The origin of this shopping centre was an unusual case of private enterprise jumping in to wrest the project from the control of the local authority. Preston was advised by a firm of estate agents from London, Goddard & Smith, and had with the Ministry of Housing's approval declared a chunk of the town's central area a Comprehensive Development Area, known in planning jargon as a CDA. This was the first stage towards a redevelopment under the guidance of a local authority. The next stage was to buy all the land inside the CDA through Compulsory Purchase Orders, or CPOs. The price at which owners were bought out under the CPO procedure was fixed by the district valuer, with the right of appeal.

In Preston the most valuable part of the CDA lay in the imperfect triangle between Fishergate, Friargate and Lune Street (see the map opposite). Fishergate and Friargate were the two busiest and most important streets for shopping in Preston and if the two could be joined up across the backland in between, another traffic-free street of shops could forge a natural link. Goddard & Smith saw the logic in this. So did Preston Corporation. But so also did some of the owners on the site and their adviser, a particularly bright solicitor in Preston named Carl Eastwood. He had a special interest in the redevelopment, as his own offices were on this seedy but potentially lucrative triangle. Eastwood realised that if he could collect together a group of owners to act together, they might well find a developer prepared to buy their land for significantly more than the district valuer would sanction.

This was exactly what happened. Once the district valuer had indicated to a few owners what price he was prepared to pay for their land, Eastwood made contact through another firm of estate agents, Bernard Thorpe, with Walter Flack and Murrayfield. Flack immediately jumped into what was for a while a highly risky situation. He offered Eastwood and any of his clients 15 to 20 per cent above the district valuer's price. They were delighted. But the Corporation was less pleased. Its original idea had been to buy the freehold of all the land and then lease it to a selected developer. Flack was forcing its hand. He suggested that the Corporation should forget its CDA as far as this particular triangle was concerned and leave him to buy the land and carry out the development without any cost to itself. The argument about cost was a

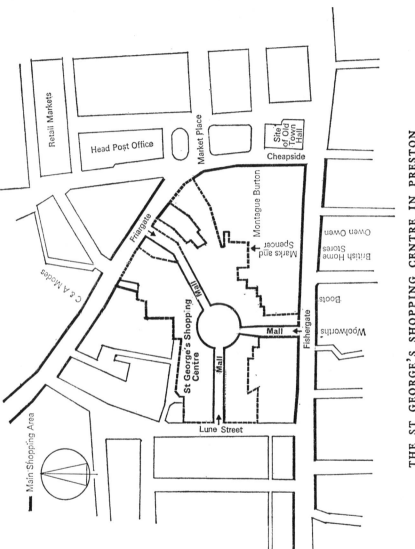

THE ST GEORGE'S SHOPPING CENTRE IN PRESTON

poor one, since the Corporation would have made an excellent profit in this area. The one genuine advantage was that with Murrayfield's money at risk the development would probably be built much more quickly than if the Corporation was the initiator.

After a struggle it was decided that Flack would continue with his 100 per cent free enterprise operation. The Corporation would give him planning permission and would not compulsorily acquire any of the land, provided, and only provided, Murrayfield's had finished the shopping centre within five years. It had.

Seymour, Harris, the architects who designed the St George's Centre, were helped by the lie of the land. Fishergate was about 12 feet higher than Friargate. This made it possible to build two levels of shopping over most of the precinct; shopping on more than one level has proved sticky almost everywhere else since it usually involves an unnatural effort for the shoppers to walk past more than one level. However, in Preston the shops were designed so that the pedestrian entered the precinct in Fishergate and came into a circular piazza at an upper level. From this central focus it was possible to walk left down an escalator and either out past more shops into Lune Street or around the bottom level of the circle and along the longest arm of the precinct into Friargate; or, instead of using the escalator, the alternative was to walk along the upper level of that long arm and down a slight incline at the end into Friargate.

The beauty of this design for Murrayfield was that it enabled about 35 per cent more shops to be crammed on to the site. That transformed the economics of the scheme. And it turned out to be justified in commercial terms once the shops were let. By the opening day in December 1964 some 95 of the 120 shops were let. It was one of the few mistakes in this development that there was something of a rush to open in time for the Christmas trade of 1964. Several of the shops which were let were not by that time shopfitted and open. Although Murrayfield would have lost some revenue through not opening by Christmas, it would have gained through delay since more shops would have been open and the greater the impact on the shopper at the beginning of a shopping centre's life, the better for its morale and chance of prosperity. Marks & Spencer, for example, were persuaded by Murrayfield to extend the back of their store in Fishergate into the lower level of the precinct. This was a great triumph, and the best evidence of all that the St George's Centre would serve Preston well. But the first couple of years would have been much easier for the traders if Marks & Spencer had opened that back entrance to their store on the opening day rather than several years later. Perhaps Marks and Spencer tend to take a rather aloof attitude to the world outside M. & S. A year and a half ago I asked a director of M. & S. who he considered its chief competitors. He replied solemnly: 'Mr Marriott, we have no competitors.'

The essential and simple reason for the success of this centre was that it was in the right location, sandwiched between two flourishing streets. And the reverse of this coin, that the location was wrong, was largely responsible for the white elephants of the shopping centre world discussed in chapter 15. The extent to which the local authorities were to blame for the failures, or to take credit for the successes, is vague. But they certainly had considerable influence over what was built and where through their planning powers, and some certainly tended to be keen on redevelopment for its own sake. When the Mayor of Preston formally opened the St George's Centre in March 1966, unveiling a plaque with his own name on it alongside that of Field-Marshal Sir Claude Auchinleck, chairman of Murrayfield, he voiced a feeling of many other local politicians in similar situations, though most are less open about it. 'I do believe', he said, 'that in years to come posterity will pass this plaque and will remember who it was who was Mayor of Preston in 1966.'

CHAPTER TEN

Cotton and Clore and Flack

JACK COTTON died in Nassau on 22 March 1964 at the age of sixty-one. In the last five years of his life he had become by far the best known to the public of all the property developers, and his photograph, with spotted bow tie and carnation, and phrases peppered with vivid exaggeration were continually in the newspapers.

Cotton's emergence during 1959 as a public figure and as a self-appointed publicist for his industry and his company, City Centre Properties, was sudden and quite unexpected to his friends. And it had some disastrous effects both directly on his business and indirectly on his personal life in his last two or three tragic years. While the burgeoning public relations industry of the 1950s was rapidly persuading businessmen into the limelight, only a handful of the men who made fortunes out of property development became at all well known. For most industrialists, especially those selling consumer products, publicity could pay dividends. For the property developer it was not only unnecessary; it was sometimes actively harmful.

Though far from a rags to riches tycoon, Jack Cotton began his career with a modest £50 in 1924. He came from a well-off Jewish family in Birmingham, where his father had founded a small firm of import-export merchants, B. M. Cotton & Co., which had done a flourishing trade in silver plate cutlery to South Africa before the Boer War. Cotton objected strongly to his father being described as a small businessman: 'There is nothing, absolutely nothing, small about my father.'

Jack was sent to King Edward's School, Birmingham, which he was later to pull down when it moved to Edgbaston and replace with an office block and shops, and to Cheltenham College. He started work at the age of eighteen as an articled clerk in a firm of estate agents and surveyors, while studying for his professional qualifications. He passed the exams of the Auctioneers' Institute. Then he set up on his own at the first opportunity. Cotton's father was deeply sceptical about his son's launching, indeed he was opposed to it. But when he was twenty-one, his mother lent him £50 and on his birthday, 1 January, he opened an office in New Street, Birmingham, with Mr Jack Cotton on the letter heading.

He was on his own for two years, collecting rents, conducting auction sales and organising his operations single handed. His office consisted of two rooms. An outer room with typewriter and stationery was connected by two doors to an inner room with his desk. When an unknown visitor called the standard routine was for a young man in shirtsleeves sitting in the outer office to ask the visitor to wait. Cotton would then go in through one of the doors, put his coat on, reappear through the other door and ask the man to come in.

Cotton had an intuitive grasp of the market's workings, and his energy soon forced the business to flourish. In the thirties, as the agency grew, Cotton started to deal more for himself, rather than just for his clients. He operated chiefly as a middleman buying farmland and selling it off for new housing estates. Apart from the profit on this operation, the Cotton estate agency would also sell the houses for the speculative builder. Signs saying 'Sold by Jack Cotton and Partners' were more and more often seen around Birmingham in the thirties. The houses were two-bedroom, ugly but solid semi-detacheds, fetching about £500 apiece and worth five times as much thirty years later.

Cotton's bank manager from this pre-war period, Norman Iles, remembers driving around housing estates to see how far built the houses were and how much the bank could lend on them. 'Whenever Jack Cotton found a way of raising money,' says Iles, 'he raised it. The result was that his affairs were always very involved. But for his banker, the big point about Cotton was that he was always scrupulously true to his word. When he said a thing would happen, it happened, and within the stated time.

'Once, in 1959, I travelled to London to see Jack at the Dorchester to discuss lending him some money towards building the Pan-Am Building in New York. Suddenly he asked me, "What is my main quality for which you've supported me all these years?" I replied, "You've always been a little better than your word." Immediately he rang a bell and a young executive came into the room. "Would you mind repeating our conversation?" Cotton asked me. I did so. "Now: get that into your head," said Cotton firmly and nodded for the young man to go.'

Though often impatient with those who disagreed with him, Cotton was a generous employer. Before the war he was paying his chief assistants £1,000 a year, which was well above the going rate for estate agents in Birmingham. He made Miss Frost, taken on in 1930 as office girl and then graduating to secretary, a partner in the estate agency. Female estate agents are extremely rare, and as partners, almost unheard of.

In the late thirties Cotton moved towards commercial development. Among his backers was the Birmingham solicitor, Joseph Cohen. Their biggest deal was King Edward House in New Street, built at a total cost of £1 million on the site of King Edward School when the din of traffic grew too overpowering for the school, which moved out to the suburb of Edgbaston. Cohen put up some of the money and Cotton, who did all the work, owned a small slice of the project, one of the most ambitious outside London before the war.

He masterminded the development of other office blocks in the middle of Birmingham, including Somerset House, Neville House and Cavendish House. This experience gave Cotton the grounding for his rapid post-war expansion, when the climate in real estate was far smoother.

Cotton also acted as agent and catalyst in the building in 1935 of Kenilworth Court close to the centre of Birmingham. This was the first time that luxury flats for sale had been built in Birmingham and it was typical of Cotton that he should have been adviser to a pioneering venture. He was never the sort of man who waited for someone else to show the way. The promoters were a syndicate of Birmingham businessmen headed by Cotton and Joe Cohen. But the flats did not sell easily and it was several years before the block was full. That hard struggle with Kenilworth Court determined Jack Cotton never to touch flats again.

In the war Cotton continued to run his estate agency, which meant little more than collecting rents. He took part in the Home Guard. Towards the end of the war he went to the United States to help emigration to Palestine and in 1945 he was a delegate in the British section of the World Jewish Congress at the Emergency War Conference.

Since the thirties, when the Dorchester Hotel in Park Lane was built by the McAlpines, Jack Cotton had always stayed there on his visits to London. Immediately after the war he made it his home and his office.

For twelve years after the war, the years of his greatest achievements, the empire grew unobtrusively. Jack Cotton was well known in his native Birmingham, certainly, and he was known and liked by others inside the property business. But to the public at large and indeed to most of those in the City, the name Jack Cotton meant nothing.

At about the time that Cotton came to live in London, a chartered accountant, Freddie Lindgren, became his closest adviser. Lindgren had known Cotton from before the war, when one acted as accountant and the other as estate agent to the developers of Viceroy Close in Birmingham; they had also worked together on Jewish charities. Lindgren fitted in well with Cotton's unconventional ways of work. His wife had died in 1943 and Cotton was separated. Lindgren used to go to the Dorchester from his office at around 5.30 in the afternoon. 'Most of our best work was done in the evenings.' They would drink and talk over the business for about three hours, then eat dinner together and go back to the suite for more discussions about property development. Lindgren usually left just before midnight.

The first step towards the eventual giant City Centre Properties was Cotton's purchase of Mansion House Chambers, a small and world-weary late Victorian company, whose one property in the City of London had been badly damaged during the war. In early 1947, Mansion House Chambers was on the point of ending its life by liquidation. But Cotton stepped in with a bid for the shares because the company had a quotation on the stock market and he and one of his partners in the estate agency tipped in some of the properties which they had accumulated before and during the war. This was one of the first 'shell' operations. Anyone realising in, say, 1954 who was the man behind Mansion House Chambers and had a vague idea of his money-making talents could have invested £100 in the company. When the shares were on the crest of the wave in 1960 that investment would have been worth £25,000.

But it was not easy to tell who was behind Mansion House Chambers. Cotton bought control through nominees. Freddie Lindgren was put in as chairman and Cotton did not even become

K

a director. Cotton was not interested in the formalities of running the company. He wanted to be bothered as little as possible with problems of law and accountancy and it was easy to leave all that for Lindgren to organise. After Cotton had agreed the principles of a deal, his usual way of ending the negotations was: 'I don't want to know about it any more. You go and see Freddie.'

Cotton was free to concentrate his talent on property development. And although he now spent most of his time in London, his earliest post-war buildings were in his native Birmingham. The first large office block built after the war in Birmingham was Cotton's, a gaunt and graceless hulk in Suffolk Street, Severn House, which mirrored the post-war shortages. The offices were leased to the Ministry of Works so that Cotton was allowed to build it while licences were still in force.

In 1954 Cotton took a big stride forward with the purchase of Central Commercial Properties, the new name for his group. Central Commercial had been founded by Stanley Edgson, one-time senior partner in the London estate agents, Hillier, Parker, May & Rowden, and had been sold to Cotton for some £2 million on his death. It owned a large number of shops in the country's main High Streets, or, as Cotton's fellow shareholders were told, '483 properties in the principal cities and towns in the United Kingdom.' With only a few additions, the income from those shops grew from £240,000 in 1954 to £475,000 in 1965.

It was also in 1954 that Cotton formed a tactical alliance with Freedman and Maynard's company, Ravenseft, to rebuild a slice of Birmingham's busiest shopping area. This was more through force of circumstance than choice. Both Cotton and Ravenseft had been buying up pieces of the same $3\frac{1}{2}$-acre island site facing New Street, High Street and Union Street, and known as the Big Top site. Cotton was keen on the idea of a joint operation with other developers—in his later years he was enthusiastic about joint companies with almost anyone. He was a 'partnership man'. But Freedman and Maynard, and to a greater degree their ally, Harold Samuel, were nervous about partnerships, lest they led to tricky complications. In Birmingham, though, Ravenseft had only managed to buy one-third of the site, so they decided that to form a 50-50 company with Cotton was preferable to giving way. The end product of this partnership at the Big Top was a fourteen-storey block of offices and some of the most valuable shops in the country—retailers in the best pitch in Birmingham take as much money per square foot as in almost any street in Europe.

As the Big Top was under way—building began in 1955 and was finished in 1959—the same partners won the competition for the huge redevelopment sponsored by the London County Council at Notting Hill Gate. They could well have competed independently. But Cotton actively enjoyed the partnership and benefited from Freedman and Maynard's greater experience of competitions, while Harold Samuel agreed with Ravenseft that in case the liaison with Cotton ever needed to be unscrambled, it would be as well to have a second counter with which to bargain.

In 1955 the name of the company was changed again. Chesham House in Regent Street was sold at a profit of £424,000 after only six years in Cotton's hands and the even more weighty name of City Centre Properties was chosen.

Not all the growth in the next years was visible—in some cases it took several years between the purchase of a site and its rebuilding. Cotton concentrated on London and Birmingham, the two cities he knew best and those where the demand for offices was fiercest in the late fifties. The impression he made on Birmingham was proportionately the greater. And as all the buildings sponsored by Cotton came to fruition in the early sixties local people began to talk about Birmingham BC—Before Cotton.

Towards the end of 1958 Jack Cotton emerged from behind the scenes. For eleven years he had in practice been the boss. He was the major stockholder and everything that the company did originated from him. But he had never been a director. He actively preferred the privacy of being unknown to his co-shareholders in City Centre and to the public at large. A man who joined the company in 1955 remembers most vividly from his interview before he was taken on that Cotton said, 'There's one thing I cannot stand and that's the Press. You must never talk to them either about the company or about me. They'll do neither of us any good.'

But in October 1958 Cotton became chairman of City Centre. One reason for this was Cotton's need to move closer and closer to the City and the insurance companies from which he borrowed. Almost the only limit on City Centre's growth seemed to be the amount it could borrow, thus Cotton's remark that 'there's not enough money in the world for me'.

In 1958 he sold 25 per cent of his shares in City Centre to the Pearl Assurance. He already had a joint company with the Pearl for individual developments and another with the Legal & General. But the effect of this deal was to make the Pearl his partners, to ensure that his interests were also theirs. One visible result was that the Pearl's investment man, E. F. J. Plumridge, more often known as Plum, was made a director of City Centre, so that he could follow its progress more closely. At the same time, in response to the conventional feelings of the insurance companies and banks, who did not like the idea of the man who was running the company not being a director, Cotton was appointed chairman.

From then on the pace of Cotton's expansion grew even more rapid and in the course of the next year his name began to appear in the newspapers more and more often. It was not just that activities such as buying Renoir's La Pensée for £72,000 ('I bought it because it makes me think'), giving £100,000 to the Royal College of Surgeons or £70,000 to Jerusalem's Hebrew University, were hard to conceal. It was also that Cotton did actively talk to the journalists now, whereas four years earlier he had told that prospective employee that he could not stand the Press. To strangers he appeared shy and he always had a slight inferiority complex, but was confident of his ability to prove himself. By the time he became chairman of City Centre Properties, his huge material success—in his company and in his buildings for all to see—made him yet more confident and open. One theory is that an incident at his daughter's wedding, in 1957, suddenly sparked off his interest in the newspapers' reports on his affairs. He had hired a special train to take his guests from London to Birmingham and had them served with a lavish meal. The *Daily Express* heard of this, took photographs and ran an article headlined 'The Mink and Champagne Express'. Though he had not organised it, many of his friends in London criticised Jack Cotton for this gaudy publicity. Perversely, Jack was stung by the criticisms into deciding that such reports were good for his image and to be encouraged. There was also a touch of rivalry which made him embrace the Press so warmly. By the end of the Savoy Hotel affair in 1955 Harold Samuel was the most celebrated property developer and he had decided that the reams of publicity which followed that encounter had, unjustly, done his reputation no good. So he resolved to do nothing to invite any publicity at all. Cotton, for some reason, interpreted the silence from the Press about his friendly competitor, Samuel, as bad publicity—certainly the general image of the property developer throughout this period could hardly have been worse—and thought that he might do better by welcoming and explaining himself to any reporters who happened to be interested. In the event this policy redounded to the discredit of his industry.

In 1958 Cotton began to look beyond London, Birmingham and his various projects in England. He made a sea trip to South Africa in September of that year with a City Centre director, Marcus Brown. They travelled by sea because they were both convalescent. This was one of Cotton's intermittent illnesses, aggravated by overwork. On the ship Cotton's disease, dermatitis, worsened and he had to fly home on arrival. But the object of the trip was achieved by Marcus Brown's reconnoitre. The next year Cotton was able to tell his shareholders that developments were proceeding in Durban and Cape Town, and in several islands of the West Indies. All these buildings were mainly to be occupied by Barclays Bank, DCO, which owned a 20 per cent slice of City Centre's overseas company. Cotton also reported in October '59 on the minor spate of acquisitions made during the previous year. The shares of City Centre were riding high in the stock market—they soared up from a low point of 7s. 7d. in 1958 to 72s. in 1959, near their highest ever. As Cotton basked in the increasing glow of public recognition, so the City, which was in any case waking up at that time to the possibilities of great profit in property shares, gave its strongest approval to City Centre. And Cotton, apart from speeding on with his own developments, used that ever more acceptable currency, CCP's shares, to buy other companies with buildings and sites collected by other entrepreneurs—for instance Union Securities and Properties belonging chiefly to Maurice Saady and Joe Green.

October of 1959 marked the turning point of Jack Cotton's career. In that month, with a double-barrelled explosion, he was launched well and truly as a figure of national significance.

The prelude to the first, quieter, half of the explosion had taken place one hot summer's evening in July 1959 at Cotton's country house on the Thames at Marlowe. A powerful builder and developer from New York, Erwin Wolfson, was meeting Cotton for the first time. Wolfson, a sensitive and highly intelligent

businessman who had started life with the intention of being a
teacher of philosophy, later described his apprehension at this
initial meeting: 'I didn't know what to expect. I was worried that
I would meet some forbidding, stiff-collar Englishman. Instead
Jack might have been a warm-hearted American Jew.' Wolfson
could not have paid a greater compliment.

After an hour's talk they shook hands. They had agreed to
develop jointly, in New York, the world's largest office building.
This was typical of Cotton's way of working. He would decide on
a deal in a very short space of time and leave the details to be sorted
out by others. Three months later, on 21 October, Cotton and
Wolfson held a press conference in New York to tell the world of
their plans. The Pan-Am Building, four times the size of the
Shell Building on London's South Bank, was to rise for fifty-
nine storeys over the tracks and platforms of the New York
Central and New Haven railway at Grand Central Station in
Manhattan. Cotton was asked if he was excited about such a big
deal. 'I never get excited. We are involved in many other large
things.'

Yet, for all his attempts to appear cool, the extent of Cotton's
euphoria in the autumn of 1959 can be gauged from his speech
to a distinguished gathering at lunch after the annual general
meeting of City Centre Properties. 'I am rich indeed in my friend-
ships and associations, and there is no wealth like that . . . it is
beyond price. . . . It is Autumn while we meet but this group of
companies is in its Springtide. And it is a joyous experience to be
in the centre of growth . . . the best is yet to be. . . .' In retrospect
those months were roughly the peak for City Centre's shareholders.

At his Pan-Am press conference, Cotton instanced just one of
the 'many other large things' in which City Centre was involved:
'the most striking project at present is the re-development of
Piccadilly Circus.'

Six days afterwards, in the inner recesses of London's County
Hall, the planning committee of the London County Council met
to discuss Cotton's *magnum opus* in Britain: already for seven
long years he had been feinting and arguing with the LCC*
over what type of building he might put up on the Monico site,

---

* The blow-by-blow details of this non-planning classic were lucidly
set out in the *Observer* colour magazine of 13 June 1965.

a redevelopment that was to become the most celebrated of the post-war era.

Cotton had bought the kernel of the development, the Café Monico, almost by chance in 1954. It belonged to the Express Dairy, which found itself ill-equipped to manage a restaurant so different from the traditional Express Dairy café. Walter Nell, chairman of Express Dairy, had been told by a prestigious firm of estate agents that the Café Monico was unsaleable and had asked the London end of Cotton's agency to find a buyer. Negotiations for a buyer dragged on for month after month. Eventually a partner in the agency was discussing the difficulties over the site with Jack Cotton one Sunday. Cotton asked for details of the site and at once said, 'if you bring the contract to me tomorrow morning, I will sign it'. He did so, at a price of just under £500,000.

Then began a long, frustrating period of plan and counter-plan, as Cotton's architects designed one building and the LCC's architects, first under Sir Leslie Martin and later under Mr Hubert Bennett, threw their own suggestions back again. As the inspector's report on Monico was later to explain revealingly: 'I do not think there was anything unusual or questionable in this procedure. Mr Bennett explained that there are very few architects who can, unaided, steer a design through all the hazards of plot ratio, daylighting, byelaws, fire regulations and other controls. What happened in this case is happening every day all over the country when planning officers and advisory panels are seeking by consultation to improve designs which are unsatisfactory for one reason or another. A great deal of good work is done in this way, but I think the fact remains that the chances of brilliant architecture emerging from this to-and-fro system are not very great. I cannot but agree with the objectors that brilliant architecture only emerges when one mind (and I include in this term the group mind of a closely-knit team) forms a design conception and has the courage and tenacity to drive it through, taking all the controls in its stride.'

But just then a stage of equilibrium in the endless modifications, concessions and drawing of new plans had been reached. The LCC was happy at last and on that afternoon of 26 October 1959 was ready to grant final detailed planning permission to the developers, Island (Piccadilly) Development Limited, a company owned jointly by City Centre and the Legal & General.

Richard Edmonds, chairman of the planning committee, said to its members at the end of the discussion: 'Is that agreed then? Permission granted subject to Section 25?' Everyone said Yes. Section 25 was some trifling technicality about car parking and but for that the clerk to the committee would have signed the permission.

Next day Jack Cotton, full of his American triumph, held his second press conference in seven days. Proudly, exuberantly—and against the imploring advice of his closest business advisers—he displayed his plans for his segment of Piccadilly Circus, what he himself called 'the hub of the first city of the British Commonwealth'.

That press conference was critical to the replanning of Piccadilly Circus. And from Cotton's point of view it was the death knell for his building. For the reaction to the plans and the model which he lovingly showed off for all to see was one of horror. Architectural critics, an assortment of individuals, Members of Parliament, peers, the Civic Trust and the Royal Fine Arts Commission—all expressed their condemnation of Cotton's building. The howl of outrage was so great that the Minister of Housing, Henry Brooke, stepped in to call an enquiry. This would have been impossible had that Section 25 technicality in the planning permission not been heeded, since the compensation payable would have been too great.

If Cotton had been able to restrain himself and had not held his press conference, the building shown facing page 87 would almost certainly be built today. Here was the ultimate case of the destructive power of public relations. The capital profit on Monico would surely have been well over £3 million.

The lobbying by the anti-developer faction to set up an enquiry —and during the enquiry itself—was intense. Monico became a national issue. And the issue, obscured by emotion at the start of the row, crystallised into a basic and relatively new problem of planning. Should the interest of a private developer overrule the interest of the community at large? Should Piccadilly Circus be replaced by Cotton pushing through a new design for his corner and the next man an unconnected design for his? Or should the private operators be forced to submit, with a particular property, to a comprehensive masterplan for a larger area? The attitude of the Royal Fine Arts Commission was ambiguous, to say the least. Whereas in February 1959 it had given virtually a blanket approval to Cotton's plan, it changed its tune completely once the anti-Cotton lobby became raucous and came out in violent opposition.

When the enquiry was over and the report published, seven months later on 20 May 1960, the Minister of Housing's inspector, Mr C. D. Buchanan, later famous for the Buchanan Report on Traffic in Towns, recognised that Jack Cotton had effectively defeated his own ends. He wrote: 'The applicants must now greatly regret that they put out the perspective sketch which they did at Mr Cotton's press conference in October 1959. This was the drawing showing the building with a crane on top, and a large advertisement "Snap Plom for Vigour" on the main front panel. Had this not been issued it is a fair guess that the building would now be in course of erection. As it was, the sketch at once focussed attention on the project, and it does not surprise me that strong feelings were aroused, for the building could scarcely have been presented in a cruder light.'

The Minister sided with the objectors and the plans went back into the melting pot once more. Even in 1967, thirteen years after Cotton had originally bought his site, no rebuilding is on the immediate horizon. But then, as the Minister's decision to reject his plan was announced, Cotton was unperturbed, although the Monico site was eating its head off. After interest charges, the project was losing money at the rate of some £50,000 a year. Cotton's comments were sublime: 'I am glad we have a decision—that is something. I am glad because I go through life trying to give happiness and pleasure to as many people as I can, and if by the Minister's decision on Piccadilly Circus more people get pleasure and happiness out of his future ideas so much the better, and I am in favour of it. So long as the eventual result is right, that is what I want.'

To help towards the eventual result, Cotton enlisted a world-famous architect, Walter Gropius. Always until then his buildings had been designed by his own firm of architects, of which he was the principal, Cotton, Ballard & Blow. It was rare for a developer to have his own architects in his pocket, but the resulting buildings were not much worse—or better—than the dim post-war average for office buildings. Apart perhaps from the Pan-Am Building, though this was fiercely criticised in New York, Cotton never sponsored a development of much aesthetic distinction. This was clearly not peculiar to Cotton. It is a charge levelled by the architectural world and critics of architecture at most developers at o ne time or another.

But, having been roundly attacked for Cotton, Ballard & Blow's designs at Piccadilly Circus, Cotton parried the shouts of his critics by producing one of the 20th century's most eminent architects as his adviser. Nothing came of this liaison at Monico for the problems at the planning level were too convoluted to allow the designer any scope. However Gropius did one piece of work for Cotton which came off. Cotton had bought 45 Park Lane, a Victorian mansion built in 1868 which had been the home of the banker, Sir Philip Sassoon, and before that of the diamond magnate, Barney Barnato, and with three houses at the top of Stanhope Gate proposed to redevelop the site as an office block. The preliminary plans had already been lined up when Cotton met Gropius, but, much to the disgust of the men at Cotton, Ballard & Blow who had designed the first scheme, the international 'name' architect was brought in on the elevation, with Professor Llewelyn Davies as consultant architect. As a result the plans went smoothly through the LCC, but virtually the only aesthetic difference was that the front of the building was faced with concrete blocks instead of Portland Stone. From the developer's viewpoint the main effect of employing Gropius—apart from the prestige—was to raise the total cost of the operation by £150,000 to £800,000. And the public hardly benefited; only a year or two after it was finished 45 Park Lane looked neither more nor less distinguished than most other new buildings in London. This development turned out well in the end for the shareholders of City Centre. The Playboy Club, making its first invasion of England in 1966, was insistent on finding a spot between the Dorchester and the Hilton for its Bunnies. 45 Park Lane was the only building between the two and Playboy paid the high rate for the time of £85,000 a year for 32,000 square feet of space. Cotton's judgment of property, despite his expensive flirtation with prestige, proved right again.

Yet during 1960 Cotton took two decisions which were not just a matter of real estate. They were decisions of a more personal kind, made at a time when Cotton's judgment was perhaps a little clouded by his fame, and in the end they turned out to be disastrous.

He joined up with two other property developers. The first link, right at the beginning of 1960, was with Walter Flack, whose company, Murrayfield, had expanded at a ferocious pace in the previous four years. But at this stage many of its projects were either under construction or were only on the drawing board, so that interest charges were high and revenue was low until the developments should be finished. Murrayfield and Flack had been running so fast that they desperately needed money and the City, nervous of the very speed of Flack's growth and suspicious of his direct, aggressive approach, had obstinately refused to produce the necessary loans. Murrayfield, in short, was up to its ears in debt and committed to the hilt. Cotton came to the rescue. City Centre bought 30 per cent of Murrayfield's shares and agreed to provide the much needed finance. Nothing was written down on paper, so that there was no specified limit to the amount of finance to be provided. The rate of interest was agreed—the favourable rate for Flack of $1\frac{1}{2}$ per cent above Bank Rate—but as to how much, no details were fixed. This led after a while to great arguments between Cotton, Flack and accountant Lindgren as to what the original agreement had meant.

However, for Flack, for City Centre and for Cotton himself, far greater problems flowed from Jack Cotton's second great decision of 1960. He decided to embrace Charles Clore.

This proved one of the most ill-fated corporate marriages ever. But when it was announced to an awed and admiring financial world on 25 October 1960 the merger appeared a logical fusion of two great property empires, a natural sequence in the boom.

The marriage broker, who suddenly dreamed up the idea in an aeroplane over the Atlantic, was Douglas Tovey, the estate agent who had adroitly advised Clore in his earlier sale and leaseback forays among the shoe shops of the country's high streets. This is how Tovey recalls the proceedings which led to the deal: 'I drove on a Sunday morning from my country house near Henley to Jack's house at Marlowe. Jack was in bed. I explained my idea that these two competitors in property in England and New York would be more powerful together, in harmony. Jack seemed to like the idea.

' "The terms of the merger should be one share of City Centre (Cotton's company) in exchange for one share of City & Central (Clore's company)."

' "No. That is absurd," said Jack, "my shares are much higher than City & Central's—and so they should be."

' "Jack, this would be the biggest property company in the world."

'He thought about it for a short while and then he said, "I will agree to those terms. But on one condition. I must be chairman of the new company. Chairman of the biggest property company in the world."

'I left Jack Cotton and drove straight off that Sunday morning to Clore's house at Stype in Herefordshire. He already knew of my plan.

' "Jack agrees," I told him, "and the terms are to be one for one— one share of City Centre worth 70s. for each of your shares. But there's only one snag."

'Charles Clore's face was impassive. He seldom smiles or shows any emotion on such occasions. But I could see his eyes glinting.

' "The snag is that Jack wants to be chairman, otherwise he won't agree to the terms. You will have to be deputy chairman under him."

' "Douglas, for 70s. a share I'll be the office boy."

'The deal was done.'

The two companies were then valued by the stock market at £65 million. Cotton's slice of the new combine was worth £14 million, Clore's was worth £10 million. These sums represented the major part of what the two tycoons had made out of property in the fifteen years between 1945 and 1960, though it subsequently turned out that the stock market had greatly exaggerated. Five years later the share price of City Centre had halved.

Size had become in its own right a great virtue in Cotton's eyes. The day after the merger was announced the annual meeting of City Centre's shareholders was held. One of the resolutions to be approved was a sanction to increase the borrowing powers of the company—already raised in 1958 from £7 million, to £20 million and in 1959 from £20 million to £30 million—by another £20 million to £50 million. Cotton told the shareholders, 'In view of the present circumstances this will probably have to be increased. It will be a very happy day when we have to call you together again for the purpose of raising our borrowing powers.' There was mutual congratulation all round.

The advantage of the merger for Clore's company was less clear. True, it gradually appeared that the financial terms of the deal had been more favourable to Clore than to Cotton. But Clore could only have capitalised on this if he had sold big chunks of his shares at the high prices current for two years or so after the merger. But although he actively dealt in the shares, he only sold a small proportion of his holding—and bought them back at lower prices. Another reason and probably the one that weighed most heavily at the time was that Clore had many other irons in the fire apart from real estate and was keen to concentrate less on that side. He wanted in a sense to get out of property. Jack Cotton, first, last and all the time a man of property, would be just the one to organise, develop and manage his property company for him.

It did not take long for Clore and his brilliant right-hand man, the lawyer Leonard Sainer, to find out that Cotton in fact had virtually no organisation at all. The idea that City Centre had an organisation capable of running a much bigger group was a myth. At the time of the merger the corporate set-up under Cotton consisted of an accountant, a couple of typists and perhaps half a dozen clerks. They had their whole work cut out merely keeping tabs on what had taken place. The boardroom of City Centre was Jack Cotton's suite at the Dorchester. His staff had little idea of what deals were in the pipeline, for many of these were just vague details in Cotton's head. They did not even have proper access to all the company's files. In his bedroom at the Dorchester Jack had two beds. In one he slept. Spread on the other, in an order which only he understood, were many of this giant company's most important files—and only he could touch them.

So Clore and Sainer soon started to ask questions. And the deal around which their questions were most persistent was the one with Murrayfield. Clore, no doubt with the reservations of one long established self-made tycoon about another of newer vintage, did not like the boisterous Walter Flack too much. And on Flack's part the feeling was mutual. Clore felt that, with the vague agreement on finance, Flack had done too well out of City Centre, of which he was now a part, and that it would be better if the whole of Murrayfield's capital, rather than just 30 per cent, belonged to the group so that the directors of City Centre had complete control over what Murrayfield did—and spent.

Cotton, on the other hand, was not keen to force this submission on Flack. He thought that a total takeover of Murrayfield would break the spirit of that unwritten agreement which he had originally made with Flack. And Flack himself objected most strongly. It would mean that he, an extreme individualist and aged only forty-four, would no longer be master in the house which he had built in so few years. Although he would continue to be its managing director, he would have to answer to the directors of City Centre.

But Flack lost. Clore and Sainer persuaded the reluctant Cotton and by May 1961 the public were told that 'agreement had been reached in principle for the amalgamation of Murrayfield into City Centre'.

This first major action of the Cotton-Clore combine did not improve an already fast deteriorating relationship between the three main camps on the board of City Centre. Here were three strong-willed, aggressive businessmen, each used to having his own way, sitting round the same table. Flack, who was developing a minor version of the sickness of *folie de grandeur* which hit Cotton in a big way, was resentful that he should have been pushed out of full control of 'his' company. Clore was worried about the unconventional manner in which Cotton ran the huge company and was determined to check his haphazard methods. Cotton, pained and surprised in his warm-hearted way that any-one should question him, had understood that it was he who was to run City Centre after the merger and thus resented what he considered Clore's interference.

The result was an atmosphere of increasing bitterness and hostility. The formal board meetings of City Centre degenerated into three-sided battles. The usual form was for Clore's camp to oppose anything which Cotton or Flack proposed, for Cotton to veto the Clore and Flack suggestions and for Flack to try to block Cotton or Clore's proposals.

Meanwhile the public balloon of Cotton's image as the king of property was puffed fatter and fatter, actively encouraged by himself. In July of '61 he spoke about a '£70 million' plan to build an office complex above a railway station in Chicago—a deal which never came off—and he remarked: 'Someone once referred to the three Cs—Cotton, Clore and Columbus. I like that. It is how I feel.' At one time he had a grand plan to move all the hospitals out of Central London and redevelop their valuable sites.

The trouble was that for journalists Cotton was an easy, colourful and accessible character to write about and that Cotton began, as one friend of his put it sadly, 'to believe his own publicity'. At the same time he became more and more difficult, even for his friends and supporters, to work with. Both he and Clore had always had certain very close advisers. But the difference now emerged that, whereas Clore continued to take the advice of Sainer and others, Cotton continued to ask for advice, yet when it was not what he had wanted to hear, he would disregard it. He even paid less and less attention to his oldest confidant, Freddie Lindgren. And if anyone of those under him in the organisation, which at the insistence of Clore began to be collected, disagreed with him, he would not go off the deep end, as some businessmen might. He would smile warmly, lean back in his chair and laugh. Regally, he would say, 'Leave it to Daddy', intending that to be the end of the discussion. And when a piece of advice was unacceptable, he would ask someone else, and someone else again. For example, he sought out the views of Sir Solly Zuckerman (whom Jack knew well through his £250,000 gift to the London Zoo), better known in the fields of zoology and defence than real estate.

Since the board meetings of City Centre opposed many of his schemes, Cotton managed to push them through by lobbying individually those of the directors who he thought would be most in favour. After a while this lobby system did not work. So he put through deals himself and presented the board with a *fait accompli* afterwards.

As a property man Jack Cotton was by instinct and by experience a more accomplished operator than Charles Clore. Their respective deals in New York, the Pan-Am Building and 40 Wall Street, discussed in greater detail in chapter 13, give an illustration of this. But, as Cotton developed his form of businessman's megalomania, so he turned in ever greater proliferation to a form of operation which looked fine on paper but which in practice did not work out—and with which Clore strongly disagreed. This was the joint company. They were of two kinds: there was the joint company with a trading organisation, such as Woolworths or Shell, which might have spare land for City Centre to help to develop or might need premises from City Centre, or both; and there was a joint company with a body such as the Church Commissioners or various pension funds which had plenty of money to spare and lacked the know-how on real estate.

In practice these alliances turned out to be full of snags, and Clore—and Flack, too—were right to object to them. Most prominent trading companies had their own real estate departments and were quite capable of looking after their own problems or opportunities. For them the joint company might be a way of palming off on City Centre some scrag end of land which they did not need. The links with the pension funds made more sense. However, quite soon the pension funds insisted on having their own advisers, estate agents usually, to look at all sides of any joint deal before it was sanctioned—and at all stages along the line once it had started. This led to endless delays and complications—property development being quite involved enough without several extra guiding hands. The result was that very little was done. A prestigious three-way collaboration between City Centre and the pension funds of both Imperial Chemical Industries and the Central Electricity Generating Board, intended to provide up to £25 million, got no further than a letter of intent. Very few of the joint companies started by the businesslike Church Commissioners failed to make any headway, but two of the three projects with City Centre came to nothing because of a mixture of the three troubles which afflicted the group: its poor organisation, its heavy commitments elsewhere, and its warring management.

As 1961 and 1962 wore on the strain of the internal strife in City Centre began to sap the health of both Jack Cotton and Walter Flack. Both were highly emotional men and both lived for little else but their property firms. For Clore the in-fighting was less of a strain. A more phlegmatic character, leaning heavily on the canny and tough Leonard Sainer, and with many other businesses to think about, he was far more able to weather the storm. Whether Clore could have done more to lessen the differences is problematical.

Apart from Cotton, Clore and Flack there were three big institutional shareholders in City Centre: the Pearl, the Legal & General, both represented on the board, and the Prudential, which had come in at the time of the merger with Clore's City & Central.

Cotton's daily routine did not help his worsening health. He got up in the mornings at about 10.30, not bothering with breakfast. He would immediately start on business meetings in his suite at the Dorchester until about 1.30. Then there was lunch until 3, followed by a nap of two hours or so. From 5 until 8 would be a series of drinks and meetings. At about 8 he ate dinner. And then he would return back upstairs for more meetings which went on until around midnight. After that he would begin to look at the previous day's work—at maps and plans of all sorts—occasionally ringing up surprised executives in the early hours of the morning to enquire after some detail. Add frequent appearances at dinners, balls and various charity functions, plus working weekends, and the effect of this routine was to sap his strength. He was trying to do too much in a company that had grown too big for him. He also drank a great deal. He was a man who was able to drink a lot over a long period of the day without it having any effect on him, though his friendly, jovial manner sometimes deceived people. But, for a man in poor health to start with, the volume of drink had a steadily undermining influence.

In the autumn of 1962 Walter Flack had a severe attack of jaundice. This was a culmination of personal misfortunes, for along with the worries about control of his business slipping from his grasp, his marriage broke up that year. After he had recovered from the jaundice, his relationship with Cotton failed to improve. On 15 January 1963 Flack resigned both from the board of City Centre and as managing director of Murrayfield. Just before he did so he observed of the break with Murrayfield, 'It's like breaking up a marriage. You know you can't possibly live together another day; yet it's incredible to think of life without each other.'

This was only too true. Life was empty for Flack without his company. He took a long holiday in North Africa, returned home, and, eleven weeks after his resignation, in an increasingly depressed frame of mind, died on 22 March 1963. He was found by his chauffeur in the bath of his flat in Whitehall Court. Always very much given to hot baths, he had taken a dose of barbiturate, fallen asleep and drowned. At an inquest a coroner gave a verdict of accidental drowning.

Meanwhile in the same spring of 1963 Jack Cotton caught a bad bout of pneumonia. And the gulf between him and his co-directors had not narrowed. Towards the end of that June

L

one of the other directors circulated a memorandum among the
board listing the details in Cotton's running of the company of
which his fellow directors disapproved. To discuss this document a board meeting was held at Cotton's home in Marlowe,
where he had a bar paper with his collection of cartoons of himself. At that meeting it was decided that Cotton was to resign
as chairman and chief executive of the company which he had
created. The only reason publicly stated for this was his ill-health,
although by then word of the internal disagreements had leaked
out.

Cotton remained a director of City Centre, but he never attended
another board meeting. The quarrel simmered on. In September
there was a rumour that he would bow out completely from City
Centre by handing in his resignation as director. Partly recovered
from his illness, he was bouncy again. 'Resign! Of course I'm not
resigning. You don't resign overnight from an empire like mine.
It's my baby.' But in November he arranged for almost all his
shares in City Centre, held by family trusts, £8·5 million worth,
to be sold to Sir Isaac Wolfson and trusts represented by the
banker Kenneth Keith, announcing the sale, most inconveniently
for the other directors, in the early hours of one morning.

Later that day the shareholders gathered for the first annual
meeting in the Clore-built Hilton. The new chairman, George
Bridge, the stolid, trusty representative of the Legal & General,
told the meeting, without the expected flourish of secrecy, of the
sale of Cotton's shares to Wolfson and Keith, and that they would
join the board. This, Cotton's last big deal, turned out also to be
one of his best, for the shares, which had already been falling in
price bit by bit for over two years, as the stock market realised its
excessive enthusiasm for property shares in general, as Walter
Flack sold out and as news of the boardroom battle came to light,
continued to drop heavily. Bridge also proposed that Jack Cotton
should be elected first president of City Centre. With polite
murmurings, in Cotton's absence, this was done.

Cotton remained ill and deeply unhappy. One of the greatest
ambitions of his last few years—to be Sir Jack Cotton—remained
unfulfilled. He was a man out of a job, the job which he had
carved for himself and which meant everything to him. After three
months he threw back the empty office of president in his fellow
directors' teeth. He resigned in February 1964, cutting his

last link with City Centre. The following month—by an un-nerving coincidence on the same day of the same month as the death of Walter Flack: 22 March—Jack Cotton died of a heart attack.

CHAPTER ELEVEN

The Euston Centre: Joe Levy and Robert Clark

JOE LEVY is a small, jovial man in a large, rectangular office. Inside a faceless Portland stone building in the Haymarket, it is unremarkable except that it has had a great deal of money spent on it. The walls are of neo-Georgian panelling. On either side of the fireplace are two domed recesses with glass shelves scattered with precious ornaments and photographs of his family.

'Will you have a drink? I must show you my little gimmick,' said Joe Levy, bouncing up from behind his desk with a genial grin. He pressed two of a battery of switches beside his desk. Across the room the two alcoves began to revolve. One turned into an array of glasses and bottles of liquor. The other was a television set. 'I have that so that I can watch my horses when they are racing.'

Joe Levy is a tycoon with an uninhibited pleasure in the material results of great wealth. Both as an estate agent and as a developer, he was a prime mover behind the office blocks which have sprung up in central London since the war. His firm of estate agents, D. E. & J. Levy, claims to have handled for clients some 9 million square feet of new offices in London, which, set against the total stock of old and new offices of around 140 million square feet, is an impressive feat.

Joe and his brother David were sons of a London bookmaker. In 1924, when David was nineteen and Joe thirteen months younger, they both went to work for the famous pre-war office developer and estate agent, Jackie Phillips, discussed in more detail in chapter 4. The direct influence of Phillips, whom Joe Levy deeply admired, is evident in Levy's post-war career. He remembered the dictum which had guided his business. 'Once,

when I returned from the suburbs after letting a shop for a commission of £40, Jack Phillips said to me, "If you can't make a
damned good living within three square miles of Piccadilly Circus
and the Bank of England, don't try in this profession. And never
go into a back street." '

After the lavish Jackie Phillips had run into heavy debts, David
and Joe took over his agency in 1939. Although they changed the
name of the business to D. E. & J. Levy, they kept the special
style of the 'TO LET' and 'FOR SALE' notice boards, which were
painted in the Zionist red and white. 'As there was a lot of anti-
semitism at the time, several people, including an uncle who was
a director of the well-known caterers, Levy & Franks, asked us not
to use the red and white and to trade under some non-Jewish
corporate name. So I asked that uncle why he didn't change the
name of his public company. "Oh," he replied, "it's well established and known all over London." ' So indeed was the name of
D. E. & J. Levy twenty-five years later.

Though they were not then to know it, David and Joe set up
on their own just at the right moment. After a few months, war
broke out. The Levy brothers were both in the fire service. Every
three days they had forty-eight hours off, and in that time they
managed to keep their estate agency open. There was plenty of
buying and selling to do as the bombs fell. Joe Levy reckons that
this experience was basic to their post-war success. 'We were on
the spot and we could see that if this country came out of the war,
London would have to be rebuilt.'

After the war David and Joe Levy naturally had a long start
over their competitors specialising in London offices, in the same
way that Healey & Baker, also open and active through the war,
did in shops. The Levys had built up a fund of experience, they
had collected clients around them and their practice did not have
to be started up again from scratch, like so many others. They
were in touch with the way conditions in the market had changed,
they were in touch with the new sources of finance and they
understood all the ins and outs of the problems arising out of war
damage. Those who came back from the war to start up in
business afresh had much to learn and were at a great disadvantage.
To cap this good fortune, the Levy brothers had a natural flair for
judging the merits of real estate.

As they guided their estate agency towards its snowballing

post-war success, David and Joe Levy began more and more to act as promoters themselves rather than just as agents. In this they had a shrewd partner, Robert Clark. The Levy brothers had first run across Robert Clark in 1937, when they were looking for finance for their first development on their own, three depots for Dunlop, one in Greenwich, one in Brixton and one in the Mile End Road. They had about £1,000 between them and they needed another £50,000. Through the introduction of a friend, they met Clark at his modest house in Hendon, which he lived in for many years after the war when he was an extremely rich man. Clark agreed to lend the money, but he did not, to the Levys' surprise, participate in any profit from the deal as he might have done. He reasoned that it would be better to take a more limited risk in his first deal with the Levys and see how the two sides liked one another.

Robert Clark was a careful Scot from Paisley. He had qualified as a lawyer just after the First World War and joined the firm of solicitors run by John Maxwell in Glasgow. Maxwell came to London to retire in the late twenties, but instead salvaged the financially rocky British International Pictures, a major producer of talkies, and merged it in 1933 with a cinema chain into Associated British Picture. At the same time he brought Robert Clark from Glasgow to work for him in London. Even before he met the Levy brothers, Clark had himself dabbled in property. He promoted a small office building in his home town, Paisley, on the site of a burnt-out cinema.

When war broke out the Levys' three depots for Dunlop were not quite finished and no permanent finance had been fixed up to repay Robert Clark. He carried the debt for six years. After the war it was possible to find a mortgage again and Clark was repaid. Then, as the Levys began to single out some plum sites for themselves after the war, they usually enlisted Clark, who was invaluable with his solid Scottish caution and knowledge of finance as a brake on their enthusiasm. In each company formed specifically for one building David Levy would have one third of the shares, Joe Levy one third and Robert Clark one third, but so that control should not be in the hands of the Levys through voting power, they both held 'B' shares with one vote each and Robert Clark held 'A' shares with two votes.

Joe Levy is lyrical about the unlikely partnership between himself and Robert Clark. 'You never know what can happen when a

Scotsman and a Jewish boy get together. Why does it work so well?' Before there was time to think, he replies with a roar of delight, 'Because they would go blind watching one another if they weren't together.' What did in fact happen was that Levy and his family made about £5 million and Clark and his family also made £5 million.

David Levy died suddenly in 1952 at the age of forty-seven, 'just as we were making the grade'. In the same year Joe Levy first ran across a property which was to become the key to his most celebrated deal and the biggest single redevelopment in the country since the war pushed through by private enterprise.

A Mr Young called on D. E. & J. Levy, asking if the firm could sell for him a 1-acre corner site, facing the Euston Road and Stanhope Street. He wanted £400,000 for it. To lever up the value of this site, Joe Levy brought in the architects, Lewis, Solomon Kaye & Partners, to draw up a scheme for a 120,000 square foot office building. This was sent in to the LCC and granted outline planning permission. However, at the last moment Mr Young discovered that he would have a tax problem if he sold the land. Joe Levy told him, 'If you ever want to sell in the future, come back to me again.'

Four years later Mr Young did come back. He still wanted the same price for the land. Joe Levy asked his most important client, Charles Clore, if he was interested. Clore was. In order to make sure of what could be built on the site before any contract was signed, Joe Levy and architect Sidney Kaye then trotted off to the LCC to discuss the detailed planning permission. They met the valuer to the LCC, Jo Toole, and an under-valuer, Ernie Sames.

Joe Levy recalled this meeting. 'Jo Toole produced a huge map and shook his head when he saw our plans. "No. I'm sorry, you can't have permission to build on that site. We have a plan to build a main East-West road there and we shall need most of the site for part of the road widening."

' "That's interesting," I replied, "but I happen to have a little piece of buff paper and if it isn't an outline planning permission for a 120,000 square foot office block, you're not valuers of the LCC. And if you intend to acquire that site compulsorily, it will cost you some £1 million in loss of development rights." ' Curiously, the LCC's valuers had forgotten the outline permission. Sames was sent out of the room to look up the file.

Joe Levy's threat that it would cost the LCC £1 million to purchase the site compulsorily was based on the following sum: the site itself might cost £440,000 including costs and an office building of 120,000 square feet would then have run out at some £4 a square foot, or £480,000, a total cost to the developer of £920,000. A possible rent would have been 17s. 6d. a square foot, giving a rent roll of £105,000 a year. The end product should have had a value of £1·9 million, so that a purchaser would be buying the building on a yield of 5½ per cent. The difference between £920,000 and the value of £1·9 million, the developer's profit, could be claimed in compensation as loss of development rights under the Planning Act of 1947 if the site was compulsorily acquired after outline permission had been granted.

Mr Sames, the under-valuer, returned to the room with the news that outline consent had indeed been granted four years before. This set the LCC a serious problem. It just could not spare almost £1 million to buy off Joe Levy or his clients as an incidental cost in a road-widening scheme when its first priorities were housing and schools. Joe Levy asked the valuers what they proposed to do about their unpalatable dilemma. The answer was that the LCC dreamt of a single, co-ordinated scheme to rebuild the shabby area to the north of the Euston Road, where it would be truncated by the underpass. But it was only a dream, since the LCC was not able to finance what under the rules of zoning would be predominantly a commercial project. What the LCC needed was a private developer who would fit in with its own plans. The bargaining counters between the two sides were money and land in the hands of the developer and planning permission up the sleeve of the local authority. If Levy or his clients were prepared to give the LCC for free that slice of Mr Young's site needed for the new road, the LCC would in return grant planning permission on the rest of the site to the same density as though the entire site was being built over.

Joe Levy pondered the huge opportunity. Although the LCC would not use its powers of compulsory acquisition, it would actively co-operate in giving planning permission to the developer over an unusually large area. There was the risk that offices would not let easily north of the Euston Road, where no important development had been built up to that time. This would be compensated by low land costs in a seedy, untried area. But the major imponderable was: would it be possible to persuade all the many owners on a fragmented 13-acre site to sell?

Joe Levy then returned to Charles Clore to make a deal for Mr Young on the original site and to recount the grandiose proposition of a possible 13-acre development. Clore remained keen to buy. But at the last moment, just before the contract was to be signed, Clore telephoned Levy, explaining that he wanted to have a meeting with Levy and somebody else about the site.

Much to Levy's chagrin, the somebody else turned out to be Clore's adviser on shops, Douglas Tovey, who was to give a second opinion. Levy complained strongly that Tovey was a shop man and to take his advice about shops was fine, but that this was to be a block of offices, which he and not Tovey understood.

However, the three of them drove in Douglas Tovey's Rolls Royce to the Euston Road, and stood about sizing up the deal. Tovey gave the thumbs down and next day Clore sent back the contract, unsigned.

Tovey maintains that his reasons for advising against the project were not that it might not make money but that it would not suit Mr Clore's temperament.

To turn the scheme into a full-blown success, it would be necessary patiently to acquire corners of the larger area bit by bit, over a number of years, never knowing until the final corner had been bought whether the jigsaw could be fitted together or not. Tovey said, 'I knew that Charles Clore couldn't stand the strain of such a long drawn out speculation. He would never have given me any peace. I would have had to comfort him for years. It wasn't worth it.'

There is a difference of evidence on this point, with which the LCC was not involved. Levy recalls that Clore, with the help of Tovey, turned down the scheme while it was still a single building, before the idea of a large operation arose.

After Bernard Sunley had also turned the proposition down, Levy took the idea to his partner Robert Clark. They decided that they could not tackle a project of this size, which might cost a total of £15 to £20 million, on their own. So they put the proposition to two big firms of contractors with whom they had already formed alliances on other developments: Wimpey and Wates. Joe Levy had been at school, Emanuel School, Wandsworth, with

Ronnie Wates. They agreed that Clark and Levy's company, Stock Conversion, should have one-third of a new company formed for the Euston development, that Wates should have one-third and Wimpey one-third. On the basis of the guarantees of all three parties, their bankers, the Clydesdale Bank and its parent the Midland, were prepared to lend money to pay for the land and the cost of construction.

The next step was to buy all the land as quietly as possible. The site stretched for a quarter of a mile between the underground stations at Warren Street and Great Portland Street, along the north side of Euston Road, which until the 18th century had been the northern boundary of London and a military road for soldiers skirting the city. Behind the frontage to Euston Road, bounded at one end by Hampstead Road and the other end by Osnaburgh Street, was a collection of decaying late Georgian terraces and sad little shops, an area which Joe Levy extravagantly describes as 'a derelict bloody den of disease'.

At the same time as Sidney Kaye was finding out what density of offices and of shops the LCC would allow and was putting in a planning application, which was then possible though the client did not own the land, Joe Levy was forming a consortium of estate agents. He knew that if his firm alone were to attempt to buy from all the many different owners, freeholders, leaseholders and sub-leaseholders, his intention might become apparent and there would be two great dangers. Owners might dream up an exaggerated idea of the value, to him, of their properties or some small-time property dealers might compete against him in order to hold him to ransom. In either case his ultimate profit on the redevelopment could be either sharply slimmed down or wiped out entirely. Levy brought in three other agents to help his strategy. With his eye on the shops facing Euston Road and Hampstead Road, he enlisted Aubrey Orchard-Lisle, the senior partner of Douglas Tovey at Healey & Baker. As the front runners among agents in shops and with access to the estate departments of the multiple retailers, some of whom had shops on Euston or Hampstead Roads, Healey & Baker would be the firm best able to buy up the shops. Two other firms with special connections in the Euston Road neighbourhood were brought in: Davis & Co., and Perkins & Ballard. Levy agreed to pay these firms a percentage above the normal fees for their vital role in the operation; after the last deal had been

clinched the three agents had shared a total commission of some
£200,000.

Joe Levy never put up an 'Acquired through D. E. & J. Levy'
notice board on the site at all. He dictated the policy and held the
reins, while the other three agents reported to him. They hoisted
their notice boards as they bought.

The bulk of the properties was bought in a four-year period
between 1956 and 1960 and the total number of separate deals
added up to around 315. If any of these had foundered Levy and
Clark could have lost a packet sitting on land with a negligible
return, since the LCC were not prepared to use their powers of
compulsory purchase except on the land they needed for the road.
But throughout the LCC was otherwise exceedingly co-operative
with Joe Levy. It was almost like having a fourth estate agent in
the consortium. Ernie Sames, the valuer involved all along the
line, recalls that when owners from within the 13 acres on which
Levy had his eye came to the LCC for planning permission or
with any queries, he would suggest to them politely that they
ought to have a talk with Mr Levy. 'For instance, Sir Jonah
Walker-Smith (father of the Conservative Minister of Health
from 1957 to 1960) owned a slice. He had already built a small
office for his firm and wanted to develop the next-door site. I told
him "Go and see Joe Levy, you may hear something to your
advantage." I used to meet him afterwards at Joe Levy's annual
cocktail party and he always said to me, "Well, Sames, that was a
good turn you did me." '

The prices paid for the land varied wildly. In Diana Place were
two adjoining semi-derelict cottages, worth in themselves about
£1,000 apiece. One was bought for £1,800. The other, owned by a
shrewd Cypriot, cost Joe Levy £45,000. A small factory belonging
to a cast-iron welder cost £360,000. Levy had a worrying tussle
with the owner of one small shop, an investor, not a shopkeeper.
As a shop it was worth £25,000. Levy was prepared to give
£40,000. The owner wanted £80,000. 'From the start I could see
that I would have trouble with that shop, that the owners were
going to bleed me,' said Levy. Then one day the LCC rang him up
to say that they had decided to widen Hampstead Road deeper
than on their original plan and take in another shop. This meant
that particular shop which was proving tricky and whose owner
Levy had broken off negotiations with, 'to let him cool off'. Levy

replied that the LCC could not have done him a greater favour. The owner would have to sell either under compulsory purchase or under the threat of compulsory purchase. The price would then be £25,000 plus a small percentage.

Levy managed to buy about 80 per cent of the front land needed by the LCC. With the remaining 20 per cent the LCC used the force of compulsory purchase. But the developers paid for all of it and handed it over to the LCC for free. In this way the local authority received perhaps £2 million worth of land for their road and in return, in the notional deal, allowed the volume of building, which would have stood on the new road, to be heaped on to the rest of the site.

Some of the tenants on the site posed special problems. One was a church, one a hospital, another a school. All three were rejuvenated at the expense of the developers. The Stanhope Institute, a school specialising in evening classes, and the church, St Anne's Chapel, were rebuilt in different spots on the same site. St Saviour's Hospital moved to Kent. It had stood on a piece of land owned by the Crown facing Osnaburgh Street. The Crown Estates Commissioners bought the lease from the hospital and sold a new lease to Levy's company. But the price from the Crown was not enough for the new hospital in Kent, so the developers gave an extra £40,000 to make up the balance. Joe Levy was particularly proud to have been asked by the nuns of St Saviour's to the opening of the new hospital in Kent.

In some of the more squalid residential parts of the site, the LCC made closing orders on houses and flats. This meant that the LCC had to rehouse about 150 rent-controlled tenants somewhere else. Joe Levy made a pact with the local authority, St Pancras, which was short of land for housing. He gave them a chunk of land for a block of flats towards the back of the site as a *quid pro quo* for rehousing controlled tenants.

Not long before final planning permission for the entire site was passed through the LCC in September 1959, Wates withdrew from the trio of developers, deciding that the waiting period and the risks were too great. This left Wimpey and Stock Conversion each with 50 per cent of the company, Balgray Investments, specifically formed for the 13 acres to be known as the Euston Centre.

Meanwhile, as Joe Levy quietly pencilled in the captured spaces on his master plan, Stock Conversion was on the brink of an amazing performance as one of the wonder shares of the property boom. Robert Clark and the Levys had in 1951 caught hold of a tiny 'shell' company with a propitious link to one of the great industrial booms of the 19th century: railways. In 1954, the year in which building licences were finally scrapped, Clark and Levy tipped into Stock Conversion most of the properties and investments which they had bought since the war.

This was only the beginning of a phenomenal 13 year expansion. In 1957, at the mean price for the year, the stock market valued the company at £360,000; by 1964 this valuation had soared to £14,400,000, yet during this period the shareholders did not put up a penny of new capital. Finance came from banks, insurance companies and building contractors. But for several years, while Stock Conversion was buying sites and sprouting office blocks at a tremendous pace, the investing public had no idea of the money-making capacity of this company with the irrelevant name.

Robert Clark deliberately gave few clues. He was the chairman and a Scottish accountant was the only other director. Since Clark was known mainly for his work as a director of Associated British Picture and the full-time property man behind Stock Conversion, Joe Levy, was nowhere to be seen, it was impossible to draw any conclusions from scanning the board of directors. When a separate property section was listed on the Stock Exchange in 1957, Stock Conversion was still misleadingly labelled as an investment trust. Clark's statements as chairman were terse and contained a minimum of information to guide the minority shareholders. Certainly there was no hint that one of the busiest estate agents in London was picking out choice sites for Stock Conversion to develop, nor that it had powerful partners. It had alliances with Wimpey just behind Marble Arch (ATV House) and in Hanover Square (Vogue House), with the Yorkshire Insurance in the Haymarket and Dover Street, with the Royal London Mutual Insurance and Trollope & Colls in Red Lion Square.

The extreme reticence of Stock Conversion was due partly to Clark's fear that even a breath of disclosure might somehow interfere with developments being planned, where the site was not finally bought. It was also normal to treat shareholders with a good deal of disdain in the fifties, as far as giving them information was concerned. Besides, Robert Clark was a very cautious businessman and deeply reluctant to say that something might happen before it actually had happened. The accounts of Stock Conversion were prepared on some ultra-conservative principles. By 1960 a writer in the *Investors Chronicle* had laboriously dug around behind the published figures and came up with what then seemed the rather wild estimate that the net asset value backing each ordinary share was not 3s. 6d., as the figures showed, but closer to 120s. Robert Clark was asked about this by a shareholder soon afterwards at the company's annual meeting. All he would reply austerely, in his clipped Scottish accent, was that the estimate was 'very enterprising'.

By 1960 insiders and students of obscure companies had woken up to the possibility that Stock Conversion might be a vast iceberg. One clue had been a dramatic and regular increase in the company's borrowing powers. In 1954 these had been raised to £1 million. In 1957 they were lifted to £2 million, in 1958 to £4 million and in 1960 they were doubled again to £8 million. 1959 was the year in which the share price began its long climb, having drifted for two years between a bottom of 6s. 4d. and a top of 20s. In 1959, year of Harold Macmillan's Never Had It So Good victory at the polls and the take off in the property share market, Stock Conversion leapt from a low of £1 to just over £3. The next year, despite Mr Clark's noncommittal remark, or perhaps spurred on by it, the price shot on up to £12. In 1961 it hit £25 10s. In the space of three years those with capital in Stock Conversion had seen their shares multiply in value by a cool twenty-five times. Later, when Robert Clark was shown a chart of his company's share price, he allowed himself a smile and observed dryly, pointing to the more prominent upward spurts, 'Those must have been after Joe's visits to Monte Carlo,' meaning that Joe Levy would not have been able to restrain himself from telling his friends on holiday that Stock Conversion was a good thing. One budding stockbroker put his shirt on Stock Conversion, and retired on the proceeds, so great were they, at the age of twenty-seven.

The great unveiling of Stock Conversion started in 1961. An investment analyst, Patrick Heath-Saunders, working for a small firm of stockbrokers in the City, delved into the intricate web of companies—some daughters, some cousins of the master Stock Conversion—charted them all on a family tree and searched out the statistics of each. They were not always possible to find. But after about a year's financial detective work, he had a rough picture of the whole operation. He persuaded his clients to buy Stock Conversion's shares and the rumour soon buzzed around the Stock Exchange that the dull old investment trust was an iceberg of valuable real estate. Finally the Press wrote up Heath-Saunders' masterpiece.

The mystery was unwrapped. Early in 1962 Joe Levy joined the board and in his next annual report Robert Clark let his hair down to the extent of publishing photographs of a few of the completed developments. But even then the public at large knew nothing of the grand project for the north of the Euston Road. Clark avoided any mention of that, no doubt lest the last few gaps on the jigsaw might become more expensive overnight. However, in the winter of 1963–64, when the demolition men swung their sledgehammers and bulldozers began to crawl about, gouging out foundations along the quarter mile between Hampstead Road and Osnaburgh Street, the Press could hardly fail to notice that something fairly colossal was about to emerge. By July 1964 Judy Hillman of the *Evening Standard*, almost the only journalist who attempted the frustrating job of reporting in depth on planning in London for a mass circulation newspaper, had uncovered more or less the whole story. The *Evening Standard* lived up to the occasion. Paragraph one pointed out that activity in the Euston Road showed that the LCC was preparing an underpass. Paragraph two was in capitals and read: 'BUT THERE IS NOTHING TO SHOW THAT THE AREA ALONGSIDE IS BEING TRANSFORMED INTO WHAT AMOUNTS TO A MINIATURE NEW TOWN.'

Joe Levy has a model of the Euston Centre, which he likes to show off to visitors, explaining that it cost over £2,000 and is lit by 800 individual bulbs. He flicks the switches with unconcealed pleasure, lighting up each building in turn. The development is 'comprehensive', that is, it provides a bit of every type of use, in line with the fashion in planning. The old streets and alleys, Diana Place, Fitzroy Place, Eden Street, Seaton Place and a slice of Stanhope Street, have disappeared entirely. In their place rise a series of high buildings with pedestrian paths all over the site below. All around the foot of the buildings are shops, 100 of them, and on the first floor above the shops a large volume, 160,000 square feet, of showrooms. A bulky, square factory sits at the back of the site, luxury flats at the corner nearest Regent's Park, and a car park for 900 cars underneath the whole scheme. Then, above the shops and showrooms on the Euston Road frontage are the offices, the most profitable part of the project, mostly crammed into one seventeen-storey and another giant, thirty-four-storey tower. As one developer observed—almost all his rivals greatly admired Joe Levy's artistry in pulling off the Euston Centre deal—'The cake is upstairs at the Euston Centre, everything else is just bread and butter.'

Unless there is some drastic recession in the economy, the Euston Centre will be worth about £38 million when it is finished in 1970. It will have cost £16 million, giving the staggering capital profit of £22 million* on one single development. Of this, £11 million will be Wimpey's share and £11 million will be Stock Conversion's.

Sidney Kaye, the architect, produced a design for the office blocks very different from his original intention. He had designed three symmetrical blocks spaced at equal distances from one another along the side. But the Royal Fine Arts Commission jumped on this, objecting that the block nearest Regent's Park would offend the principle that tall commercial buildings should not overlook a Royal Park, a principle which the RFAC failed to thwart with Sidney Kaye's design for the Hilton.

The change in design did not alter the value of the Euston Centre. What did boost its value, perhaps by as much as £10 million, was the delay in starting construction and Mr George Brown's ban on offices in November 1964.

The start was delayed for some three years, partly by the LCC, which was short of money and did not know exactly how much of Joe Levy's land it would need for the underpass. Between the end of 1961 and the end of 1965 rents for office space in the Euston Road climbed from around 27s. 6d. a square foot to 55s. a square foot, given a sharp shot in the arm by the office ban. Joe Levy has no illusions about the developers' luck in this delay, and in the signing of the building contract for the entire job five months before the ban. Since there can be no other large new office blocks on the market by virtue of the Brown ban, Joe Levy gleefully labels the vast tower opposite Warren Street tube station 'Monopoly House'. It will be finished in late 1968, and by then

* For detailed analysis behind these sums, see Appendix 8.

rents will probably have risen even further. Even though some of the shops at the Euston Centre may prove sticky to let, any effect of this on the scheme's value will be swamped by the bonanza with the offices.

Not content with the Euston Centre, in April 1967 Levy and Clark pulled out of their hats an even more dramatic project, which they had been accumulating for 15 years. This was four acres on the edge of Piccadilly Circus, an island site bounded by Shaftesbury Avenue, Rupert Street, Coventry Street and Great Windmill Street. Within about three years a hybrid building with cinemas, shops, offices and other uses will rise on the site at a total cost of £10 million. When the scheme was announced Joe Levy remarked, 'The Euston Centre is three times as big, but this one is six times as important.'

Joe Levy's fortune has been made with the help of inflation and a prosperous economy. He himself radiates optimism. When he was expounding to me on the virtues of bricks and mortar as an investment in good times and in bad, he forgot an important word which has not troubled the post-war developers: 'First of all you have a boom,' he said, 'then you have a . . . what's that other word?' 'Slump?' I said. 'Yes, that's the thing.'

It was probably the secret of the Levy and Clark combination that Robert Clark might possibly forget the word boom, but never slump.

M

CHAPTER TWELVE

'The Evil of Congestion'

CONGESTION was the fashionable word used to describe the main problem of London throughout the post-war period. It was a problem which the planners dismally failed to cope with. The accepted cure for congestion, decentralisation of office employment and dispersal all over the country, may have been wrong; it might have been better radically to improve the public transport and road systems and allow workers and employers to enjoy the pleasures and benefits of central London as they undoubtedly wanted to. But the Government fell incompetently between the two stools. It was ineffectual in introducing the accepted cure until much too late, and it did not improve the transport networks nearly fast enough to service the mushrooming increase in new offices.

The hazards of too many offices in London were officially recognised as long as twenty-seven years ago. Harry Hyams was only twelve when Sir Montague Barlow's Commission reported in 1940 on the Distribution of the Industrial Population. Barlow was concerned only with the dispersal of industry, but he suggested that as manufacturers moved out of central London, office employers would take their place and intensify congestion. This is exactly what happened after the war* and it was not surprising: an acre of floor space used as offices houses seven or eight times as many people as an acre of factory, and offices are built with more floors on a given site.

In spite of Barlow's warning, early post-war planning assumed that employment in London would be static. The planners realised that manufacturing industry had to be forcibly dispersed if it was to be kept out of the centre, but they entirely failed to foresee the

---

* An excellent pamphlet on office employment in London was published by the Town & Country Planning Association in 1962: *The Paper Metropolis*.

continuous rise of the white collar worker. Industrial development certificates controlled the building of new factories, but no provision was made for regulating offices. Sir Patrick Abercrombie's plan for London, first completed in 1943, was modified several times and finally turned into the County of London Development Plan. The one important recommendation of Abercrombie to be dropped was his scheme of arterial ring roads. As he himself complained prophetically in December 1951,* when the Development Plan appeared, 'London is faced, instead, with the expenditure of many millions on tinkerings which will eventually be ineffective. The fault is not that of the LCC but of the Ministry of Transport.' Part of the blame for the chaotic post-war policies for London's roads must in turn be passed up to the Treasury's deadening hand on the purse strings.

By the time Duncan Sandys, as Minister of Housing and Local Government, eventually came to approve the Development Plan in 1955, the false premise of a static level of office employment was plain for all to see. Between mid-1948 and the end of 1954 planning permission had been granted for 22·3 million square feet, and permission to change buildings to office use for another six million square feet, a total virtually three times as great as the loss during the war. Duncan Sandys' advisers realised that the situation had changed drastically during the long period of gestation of the Development Plan. Sandys fiercely denounced the 'evil of congestion' and re-zoned 380 acres of land allocated to factories and offices as residential use. This was a minor reform in relation to the 6,720 acres of the central area. (Sandys also suggested that the scheme for turning Park Lane into an eight-lane highway, known in County Hall as the Park Lane Boulevard, should be renamed. 'I cannot believe that it is really your intention to import foreign expressions of this kind into London's street names.')

Already in 1955 the dangers of too many offices in central London were worrying both the Ministry of Housing and the LCC. But it took another nine years, a consistent spate of planning approvals and office building,† and a change of Government from Conservative to Labour before the problem was finally stamped on. By then market forces had in any event run the boom dry. The market was ahead of the legislator.

Between 1955 and the total Brown Ban of 1964 various wavering

* Article in *The Times*, 22 December 1951.　　　† See Appendix 3.

attempts were made to control the unforeseen boom. The first was the LCC's Grey Book of 1957. Its official title was *A Plan to Combat Congestion in Central London*. This altered the densities allowed in different areas under zoning by plot ratio. Thus some of the more dense zones, plot ratios of 5 : 1, were reduced in area and in others the commercial content was slimmed down and more residential building was allowed. The effect of the Grey Book was bound to be extremely long term. It meant that if there was a strong demand for new offices, more buildings, each containing fewer offices than before 1957, would be promoted by developers. In the long run, a matter of decades, central London's potential density was reduced. But the LCC appeared to be concerned with the immediate problem.

What the Grey Book did not mention were two pieces of planning legislation which together enabled office developers to make a mockery of the LCC's plot ratios. The nigger in the woodpile was known as the Third Schedule: it was in effect a mistake in Schedule 3 of the Town & Country Planning Act of 1947. Lord Silkin's recollection of the Third Schedule was that 'we did not realise that it was capable of being abused. It was sheer ignorance.' The Third Schedule laid down that a building could be enlarged by up to 10 per cent of its cubic content, the purpose of this in 1947 being to allow owners to make minor improvements to existing buildings without having to pay the development charge. But when Mr Macmillan abolished the development charge, the Third Schedule was effectively unchanged.

The trouble began when old buildings were pulled down and rebuilt on a large scale. Until 1957 developers were too busy operating on bomb sites and pulling down small buildings to bother with rebuilding large and out-of-date offices. But from 1958 onwards the trend was increasingly towards pulling down Victorian office blocks, as these figures show:

Planning permissions for offices in central London*

	1948–56	1957	1959	1961	1963	1948–63
			(000's omitted)			
Gross sq. ft	31,898	4,753	4,379	4,796	2,063	59,858
Net new sq. ft	30,505	4,499	3,297	2,422	401	49,326
Percentage of net new space	95·75	94·7	75·3	50·5	19·5	82·4

* From the survey quoted on page 6 and partly detailed in Appendix 3.

These figures also illustrate my point that by 1963, shortly before the ban, the urge of developers to build new offices had fallen sharply; the net addition to all the offices approved in the central area—410,000 in relation to a potential stock of roughly 130 million at the time—was a mere 0·3 per cent.

When an existing building was redeveloped, the developer was allowed to put up a new building with 10 per cent greater cubic capacity than the old building, by claiming his rights under the Third Schedule. This did not mean that the new building was 10 per cent larger than the old, or that it housed 10 per cent more workers. Far from it. There was usually an increase much greater than 10 per cent. Old buildings have higher ceilings, thicker and more numerous walls, more space for passages, staircases, cupboards and directors' lavatories than new buildings. Thus the space actually used for work could be substantially increased by building a modern office box within the cube plus 10 per cent of the old. The modern building would also tend to have a floor area much greater than the maximum plot ratio permitted by the LCC.

A classic Third Schedule job is a huge office in Victoria Street, developed by the Westminster Trust and designed by Chapman, Taylor, Partners. It is now let to New Scotland Yard and helps to cover the losses of the struggling shopping centre at the Elephant & Castle (see chapter 14). Until 1960 this site was graced by four Victorian buildings, all linked; it was a quirk of the Third Schedule that if more than one old building was being replaced by a single new one, the old had to be interconnected, otherwise the 10 per cent 'bonus' could not be claimed. Victoria Street was laid out under a 19th-century scheme for improvement—it had previously been a slum too close to Buckingham Palace for comfort. The sites on either side were leased to Victorian developers and were slow to find takers. But after a while the new 'chambers' did gradually fill up with civil engineers, who were either building railways or advising railway speculators; they had to be near Whitehall and Parliament in order to lobby for the Private Acts needed to push through each new railway. When it came to pulling down the chambers on Westminster Trust's site, Chapman, Taylor found that by adding 10 per cent to their cubic content, the new building would have a net floor area of 400,000 square feet, giving a ratio of site to floor space of 7 : 1. The maximum allowed by the LCC's zoning rules was 3·5 : 1. In short, the new tenant, New Scotland

Yard, was able to employ exactly twice as many people on that site as the LCC thought was desirable.

Why did the LCC allow its rules to be flouted so laughably? Quite simply, it was not rich enough to deny the developer his rights under the Third Schedule. This resulted from a curious contradiction between the authority of the Government and the local council on planning, in this case between a Conservative Government and a Labour local authority. Under Labour's 1947 Act a local authority which refused or revoked a planning per-mission could be obliged to compensate the developer for his total abortive expenditure up to the time of revocation. In 1954 the Conservatives changed the law so that compensation had to in-clude the hypothetical development value lost, profit and all. This made it prohibitively expensive for the LCC, or any other planning authority, to refuse an application of any size. If the LCC had refused the Westminster Trust its 400,000 square feet in Victoria, it could have lost £7½ million as a total write off. It was desperate to turn this particular application down as an earnest of its tough-ness on offices, but it took Counsel's opinion and decided that it was too dangerous to do so. The LCC might apparently have been liable to buy the scheme from the developer at £15 million, the full value of the finished New Scotland Yard building, and if it had then itself promoted an office building at half the plot ratio, the end result would only have been half as valuable. The LCC could not dream of throwing away millions in compensation for the sake of its principles, however enlightened, on density.

Not until 1963 was the Third Schedule absurdity revoked by the Government. By then several million square feet of extra offices must have been tacked on to London through this developer's delight. Since it had been the Government's policy to discourage offices in central London since 1955, it is amazing that action was not taken sooner, or that the LCC did not lobby more vigorously to protect their standards. Richard Edmonds, chairman of the town planning committee, said that 'the Committee was com-placent until the full threat of the Third Schedule emerged through developers taking advantage of it. Also, given the Develop-ment Plan and its intention not to affect the commercial buoyancy of London, I always had a particular feeling that I mustn't antagonise Big Business.' For a Socialist, on a Socialist council, Edmonds, an ex-journalist, tended to follow a moderate, let's get-on-with-it line on planning. But if the LCC had wielded that eminently Tory instrument, public relations, it could probably have forced through a revocation of the Third Schedule much earlier than 1963. As it turned out, it may not have been all that important in the public interest that the restrictive policies of the fifties and sixties were not successful, for, as I discuss later in this chapter, those policies were largely based on incorrect data!

Sir Keith Joseph, himself a director of the building contractors Bovis when not in office, was the Minister of Housing to repeal the wart on the Third Schedule. He observed: 'The reference to cubic capacity in the schedule enabled a developer to drive a coach and horses through the original legislation . . .' For three or four years before this developers had been rushing through their Third Schedule applications, sensing a change in the law. Joseph's Bill allowed the local authority to refuse an addition of 10 per cent to the cube without having to pay compensation. But an extra 10 per cent on the gross floor space was still possible and even that could be made to yield a useful increase in net floor area and potential number of staff by an ingenious architect. This extra 10 per cent in floor area applied to buildings which were not pulled down, so that often old office blocks had workmen on the roof adding a couple of floors. The Silkin Act of 1947 specified that only pre-1948 buildings should qualify for this bonus, but the Macmillan Act of 1954 extended this to modern buildings. The officialese of the White Paper for the Joseph Act of 1963 toned down its comment on this stupidity: 'It is, in the Government's view, wrong that a local planning authority or the Minister on appeal, having settled the size of a new building, should be compelled to authorise a 10 per cent increase in its size under threat of compensation as soon as it has been erected.'

One month before the Third Schedule was amended, planning permission was given by the LCC to a textbook example of a Third Schedule building, Cleveland House, on the corner of St James' Square and King Street. This was a Victorian block of flats, which had been requisitioned by the Government, first during the Boer War, then in the First World War and again in the Second World War. The promoter of Cleveland House was only 28 in 1963, a precocious and untypical developer named Nigel Broackes. Son of a country solicitor, Broackes was one of the few developers to have been educated at a public school, in his case Stowe. He joined a firm of insurance underwriters in the City as his first job for the comfortable reason that the father of a friend from Stowe was the boss. He did not enjoy life as a glorified insurance clerk. 'I felt fearfully cramped and restricted and had a sense of claustrophobia.' He spent only two years in the City, interrupted by a spell of National Service; Broackes was unquestionably an officer, while few of the senior property tycoons who had ability enough to amass great fortunes had managed to rise from the non-commissioned ranks during the war.

Broackes started on his own by buying two houses in Chelsea. He was on the point of inheriting £25,000 from his grandfather. The houses took longer and cost more to modernise than he had expected and at the end of two years he recouped his investment, £14,600, plus £100. Then he tried the hire purchase business, which was becoming fashionable at the time. Broackes put up £10,000 and everything went well until one bad debt wiped out the firm's profits and most of his investment. He sank another £15,000 into a toolmaking and plastic moulding business. From that he recovered £4,000.

By that point he had lost almost all his capital. He was only twenty-two, he had just married and he realised that he needed to stop being an amateur and stop doing things which he understood virtually nothing about. He joined a West End estate agency to learn thoroughly about property. (During his few years spending his birthright he had briefly owned a tiny estate agency in Chancery Lane, which he bought for £100 and sold for £70.) While he was learning his way around estate agency, Nigel Broackes formed an alliance with a financier from the City, David Fremantle, a friend of his mother's. Fremantle wanted his company, Eastern International Investment Trust, to diversify into property. Having lost almost all his own money, Broackes started the link with Fremantle by managing a development for him on the corner of Half Moon Street and Piccadilly, which went like clockwork. Not long after that development was finished Broackes left the estate agency and participated directly in a company with Eastern International as co-owner. 'It was obvious to me that if I didn't break out, I would remain unfulfilled. I was an innovator and manager of events rather than of routine.'

At about the same time Sir Geoffrey Crowther, eminent ex-editor of the *Economist* and acquaintance of Fremantle's, liked the promise of the Broackes-Fremantle company, Eastern International Property Investments, joined the board and later became chairman. Broackes was in the process of negotiating a development in Sackville Street, which was to elevate his company into the big time. The Sackville Street project was a success and Broackes was then offered the chance of a second development next door. Because of existing commitments, finance was a barrier to this second development. But through Sir Geoffrey Crowther, who was a director of the Commercial Union Assurance, Broackes persuaded that insurance company to finance it by what was then a relatively daring method: to lend up to £550,000 on a debenture and simultaneously to buy 28 per cent of the company's ordinary shares, £56,000 worth at the time. Geoffrey Crowther, who as honest broker was probably the key figure in the most important link in the short life of Broackes' company, made a respectable nest-egg out of his vital role. He bought £5,500 worth of shares from Nigel Broackes at an early stage, which today, if he has kept them all, would be worth £50,000. Broackes, on the other hand, put up £15,000 in 1959 and by the end of 1966 had turned that into roughly £1 million. The Commercial Union and Eastern International also did extremely well.

The breakthrough which was to transform the company from one with assets in the hundred thousands to one controlling several millions was a chance conversation in 1961. Broackes visited the Commercial Union to pick up the cheque for their loan on the property in Sackville Street from the CU's secretary, Leonard Cooper. On the same day Cooper was to join the board of Eastern International Property. He asked Broackes if the appointment would be sent to the Directory of Directors. He explained that he was already a director of one other company, a subsidiary of the Commercial Union, named Westminster and Kensington Freeholds.

This company was not new to Broackes, and he was deeply interested. He asked Cooper if he had a few minutes to discuss it. They talked for an hour and a half. Nigel Broackes had come across it in 1958 when discussing buildings suitable for the Third Schedule treatment with his architect, Bob Chapman of Chapman, Taylor. Chapman had explained that one building which would lend itself ideally to reconstruction under the Third Schedule was an old block of flats in Kensington called Rutland

Court. In case it might be for sale Broackes had found out who it belonged to by the simple expedient of looking it up in the telephone book, which gave the name of the company as well as the building. It was then possible to search for the company at Companies House and discover that it was the subsidiary of a big insurance company. That was a full stop. Broackes had presumed that it would not be for sale and had forgoteen about it.

His talk with Cooper revealed that the company might indeed be for sale. Westminster & Kensington had been started just before the First World War by the Prudential and the North British & Mercantile, later merged with the Commercial Union, to look after properties on which either of the two insurance companies had foreclosed. By 1961 it was wholly owned by North British, but had become an embarrassment to the insurance company. It mainly owned blocks of flats, most of which were let well below the market rate to some extent because the insurance company was not fully in touch with the market and tended to err on the generous side. Its income from the company represented less than 3 per cent on the true values of the properties, but it could not face the odium and possible bad publicity from doubling the rents on average. Nor would it look good to offer the properties for sale on the open market.

Broackes expressed the keenest interest in buying Westminster and Kensington. The Commercial Union decided that the fairest way to sell the company without giving Broackes preference was to invite three tenders, including one from him. Broackes won. He offered £3,345,000, which was about £500,000 more than the nearest bidder. But this was not over the odds. Nigel Broackes had not spent his weekends sizing up each property in the greatest detail in vain. On one building alone, the Third Schedule operation in St James' Square mentioned earlier, the capital profit will have been around £2·2 million for Trafalgar House, the new name of Broackes' company after the takeover of Westminster & Kensington.

Broackes managed to take over a company much larger than his existing one by an ingenious and almost insolent method of financing. Each individual property was to be transferred by Westminster & Kensington to a new company, with the effect that the group would have a total share capital of £10,000. The Commercial Union subscribed for £9,000 of this in preference, fixed interest shares, plus £450 in preference shares convertible into £450 ordinary shares. Broackes' Trafalgar House had to put up only £550 in ordinary shares and thus controlled 55 per cent of the company. The remaining £3,335,000 of the purchase price was lent by the Commercial Union. It is a measure of the insurance giant's faith in the 27-year-old developer that it was prepared to give up control of Westminster & Kensington and simultaneously lend virtually 100 per cent of the purchase price, its value at the time. Insurance companies tend to lend only around two-thirds of value.

Normally, when shares are transferred in a takeover, stamp duty of 1 per cent (before 1963 2 per cent) on their value has to be paid. In this case, by the system of W & K forming new subsidiary companies for each property and Trafalgar House later subscribing for new shares, stamp duty of around £67,000 was saved. Broackes also congratulated himself for having pushed ahead with unorthodox speed on the development in St James' Square, Cleveland House. In his analysis of each property in Westminster & Kensington, Broackes realised that with the chance of redevelopment at a high density, Cleveland House was the plum. Even before he put in his bid for the company, he persuaded the Commercial Union to let him apply for outline planning permission to redevelop for the benefit of whoever won the tender. But for that extra floorspace above the LCC's normal maximum under plot ratio zoning might not have been granted before the Third Schedule was amended. But because it could claim its weird rights under the Third Schedule, Cleveland House has been built at a plot ratio of 7·6 : 1 in an area which was zoned at an upper limit of 5 : 1.

As the political climate looked increasingly chilly for office developers in London, Broackes moved fast. Trafalgar House absorbed Westminster and Kensington in March 1962. While that was being digested, Trafalgar was publicly floated in July 1963. At the time Broackes was warming up for an even more ambitious takeover. Again by chance, he had been visiting the office where W & K was registered and had noticed the name plates of three other companies: City and West End, Consolidated London and Metropolitan. He decided to investigate them property by property. They were all publicly quoted companies run by the same highly respectable but sleepy management. The assets sat in the balance sheet at well under true values, no attempt had been made to develop old properties and the capital structures were archaic.

The management of the three companies was unreceptive to a degree to Broackes' acquisitive approach. It was clear that any takeover would be resisted all along the line, and it turned out that the companies had already turned down twenty-three previous bidders. Broackes was not so easily put off. He began by buying shares in the companies through the stock market to reduce the cost of the takeover or to pay for his expenses and a bit more should the boards decide to embrace an alternative bidder. Then he arranged to borrow up to £8 million from Barclays Bank on the guarantee of his merchant bankers, Kleinwort Benson. When Trafalgar House did make its bids for the three companies in November 1963 a bitter fight developed. Broackes thoroughly enjoyed the ins and outs of the takeover battle—it gave him great pleasure when advisers to one of the three companies prematurely organised a champagne dinner to celebrate victory just before Broackes proved the winner; he was also adept at the financial manoeuvring needed. But he was worried lest his aggressive tactics might be used against him by the defending management, which was essentially the organisation of a third generation family, to brand him as a reckless pipsqueak of a developer. Broackes was highly conscious of his image at the age of thirty. In the end Trafalgar House only managed to collar one of the three companies, City and West End, but even that served to send up the value of properties owned by Trafalgar from £5,142,475 to £10,472,592 in its next balance sheet. Broackes paved the way for two other property companies, one run by Mr Leslie Marler, the other by Mr Osias Freshwater, to eat up the other two of those three staid companies. Broackes helped to pay the £4·6 million for City and West End by selling his shares in the other two companies to Freshwater and Marler at a profit of £600,000.

In the years from 1958 to 1965, the years in which Nigel Broackes expanded as fast as he could in real estate in central London and broke through into the ranks of the millionaire developers, an entirely new movement was gathering pace on the periphery of London. This phenomenon was known in the property business as 'decentralised offices'. It was a trend which in the remarkably short time of around seven years was to scatter the outskirts of London with a host of banal and unrelated office blocks, and radically to alter the townscape along the main roads and railway lines out of London.

Before the war there was no such thing as a decentralised office. There were offices in the suburbs and in small provincial towns, but they were mainly occupied by firms with local ties, by solicitors, estate agents or accountants. They were located above rows of shops or in converted houses. In its modern meaning a decentralised office is a purpose built block with the same characteristics as that in the City of London or any big provincial hub like Birmingham or Glasgow. It is let as the headquarters of some international or national company, or to a number of big companies. The only difference was that instead of being next to the Bank of England, or in the shipping quarter of the Big City, or huddled next to the headquarters of other companies in the same industry, the decentralised offices sprang up in lonely ones and twos alongside main arterial roads into London, next door to underground stations or in groups in the middle of the capital's denser suburbs.

The movement was caused in the first place by the spiralling cost of land and rising rents in central London. It began in the middle fifties. Some firms had been obliged to move out of London during the war, found it just as convenient not to be at the centre of things, and stayed. So when rents went up consistently year by year, companies were able to find some precedent for an alternative to the traditional office pitches. It was usually firms commissioning their own offices which started the ball rolling in a given area, since they had much less to lose than the speculative developer if the site proved to have its drawbacks. It took a great deal of courage for a developer to try out a new part of London and it is easy to forget in retrospect just how conservative are the ideas of the public and of users as to what should be built where. As London uncoiled itself westwards, with industrial development concentrated along the axis of the Great West Road and in sympathy with the boom in traffic at London Airport, the office blocks followed. For some years after the war the property world was firmly convinced that there was no demand for offices of any size west of Hyde Park Corner. When Sir Harold Samuel announced in 1956 that his company was to promote an office block next door to the Hyde Park Hotel, opposite the top of Sloane Street, the doubters had a field day of scepticism. It must be a white elephant. But Bowater Paper leased the entire, 321,000 square foot building before it was started. A bevy of office blocks soon sprang up in that neck of Knightsbridge once the fashion was established.

Fashion, a surprisingly strong force in the hard-headed world of business, played a leading role in the dissemination of decentralised office blocks. In the same way, once Felix Fenston's efforts to replace the St James's Theatre with offices, and his success, became known, the LCC had to resist a spate of applications to snuff out theatres and run up office blocks. Permission was refused for the Palace, the Adelphi, the Princes, the Aldwych and the Saville. Both the Stoll and the Gaiety fell.

There was no question of resisting the trend to decentralisation. It was almost equally welcomed by the local authority graced with the developer's work, by the LCC and by the Government. Middlesex was the first planning authority to attract decentralised offices in any volume. In 1956, the year after Duncan Sandys' famous 'evil of congestion' letter, the County of Middlesex plan catered for an emigration of offices to its territory beyond Hammersmith and the North Circular Road. In the following four years, up to the end of 1960, Middlesex gave permission for 9 million square feet of offices, almost the same footage as was destroyed by bombs in central London during the war. The buildings were scattered around the main roads of Willesden and Wembley, Finchley, Ruislip and Southgate, Harrow, Hendon and Brentford, Chiswick and Ealing. In line with the national average,* about half of the offices were deliberately commissioned by firms for their own occupation, the rest were built on spec.

Although the shock of seeing towers of offices climbing out of quiet and totally unexpected suburban spots gave the impression that their locations were based on entirely haphazard whims of the developers, there was in fact a rational pattern behind the spread. Access to transport and to pockets of white collar workers were the two decisive factors. Decentralisation began to the west and the north-west of London. It was in these areas that the most concentrated supply of office workers lived and could be tapped. When a firm moved from the West End to Wembley, it could not count on all its staff being prepared to follow, especially the more routine, clerical staff who found it easy to move from job to job. Transport was vital, and the blocks which stood unwanted by tenants as

---

* Statistics here are limited. But the Pilkington Research Unit suggested this 50/50 split.

NEW OFFICE BLOCKS OUTSIDE CENTRAL LONDON.
ALL HAVE BEEN BUILT SINCE THE WAR,
ADDING A NEW DIMENSION TO THE SUBURBAN SCENE

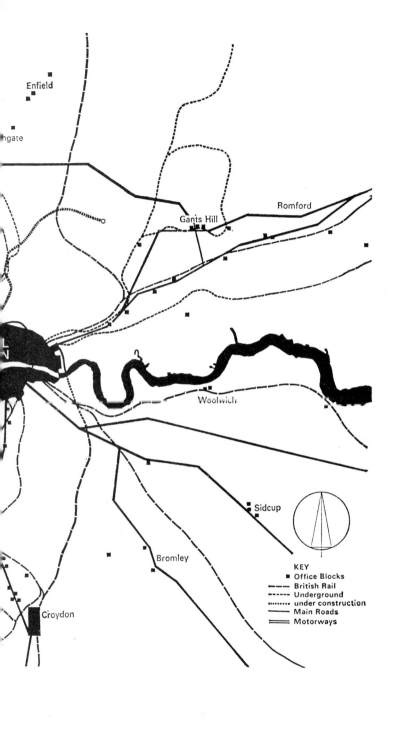

Enfield

hgate

Romford

Gants Hill

Woolwich

Sidcup

Bromley

Croydon

KEY
■ Office Blocks
– – – British Rail
- - - - Underground
••••••• under construction
—— Main Roads
═══ Motorways

saturation arrived in some areas in the mid-sixties usually failed to meet this criterion. Ideally, there had to be inter-suburban links to ferry office workers to and fro by public transport, and links of road and underground train with the West End or the City, or both. The grouping of the decentralised office blocks shown facing page 180 can be explained almost entirely in terms of their relationship with main roads or underground lines. Shops near by for office workers was another important factor which developers now and then overlooked, but seldom suffered for due to the strength of demand. The speed with which the Post Office could cope with the demand for more telephone lines also influenced the trends.

After the LCC had tinkered about with plot ratios via the Grey Book of 1957, official policy relied mainly on exhortation to achieve decentralisation. Typical was a letter from Henry Brooke, then Minister of Housing and Local Government, to some 200 companies with offices in central London. It began: 'I think we must all be concerned about the way in which central London is becoming more and more congested.' He went on to point out the charms of the suburbs and the new towns, in case those particular businessmen had not noticed, concluding with an appeal to the instinct for bandwagons: 'I have not yet heard of an organisation which after moving part or all of its office work out of London in the last ten years, has regretted its bold decision. I believe this movement is going to grow, and grow rapidly.'

The movement was already well under way by that time, as the figures for Middlesex showed, and permission was given for a rather greater volume of offices in the conurbation outside central London in the four years to the end of 1961 than in the central area. It is impossible to judge what part was played by the Government, but since the sanctions were minimal, the movement was no doubt a natural one and only fractionally influenced by official exhortation. In spite of the inter-related problem of transport for the entire region of London which was affected by the new pattern of offices, there was a remarkable lack of co-operation between one local authority and another. Virtually no attempt was made to knit in the office policies of the local authorities on the perimeter of London to one another or to the decisions made at the centre. Richard Edmonds, at the hub of London's planning as chairman of the LCC's town planning committee from 1955 to 1961, recalled that he had only had two visits from the planners of Middlesex in those vital six years. Only in 1962—to a large extent after the event —did the planning authorities of the London region band together, in the absence of any initiative from the Government, to form the Standing Conference on London Regional Planning and find out what one another was up to.

The Government returned to attack the 'evil of congestion' in February 1963 in a White Paper, in March 1964 in the fat, glossy South-east Study and a White Paper, and in November 1964—one of the first measures of the newly elected Labour Government—in yet another White Paper. Apart from the overdue repeal of the absurdity in the Third Schedule discussed earlier, the White Paper of 1963 recommended greater dispersal of the Civil Service from London's centre, new office centres in the suburbs and right away from the London region, and the creation of the Location of Offices Bureau. LOB, sitting conveniently in central Chancery Lane, was to act as a sort of a Government estate agent of decentralisation and as a general propagandist for its aims. The Southeast Study was forced to take a more forward looking line. After bemoaning the remorseless 15,000 a year rise in office jobs in central London—from 1955 through to 1962—the same annual average was flourished in 1963 for the decade 1951–61—the Study predicted a 3½ million increase in the population of South-east England between 1961 and 1981. It recommended more office blocks in peripheral centres like Croydon or Uxbridge or Surbiton, and more independent centres way out at Southampton, Newbury, Swindon, Northampton or Peterborough.

The White Paper of 4 November 1964, perhaps the official close of the office boom ten years almost to the day after it had been unleashed by Mr Nigel Birch, was better known as the Brown Ban or, to some, as the Night of the Long Pens. It amounted to a nearly total ban on further office building in the area of the Greater London Council; Office Development Permits would have to be obtained for any new projects. Mr George Brown announced this proposal in mid-afternoon on 4 November, exempting any developments for which the contract was signed by midnight on the same day. Naturally enough, developers started to sign every possible contract with their building contractors. One large and respectable property company happened to be giving a cocktail party that evening to celebrate a move to new offices overlooking Hyde Park and generally scatter goodwill. Building contractors who were there are said to have taken a record volume of business via some unconventional contracts. Nigel Broackes signed three contracts on 4 November. Other developers hastily buttoned up contracts over the next few days which were quietly backdated.

The Brown Ban, paradox of Labour legislation, did most developers a power of good. By artificially restricting supply, it helped to fill up the unlet blocks which were becoming more frequent in and around London. It also sent rents soaring merrily upwards with a fresh burst of strength; whereas 50s. was a common rent for a new office building in central London at the time of the ban, 70s. was nearer the average two and a half years later. Those with unlet buildings, with buildings under way, or with hurriedly signed contracts, all had the Labour Government to thank for saving them from any problems of over-supply. Later, during 1965 and 1966, this stringent control of office building was extended outside the GLC area to Birmingham, which had a minor glut of offices, and finally to all the South-east, the East and West Midlands. Given the economic crises of those two years, offices were first for the squeeze.

Governments may have been right gradually to restrict office building in central London more severely from the middle fifties to the middle sixties.* But if they were right, they were right for quite the wrong reason. One main plank of successive policies was based on a colossal misconception. Each time the screw was tightened in 1963 and 1964, the bane of the extra 15,000 a year employed in offices in central London from 1951 to 1961—150,000 in all—was rubbed home. This turned out to be a false statistic. When that figure was being flourished, information from the 1961 Census was not available. In November 1966 the Standing Conference on London Regional Planning usefully analysed the data from the 1961 Census and showed that the total increase in jobs in central London from 1951 to 1961 was 55,000, and not 150,000 as given in all the Government's anti-office propaganda. This 55,000 was split between 50,000 in the City of London itself, and a mere 5,000 in the other five central London boroughs.

Another figure shows how very wide of the mark were the statistics with which the planners attempted to plan. Total employ-

* I am grateful to the Economist Intelligence Unit for permission to see a privately commissioned study on official policy on offices in the South-east.

N

ment in the area covered by the Standing Conference increased by some 600,000 in 1951 to 1961; 157,000 of these extra jobs were in Greater London, whereas the previous estimate had been that 450,000 new jobs had been created in Greater London. The Standing Conference's paper of November 1966 made a frank admission, and neatly undermined the prestigious South-east Study: 'Our earlier attempts at analysis of the employment changes within the country and within the Conference area (and indeed those of others, including the authors of the South-east Study) have suffered from lack of later information directly comparable with that provided by the 1951 Census.'

Had the true figures for the rise in office employment been known—only one-third of earlier assumptions—it is possible, as the Standing Conference observed, that '. . . significantly different conclusions about the trends in the region, and proposals to meet them, would have been made.' What was clearly not appreciated was that the great increase in new building did not bring a proportionate increase in office workers, as old buildings were occupied much more densely than new. The Government must also have failed to realise the extent to which congestion was caused not by more office workers in the central area, but by more of them moving out of the central area to live and burdening the transport system with commuter traffic.

One solution, never put into effect, ought to have been a radical improvement in roads and railways. Another answer must be to increase greatly residential accommodation near the central area, as the City is doing at the Barbican, instead of driving out employment from the hub which both employers and employees seem to prefer. It seems archaic and a confession of failure to attempt to drive out employment by limiting modernisation, when the renewal of old office buildings into new does not appear to raise significantly the total number of workers. There may not in the event be any great change in the number of office workers in central London over the next decade, or decades. There may even be a mild long-term decline. Mechanisation of office work, and the replacement of the clerk by the computer, could see to that. The computer does in fact take up more space than the clerk. But it does not need to be housed in the same place as the rest of an office. If an insurance company has to have its executives and the core of its staff in the expensive insurance area of the City of London, there is no reason why the computers doing the work of batches of clerks should not be located miles away in Southend in office space costing one third as much as that in the City. It is possible to communicate with a computer miles away just as satisfactorily as if it were in the next door room. Some companies do not seem to have appreciated this fully; both the National Provincial Bank and Lloyds Bank have computer installations in extremely expensive modern space in the City. But the trend has set in to remove machines from land of high value and this will in the long run ease the demand for office space in the centre. It will not cancel out the need for developers to replace obsolete buildings, of which there is a huge stock in London, with new and efficient ones.

The most sensational phenomenon thrown up by the office boom in South-east England was the development of Croydon. The commuters who rattle on Southern Electric through East Croydon station, the busiest station in the whole of England outside the main London termini, have watched from 1958 to the present day the cranes over Croydon rapidly transforming this proud, commercial borough into a mini-Manhattan of offices. There has been much talk of decentralised offices and of decentralised office centres, but Croydon is the only centre worthy of the name.

The office boom in Croydon was set off and fostered throughout by Croydon Corporation. One of the first office blocks, developed by the Norwich Union and Myton the contractors, was the by-product of the Corporation's road widening in George Street, which ran between North End, one of the country's busiest shopping streets, and East Croydon Station. The Corporation already owned the key site, an old public hall, but to smooth the way for the purchase of the remaining sites and to avoid the bureaucratic delays of a Comprehensive Development Area plan, Croydon promoted its own private Bill through Parliament. This was passed in 1956 as the Croydon Corporation Act and gave the local authority the power to acquire land compulsorily without having to justify itself to the Ministry of Housing.

This practical approach to the replanning of Croydon reflects the driving force of one man, Sir James Marshall. Sir James, a councillor in Croydon since 1928 and now aged seventy-two, was chairman of the town planning committee throughout the formative years of the office boom. Although an elected representative rather than an official, this hard-headed autocrat was in a sense comparable to an American-style town boss. What Marshall said, went. Extremely commercially minded and an orthodox Conservative, he was as it were the managing director of Croydon. He got things done quickly—and they worked. When I talked to him about the transformation of Croydon he remarked wryly that 'the best committee is a committee of one'. A property developer who had operated in Croydon recalled that 'one didn't get anywhere if Sir James disapproved of one'.

Once the Corporation had bought the land needed to widen George Street, it leased the adjacent plot to a partnership of Norwich Union and Myton, who softened what seemed to be the rank speculation of building 225,000 gross square feet of offices in Croydon with the surer prospect of shops along the street front at the bottom of the buildings. The adviser to Norwich Union/Myton was a London estate agent, Leonard Mills of Jones, Lang, Wootton, who had already co-operated with Myton on a smaller shop and office block named Surrey House, the first in Croydon and one of the first decentralised blocks anywhere. Mills was one of three estate agents who specialised in Croydon and between them acted for the great majority of the offices built there. The second from London was called John Croydon, his real name, not a *nom de commerce*; the third was a local agent named Geoffrey Pollard.

As soon as it was apparent that the three blocks pioneered in George Street—Norfolk House, Suffolk House and Essex House —were readily filled up with tenants, developers began to see the potential in Croydon. Site values and then rents started to rise in leaps and bounds. One of the first pure office blocks was built on the site of ten Victorian houses and subsequently let to the RAC; the site cost £50,000, or £5,000 a house. About three years later a similar site with three old houses on it was sold for £340,000, or £113,000 a house. Norfolk House was let at 9s. a square foot in mid-1959. By the end of 1960 the RAC had to pay 14s. a square foot and within a couple of months the RAC was itself able to sub-let some of its space for 20s. a square foot.

This sudden popularity and demand for Croydon's offices was based mainly on three assets. Transport was the key. It was only minutes from Victoria, and the first stop on fast trains. There was good lateral train service with near-by suburbs and a huge pool of white collar workers within a fairly small radius. Trains from the south brought in higher-paid workers from executive countryside.

Secondly, Croydon was already a large town in its own right, not just a dormitory suburb, and it had services to match: one of the best southern shopping streets and, built on the back of the rates from the office development, the Fairfield Halls, a modern theatre, concert hall and art gallery. Thirdly, rents were between one-half to one-third of those in central London.

It was only just that the rush of offices should indirectly pay for new cultural facilities, since the Grand Theatre, the old local repertory, and the Davis Cinema, one of the largest in Europe, both underwent the change of life from show business to office development. The passing of the Davis Cinema, which was greeted with a burst of protest in Croydon, startled the Corporation into action. Like almost everyone else involved, it was quite taken aback by the extent and speed of the boom. It decided to limit the area in which offices could be built to 45 acres and, instead of a comprehensive architectural plan, to set up a panel of architects to advise on developers' proposals. It is hard to see what standards this panel applied. Aesthetically, the main area of new offices is a jungle of unrelated designs and disjointed, piecemeal positioning. Given the deliberate intention of the Corporation to attract offices into Croydon, it could be argued that it was short-sighted and boorish not to have imposed a rigid master plan to which the developers' buildings would have had to conform. But as with the City of London after the Great Fire of 1666, or after the Second World War, the virility of private enterprise was too quick off the mark for officialdom.

Not that officialdom in Croydon seems to have been particularly interested in the finer points of the new environment. The commercial side of it, the number of square feet built, and the prospect of increasing the whole borough's rateable value by 20 per cent appeared the main attractions. The hard statistics were undeniably impressive. Whereas before 1957 virtually no office building had touched Croydon, by the time of the Brown Ban in November 1964 2 million gross square feet had been built in the central area, 750,000 square feet was under construction and another 3·3 million had been given planning permission, of which 2·3 million was outside the Ban and is now under way. Another 1·5 million square feet was scattered around outlying parts of Croydon such as Norbury, South Norwood or Broad Green. The total of 6·5 million square feet, or 7·5 million once the Ban is lifted, is roughly equal to all the offices, by no means built in the last ten years, in the centre of Manchester or Birmingham or Liverpool.

Most of the prominent office developers descended on Croydon to buy up sites within the forty-five acres designated for commercial development and put up one, and occasionally two, buildings. But it was not just they—and the Corporation via the rates—who grew richer in this suburban spree. The largest single slice of the forty-five acres was transformed from several streets of small Victorian houses and stout villas into a group of twenty or so towers of offices. Householders of Wellesley Road, Lansdowne Road, Sydenham Road, Dingwall Road or Bedford Park Road suddenly found their houses and back gardens turned into minor gold mines. One doctor developed quite a nose for property speculation and made himself a small fortune. He lived in a house in Lansdowne Road which his father, once the mathematics master at Croydon's Whitgift School, had bought between the wars for £1,800. One day in 1958 an estate agent walked in and offered him £25,000 for the house. After some competition he sold it for £42,000. That experience decided him to buy other houses which he thought would lie in the path of the bulldozers. He bought two neighbouring houses in Lansdowne Road, one for £12,000 and the other for £4,500, and sold the pair for £40,000 to a developer. He also picked up a bungalow for £4,250 several streets away from the initial pool of offices; in due course the tide advanced and the doctor unloaded for £70,000. All this was before the days of capital gains tax.

The seller is an often overlooked beneficiary of property development. Two schools cashed in on the bonanza in Croydon. The Trinity School of John Whitgift, a private school for boys, had sat in the same spot for four centuries, but in the mid-20th century that spot turned out to be the most valuable in the town. With its playing fields it occupied twelve acres sandwiched between the new office centre and North End, the main shopping street. Having Sir James Marshall's advice as a governor was no doubt a help and the school shrewdly decamped for Shirley, a quiet fringe of Croydon. The developer selected, Freedman's and Maynard's Ravenseft, paid for the brand new school at a cost of roughly £1 million in place of the drab Victorian buildings, and an annual rent, never publicly disclosed, but probably of the order of £200,000. The school will also share in the profits of the shopping centre and office blocks above a certain level. All in all, a handsome endowment. Ravenseft is covering the old playing fields with 140 shops and three large towers of offices.

This shopping centre, lying side by side with the crowded North End, where the big retailers have been itching to expand, should have no difficulty in finding tenants. But it has been an ill wind for another shopping centre, which, finished about a year before the Whitgift scheme started in 1965, grandly called itself the Croydon Centre. This was an eighty-five-shop precinct set at right angles to the High Street, an extension of North End but less vibrant with shoppers. The troubles with this precinct, which has been somewhat slow to find tenants, are that it leads the shopper nowhere in particular at the opposite end to the High Street, that most retailers wanting more space in Croydon are waiting for the Whitgift and that it is extremely draughty, a malaise of new buildings discussed on page 244. But despite the emptiness of many of the shops, the Croydon Centre will have made a large potential profit, probably in the region of £3 million, for its developers, since it included 335,000 square feet of office space, which was gobbled up by decentralising industrial companies, chiefly Nestlé.

The owners of Croydon Centre were a strange combination of an individual, an already rich heating contractor named Charles Ellis, and the Church Commissioners, who provided the finance.

The crucial stage in the initiation of this project was a meeting over drinks at the Addington Palace Golf Club between Charles Ellis, director of the publicly-quoted Ellis (Kensington), Freddie Lindgren, the accountant, and a director of Hammond and Hussey, whose headquarters used up the most important slice of the island site. Ellis and Lindgren found out that Hammond and Hussey were willing sellers. Lindgren, Jack Cotton's main adviser for many years, put up the idea of the development of the site to Cotton. In turn Cotton sought advice. The explosive growth of Croydon as an office centre had not begun and Cotton decided to leave it alone. Ellis and Lindgren then decided to go ahead on their own account.

Before the majority of the site was acquired, Ellis brought in the Church Commissioners—still at the stage when Croydon was generally considered a big risk—to share 30 per cent of the project and put up the fixed interest money. They financed the entire cost of £5,500,000.

Croydon Centre is among the biggest single developments in the country. It is also unusual for a scheme of this size to be controlled by a private individual. The other 70 per cent of Croydon Centre is held by Ilmarish Investments, a company owned 90 per cent by Charles Ellis and family, and 10 per cent by Freddie Lindgren and family. Thus Ellis's gross potential capital profit on the deal is £2,300,000 and Lindgren's is £230,000.

The other school which was touched by the developer's golden wand was the Croydon High School for Girls, just across the road from the Whitgift School, on the other side from North End. Harry Hyams' company, Oldham Estate, is replacing the girls with office blocks. That school too has pulled in a lump sum of £1 million towards completely new buildings on the outskirts of Croydon and will have an income from its site of over £100,000 a year.

Of the several huge projects to hit Croydon, the biggest, and the most dramatic, was stayed by the Brown Ban. It was a plan to build 667,000 square feet of offices above East Croydon Station. Had it been an entirely private development it would probably be half way up at this moment. But it was a development planned jointly by Mr Clore's City Centre Properties and British Rail. At the time of the Ban there was a tentative contract with Tersons, the building contractors. City Centre discussed this with British Rail, assuming that there would be no question but that the thing would go ahead. But the bureaucrats at British Rail, much to the fury of City Centre, said 'We'd better show this contract to the Board of Trade'. And the Board of Trade, given the opportunity, of course said 'no'.

After the Brown Ban, there were two more twists of the restrictions on developers. In July 1965 no commercial projects of over £100,000 were allowed without a building licence, with the exception of development areas. In July 1966 the value of the contracts covered by this restriction was lowered to £50,000. Once acclimatised to restrictions property developers were not greatly surprised by either of these measures. With the precedent of the Brown Ban, developers were careful to sign any building contracts as soon as they possibly could. A few weeks before the July 1965 measures there was in any case a strong rumour in the property world that restriction was imminent. On a Thursday exactly three weeks before the event, one young developer, Ronald Gerrard, partner with Bernard Berwick in a successful small company, London and Provincial Shop Centres, was at home in the early evening, in his garden pruning roses. He was fetched in from the garden for a telephone call from his architect. The architect told him anxiously that building licences, so rumour had it, were to be introduced later that evening with a statement in the House of Commons. Gerrard immediately drove into the centre of London from Finchley and signed every possible building contract.

CHAPTER THIRTEEN

Overseas

AT home the property developer had it almost all his own way in the first twenty post-war years. But abroad he had a more bumpy ride. This was partly the result of inevitable over-confidence. As the boom crescendoed towards the end of the fifties, rapid riches tended to turn the heads of some of the participants. The *Investors Chronicle*, voicing the feelings of the commercial property market in London, wrote in June 1961: 'Clearly our property groups will colonise on a tremendous international scale . . . The British property man has no peer,' and in October that year it observed, 'Putting truth before modesty, it can be said that the British property developer is among the most versatile in the world.'

Put to the test the experience of British developers overseas proved less glorious than this suggested. Before the war, and before the First World War, there was no deliberate exploitation of commercial property by British owners outside the country. Vast tracts of land were in British hands—from mines to sheep farms to tea plantations—but these were the commercial reflections of the Empire, and they seldom extended to real estate operators specifically buying sites in foreign cities and creating investments out of buildings. The great trading companies such as Hudson's Bay or the East India built their own local headquarters abroad. But the middleman operating from London was not in evidence.

When the property market in England began to take on an organised shape in the thirties, most developers had their hands too full in London and the Home Counties to bother with provincial forays, let alone branching out overseas. As the war approached, the odd developer exported himself, his skills and his money permanently, but this was hardly an overseas investment in the normal sense. Edward Lotery, the suburban shop specialist, left for California in 1938. Sidney Blum, the pre-war operator who promoted the mammoth Berkeley Square House, departed for further exploits in Salisbury, Rhodesia. The entrepreneur behind Park West and many other vast blocks of flats in the thirties, Reginald Toms, withdrew to Switzerland.

For many years after the war two barriers stopped developers looking overseas on anything more than a minor scale and intermittently. The most compelling reason was that they had more than enough to cope with at home, and the profit margins were lush. Besides this, official restrictions on overseas spending, administered through the Bank of England, frowned on vital pounds being exported for non-essential investment which would not bring a fairly immediate return, unlike, say, a chemical company building a plant near its markets in order to compete on an international level.

But occasionally British investors did stick their spades into foreign soil. They went first to Canada. It was typical of the early fifties that the first man to dive at all deeply into Canadian real estate was not exactly a property developer. He was the late Hugh, 2nd Duke of Westminster. In 1950 he bought Annacis Island in the Fraser River, just off Vancouver in British Columbia. This was a continuation of the policy of the rich families, started in Victorian times, of buying estates in the Empire. The Duke of Westminster, who had fought in the South African War at the turn of the century and was full of zeal for the Empire, was allowed to export £5 million, part to Canada, in 1950 because of the good character of the Grosvenor Estate. The judge, Mr Justice Roxburgh, who gave the permission, observed that 'the Grosvenor Estate has the reputation for seeking the best advice available and being prepared to pay for it . . .' But on Annacis Island the Duke was doing more than just adding an estate to his collection. This was the beginning of the period when the Grosvenor Estate began to be run more like a vast commercial business than a passive collector of rents (see page 92). Annacis Island was to be developed as a large industrial estate of factories and warehouses. The Government of British Columbia built a bridge and causeway from the mainland to the island and the project had just started when the Duke died in 1953 and the Inland Revenue started to collect some £18 million in death duty. After that the trustees of the Grosvenor Estate took Laing the contractors into 50–50 partnership in

Canada. Annacis has been developed on the British leasehold system, as in Belgrave Square, which is unusual for industrial estates in North America. When Sherwin-Williams of Chicago, the biggest paint people in the world, wrote to ask about the chances of buying a factory on Annacis and heard that they could only take a lease, not buy the freehold, they wrote back angrily that 'we thought the British feudal system was dead'. Eventually they settled down on a lease quite happily.

Annacis turned out well in spite of some tough, price-cutting competition near by from a ubiquitous operator from New York, a Mr Zeckendorf. Grosvenor-Laing later spread its wings widely in Canada. But in 1951, soon after the start in British Columbia, the Grosvenor Estate began to invest in and build commercial properties in Australia, way ahead of the rush by the developers, who were still too busy in England.

In 1952, worried by the building restrictions in England, Berkeley Property, which had Hambros Bank and the Prudential as two big shareholders, bought a company with Canadian properties.

In the same year two executives from Metropolitan Estate and Property Corporation, a large, respectable and cautious group built up by the late Claude Leigh, visited Canada to look for real estate. Not until 1955 did they start a company there, when the Bank of England allowed them to send out $750,000 to buy a block of flats in Toronto. Both Berkeley and MEPC steadily grew stronger in Canada. Their basic caution was of great help to them in the perilous waters of North American real estate.

The first of the newer school of developers to plump for Canada were Louis Freedman and Fred Maynard, in 1956. During 1955–57 there was a great enthusiasm among British investors for Canada, both on the Stock Exchange and through the medium of direct industrial investment. Ravenseft, by then owned 100 per cent by Harold Samuel's Land Securities, bought a section of the Beique Estate, 10 miles outside Montreal, to be developed as houses. Freedman and Maynard had found that the sites in blitzed cities were running out, and there was a fierce restrictive credit squeeze in England. In due course Ravenseft bought commercial sites in Montreal, Calgary, Edmonton and Vancouver. The invasion was a flop. Freedman and Maynard were essentially lone wolf operators and they went into Canada owning 100 per cent of their local company, without a Canadian partner who knew the detailed workings of the local market.

This was unquestionably a mistake and it was the same mistake as that made by other developers who came to grief abroad. There are certain differences in any foreign market, some glaring, some subtle, which it is impossible to decipher at once. Fred Maynard, who looked after the Canadian end, also found that he spent too much time there, which could in fact have been put to better use in England. In 1962 Ravenseft pulled out of Canada at a net loss, made worse by devaluation of the Canadian dollar, of $1·8 million.

Central and District Properties, run by Johnny Rubens and Barney Shine, also jumped into Canada at the time when the business world thought that it was the new El Dorado. Oil and natural gas discoveries set alight a raging false boom in the middle fifties. American investors poured money across the border and the Canadian dollar was even at a premium over the American dollar. Rubens and Shine bought a 750-acre estate 15 miles west of Toronto in July 1957, the idea being that the land should be covered with houses, flats, offices and factories: a bit of everything. Their judgment of the land was on target. It cost $2,500 an acre and was worth $10,000 an acre by 1966. But their judgment of their local management was poor. The subsidiary built houses with an elementary defect: they cost more to build than they could be sold for. 'We would have done much better if we had just sat on our bottoms and done nothing with the land,' observed Rubens in 1966 after they had decided to cut their losses on the operating side and keep the good investments. The net result of that nine-year involvement in Canada was neither profit nor loss.

Through the fifties spasmodic investments were made in South African cities by British property men, and a few buildings in Rhodesia were picked up, even one in Nairobi. The companies of Sir Aynsley Bridgland, who was in sympathy with the policy of apartheid and distrusted the rise in rents and land values in England, were the chief operators in South Africa.

Jack Cotton's dramatic entry into Manhattan in October 1959, to participate in the building of the world's largest office block, symbolised the movement overseas and spurred rivals to set out on their own travels. What Cotton contributed to the $96 million Pan-Am Building over New York's Grand Central Station were two British ingredients in development: hunch, and an ability to persuade banks to lend money. Cotton decided very quickly to share with Erwin Wolfson in the project (see page 139), because he had the feeling in his bones that the site was right; he convinced a consortium of British bankers, led by Helbert Wagg and Hambros, to put up the finance on the speculation that the offices would find a tenant.

American real estate was far more competitive and the financiers, both banks and insurance companies, vividly remembered the slump in the thirties, which left them with empty and unsaleable properties as the borrowers defaulted on their loans. Unlike in Britain, the banks would not lend money against the construction of an office building or a shopping centre unless a tenant was signed up for a major part of the space. The insurance companies were restricted by legislation, drawn up under Roosevelt's New Deal for the financial markets, to a policy of caution on investment in real estate. Moreover, American operators, unlike their British counterparts, had not enjoyed fifteen years of a sellers' market and had been obliged to work out more sophisticated, less speculative, techniques than were normally used anywhere in Europe.

The idea of a vast building above the tracks of Grand Central Station had been floating around New York for a long while before Erwin Wolfson met Jack Cotton. But no tenant could be found and therefore no finance. Cotton's contribution to the deal was to talk the financiers into loaning the money, so that construction could be started without a tenant. It turned out that Cotton's hunch was correct. In mid-1960, while demolition of old buildings was interfering with the peace of mind of commuters at the station, Pan-American Airways decided to lease 25 per cent of the 2·4 million square feet of offices. Cotton dearly loved Grand Central City for its size. He was also delighted with the slavish publicity accorded to his pioneering coup in New York.

When it was finished and let, Cotton's City Centre was providing 45 per cent of the $10 million ordinary capital, so that it was necessary to export under $5·7 million of the $25 million sanctioned by the Bank of England and the Treasury in 1959, which would have been the largest single movement of dollars from Britain to the United States allowed by the Bank of England in the post-war period. The rest of the $96 million cost of the building came from a $75 million mortgage lent by the State of New York Pension Fund and an $11 million overdraft with American banks. At the end of 1965, the Pan-Am Building was worth $20 to $25 million more than it had cost.

Although Jack Cotton's basic hunch was so handsomely vindicated, he ignored some vital differences between English and American practice of property development and this added to the bitter friction between him and his co-shareholders in City Centre. In the US buildings are depreciated heavily in their early years in order to pay little tax and to increase the capital value. This means that little or no dividend can be paid for several years. Cotton either did not know or forgot this and in 1961 cheerfully forecast that City Centre would receive a dividend from the Pan-Am Building in 1964. He also overlooked the local custom that a land-lord often has to take over the old leases and obligations of a new tenant, and lease or sell them as well as his new space. This put up the cost of the Pan-Am project by $3 million more than Cotton had bargained for. When Charles Clore and the men from the insurance companies heard of these hidden snags, they grumbled exceedingly. After Jack Cotton had been toppled from his throne at City Centre, the new chairman, George Bridge, the worthy representative of the Legal & General, painted a gloomy picture of the stake in the Pan-Am building in his first report to stock-holders. (It is not uncommon for an incoming management to stress the gloomy aspects.) This was taken up by the Press and infuriated the American partners in the project. Juan Trippe, the forceful president of Pan-American Airways, which by now had a 10 per cent stake in the building in return for favouring the building as a tenant, at once rang up George Bridge from New York to complain strongly at the tone of his remarks. Bridge was deeply embarrassed by this unexpected onslaught, especially as he was explaining his statement to a journalist when Trippe's call rang through. Trippe's indignation crackled clearly into the room.

Clore criticised the investment in the Pan-Am Building at the time of his struggle with Cotton, but later, as it turned out better and better, and after Cotton was dead, he became very fond of this huge octagonal building which blocked the view down Park Avenue to the disgust of most New Yorkers. He was apt to take people round, saying 'Look at my building'. By then he was the largest single stockholder in City Centre.

Clore in fact had bought his own office block in New York.

This was a genuinely poor investment. In 1960, a few months before he teamed up with Cotton, perhaps from competitive instinct at the noise Cotton was making over his triumphant entry into New York, Clore bought 40 Wall Street, sometimes known as the biggest aspidistra in the world because of its spiky pyramid. 'In the headstrong atmosphere of 1960 Mr Clore had to have the biggest something to rival Cotton's Pan-Am,' said an adviser to Clore. 40 Wall Street, a seventy-storey tower, was built in 1929 and was for a few months distinguished as the tallest building in the world. By 1960 it was only the fourth tallest. Clore bought the lease from William Zeckendorf, one of the world's great salesmen, and his basic mistake was that at $14\frac{3}{4}$ million he paid too much for it. After spending $5 million on a drastic reconstruction of the building's innards, he relet it to a high-powered list of Wall Street bankers and brokers. But the six-year-long worry of refurbishing and letting 40 Wall Street only served to safeguard Clore's capital in the operation. His company had to tie up $5·5 million of capital in the project and, when he sold out in mid-1966, the profit was a mere $700,000—a paltry deal alongside Cotton's profit of $20 million on a similar capital base. Clore in fact only managed to scrape out of the 40 Wall Street deal with the honour of a profit for the technical reason that when his money was sent from London to New York there was no premium on dollars for investment; when they were repatriated there was a 25 per cent premium and thus a turn on the deal.

Zeckendorf, who achieved the feat of selling something which turned out poorly for Mr Clore, was the king of American real estate in the fifties and the incarnation of the flamboyant, huge-scale wheeler-dealer. He haunted British property men in the United States and he helped Second Covent Garden Property, an orthodox company directed by some shrewd and sober bankers from the City of London, to lose $20·5 million in one of the most disastrous investments ever made abroad by any British company.

William Zeckendorf, Senior, six feet tall, powerfully built and with an unusually large, bald, oval head, often topped by a pale grey homburg, was always overflowing with ideas. His brain was dangerously ingenious and fertile. 'If I had been a woman,' he once remarked, 'I would have been pregnant every nine months.' Zeckendorf was a compulsive dealer, and it was this compulsion, spurred on by the strident and idolising publicity reserved by the press for an extravagant example of Free Enterprise Man, which led to his undoing and to the bankruptcy of his company, Webb & Knapp. Zeckendorf adored the publicity, even when it rubbed home his mistakes. When I visited him in December 1965, a two foot square, black book lay on the table of his waiting room. In white was engraved on the cover, 'Editorial digest of the problems and difficulties facing Webb & Knapp, 1962–65.' I enquired about this frank exhibit. 'I,' replied Zeckendorf graciously, 'am not afraid to face and present the bad as well as the good.'

Long before he teamed up in the unlikely alliance with the British bankers in his attempt to solve his company's looming insolvency in 1960 and 1961, Zeckendorf had been at the centre of the real estate scene in New York. He was born in Tucson, Arizona, but his father, a shoe manufacturer, moved the family to New York when Zeckendorf was two. In 1925 at the age of twenty he started work in the New York estate agency run by his uncle. His first job was to fill up a number of empty office buildings as fast as possible. His approach was direct. He walked round competing buildings, made a note of the tenants and rang up the manager of each company, telling him that his lease would soon expire and offering a lease in one of his uncle's buildings. Zeckendorf explained his reasoning: 'Since the average lease in those buildings ran for three years, I always had a three-to-one chance of hitting a guy whose lease really was running out.'

Zeckendorf joined an old-fashioned firm of Manhattan estate agents in 1938 as an executive and at the end of the war he became its boss. In 1949 he bought out the other partners. Three years before he had pulled off one of his most famous deals. Hearing that the United Nations might build its headquarters in Philadelphia for want of a site in New York, he offered the UN at any price it chose to pay 17 acres of a 26-acre run-down quarter on the East Side, which mainly housed a string of old slaughter houses. Webb & Knapp had bought the slaughter houses for $17 a square foot while the adjoining land was selling for only $2 a square foot. This was a classic developer's operation. Zeckendorf, in a speech to an economists' club in 1962, happily talked about the slaughter houses, 'We bought the slaughter house property at $17 per square foot with our eyes open, because we thought in pro-forma terms and recognised that the sole reason the adjacent land was

o

selling for only $2 a square foot was because it was sitting next to slaughter houses, and if you removed these abominations there would be no more $2 land value—or $17 land value. And now the land value, up and down midtown First Avenue, I would say, is worth on the average $125 a square foot.'

The Rockefeller family bought the 17 acres for $8·5 million and gave it to the UN. Zeckendorf collected a profit of $2 million, claiming that if he had sold in the open market the profit would have been $20 million. 'Disappointed?' he replied to a question about the size of his profit, 'I never thought any real estate man would be able to move the capital of the world in eight days. How could I ever top that?' Needless to say the 9 acres which he kept himself benefited greatly from being neighbours to the United Nations.

Zeckendorf's judgment of a site was usually inspired. But, as Webb & Knapp took on project after project on an ever grander scale and as the image of the great Mr Zeckendorf was puffed ever more omnipotent, Zeckendorf himself seems to have developed a much worse attack of the disease which undermined Jack Cotton's last years, businessman's megalomania. Although they were usually received with wide-eyed public acclaim, many of Zeckendorf's more fanciful ideas never left the drawing board. He tried to promote an airport above the West side of Manhattan, 200 feet above street level, from 24th to 71st Streets. He planned a mountaintop community for Los Angeles. He developed a futuristic automatic car park. Always there was great enthusiasm for his ideas, but the financiers turned a deaf ear.

His wilder schemes were turned down, but Zeckendorf managed to initiate a huge volume of construction. Much of this stemmed from the Federal Government's National Housing Act of 1949, which provided generous loans to developers for large-scale urban renewal. Zeckendorf flew around the country in Webb & Knapp's private plane with his team of experts, involving his company more and more deeply in office blocks, hotels, flats and shopping centres. He was greeted effusively by local officials and politicians, who found an ambitious urban renewal scheme tended to help their chances at the polls. 'Some of these people actually seemed to think that Zeckendorf was the Saviour himself,' recalled an executive of Webb & Knapp, who experienced the hysterical atmosphere of Zeckendorf's triumphal progress around the United States.

By 1960 Webb & Knapp had the largest urban renewal programme in the US, with $500 million of construction under way.
But by then two fundamental mistakes were making Zeckendorf's
financial empire, valued by the stock market at $100 million in its
prime, look extremely sick. The first was that he increasingly forgot
about the cost of buildings. Zeckendorf proudly interpreted to me
this aspect of his troubles: 'We permitted our sense of aesthetics to
override our commercial judgment.' He did in fact promote many
buildings of a far higher quality than was usual for a developer.

'Our sense of aesthetics' came largely from Zeckendorf's
architect, the brilliant Chinese I. M. Pei, whom Zeckendorf hired
as he left Harvard. He was full time on the staff of Webb & Knapp.
Today I. M. Pei is one of the more respected architects in North
America. Unfortunately he was not over-concerned about cost and
there was no hawk-like eye on the budget, least of all Zeckendorf's.
Spiralling costs made many projects uneconomic. Zeckendorf was
forgetting a basic rule of business, perhaps even that he was
primarily a businessman. He saw himself in a loftier role. In
the speech quoted earlier he discussed the nature of a secure investment: 'In my research, however, I finally discovered the only
absolutely imperishable value. It never goes down, always stays
apace with monetary evaluations, usually runs ahead of the
economy, and has an ever-increasing scarcity value, because it has
an imperishable market. It is "beauty" . . .'

The other basic reason for the downfall of Webb & Knapp was
that Zeckendorf strayed from pure real estate into other operations
which he understood less well. One was Freedomland. This was
intended to be the world's largest entertainment centre, but
it turned out a debacle. Zeckendorf had never really meant to be
in the recreation business, but he happened to own 205 acres of
marshland in the Bronx outside New York and failed to win planning permission for a more normal development. Instead he built
a huge pleasure park, finished in 1960. With delays and costs
mounting, Freedomland was a failure from the start. By the end of
1963 the total write-off totted up to a crippling $18 million.

Zeckendorf's other disastrous operation was in hotels. Webb &
Knapp entered this industry in the mid-fifties, just as occupancy
rates in New York began steadily to fall. At one point he operated
nine hotels in New York and three in Chicago. They never made
money and their rising deficits—the losses on hotels jumped from

$2·1 million in 1962 to $4·5 million in 1963—ate into revenues from the real estate side. At the same time his buildings took much longer than Zeckendorf originally conceived. Debts and interest charges combined with the hotel deficits forced Webb & Knapp to borrow at higher and higher rates. Again Zeckendorf treated cost lightly. 'I prefer to stay alive at 18 per cent rather than be dead at the prime rate,' he said. The sound-money elements on Wall Street were appalled at Webb & Knapp's finances and shivered for fear of the crash which might follow. But Zeckendorf shrugged off any criticisms with his usual charm: 'It takes courage and imagination to make a profit after paying 18 per cent. People say, look at all the money I owe—well, let them try to go out and borrow that much.' Many banks and respected figures on Wall Street made big profits out of Zeckendorf's insatiable thirst for loans at almost any price; André Meyer of Lazard Frères was one.

Through the late fifties and early sixties, Zeckendorf was obliged to sell off properties to stay afloat. Then, in December 1961, the British rescue of Big Bill Zeckendorf was mounted. It was organised by one of London's younger and more vigorous merchant banks, Philip Hill, Higginson, Erlanger,* under its chief executive, Kenneth Keith, and director Harry Moore. The Philip Hill stable (Second Covent Garden Property, Eagle Star Insurance and Philip Hill Investment Trust) was first involved with Zeckendorf the previous year through Webb & Knapp (Canada), a partly owned subsidiary which ran into financial hot water before its US parent. In Canada Zeckendorf's illiquidity forced him to bequeath to the British three shopping centres and a $115 million chunk of offices in Montreal, known as Place Ville Marie. This project typifies Zeckendorf's great imagination. He saw a hole in the ground on railway land in a slum district and decided, against great local scepticism, that a large part of the financial centre of Montreal could be moved. He was right. Moreover, the end result is a widely praised example of commercial architecture. And although the estimates made when Second Covent Garden and Eagle Star joined Zeckendorf in Canada have proved over-optimistic, those investments will turn out highly profitable in the long run and help to recoup the losses in the United States.

The philosophy behind Second Covent Garden's plunge into North America was conventional. This was 1960 and its directors

* Later to merge with M. Samuel into Hill, Samuel.

reasoned that the property market at home was waxing exceedingly competitive: that a geographical spread of properties would be prudent: that North America was the most inviting territory to explore, since the law and language there were reasonably much the same: and that experience of shopping centres in America would help Second Covent Garden's men in their operations in England.

It was also wise to choose a local partner, rather than go it alone in unknown conditions. The chronic mistake was in choice of partner. Keith and Moore knew full well that Zeckendorf was given to over-indulgence, so they devised a formula to tie him down. But they greatly underestimated their man. One condition was that before the deal was signed Zeckendorf should sell off a bunch of properties and after the deal some more. He sold. The deal took place and Mr Zeckendorf was propped up with an extra $43·7 million. A new company was formed, the Zeckendorf Property Corporation, to own thirteen of Zeckendorf's choicest projects and was owned equally by Webb & Knapp and the British. Both Philip Hill Investment Trust and Second Covent Garden bought shares in Webb & Knapp to provide that, quite separate, company with more cash. Financiers on Wall Street were amazed at the deal, amazed that their own Bill Zeckendorf should have been so miraculously shored up after several years on the verge of insolvency, and amazed that supposedly cautious British bankers should have come to the rescue.

The alliance ran into trouble almost from the start. After the deal was signed, Zeckendorf stopped selling properties. On the contrary, he started to buy again regardless of the wishes of his new partners. One safeguard insisted on by Keith and Moore was that the directors of Zeckendorf Property Corporation should be divided in three between Zeckendorf and his henchmen, the British directors and some independent members, including an ex-secretary to the Treasury and a former ambassador in London. Keith and Moore expected these independents to vote with them if Zeckendorf proved difficult, but Zeckendorf was often able to sway them with his persuasive euphoria. After the third meeting, the board meetings degenerated into blazing rows as the British tried to restrain Zeckendorf from increasing the company's commitments. Another destructive element in the partnership was that in the spring of 1962 the real estate market turned sour and the values of the properties declined.

After a year of struggling to contain Zeckendorf the British decided that the only course was to cut loose from him completely. In December 1962 Kenneth Keith resigned from the board of Webb & Knapp over a disagreement on Zeckendorf's principles of accounting. He declared, 'I resigned from the Webb & Knapp board because I found it impossible to have control. W & K happily bought and sold property without reference to me and told me afterwards.' Seven months after that, in July 1963, Zeckendorf was out of the Zeckendorf Property Corporation.

Second Covent Garden has not fully recovered from the financial nightmare of its nineteen-month alliance with Mr Zeckendorf in the United States. In September 1963 it wrote off in its consolidated balance sheet $8·9 million against its North American operation, in September 1965 $11 million and in September 1966 another $635,000. To 'write off' was the euphemism of the balance sheet for to 'lose'. Some of this $20·5 million loss may one day be partly recouped by profits on Place Ville Marie in Montreal. In April 1967 Second Covent Garden swapped its equity for fixed interest stock in the tail end of its involvement with Zeckendorf in the USA, three vast blocks of flats in Manhattan: Park West Village, Kips Bay Plaza and Lincoln Towers. On this occasion there was a write-up to come from $5·1 million in the books to $6 million, a small compensation for its earlier net loss. Philip Hill also lost $2·5 million on its shares in Webb & Knapp, which became virtually valueless.

After Second Covent Garden parted company from Zeckendorf, Harry Moore had to spend around one week a month for three years in America, sorting out the consequences of the involvement. Another director, Peter Kirwan-Taylor, was permanently resident in New York on this one job for over two years. At the time of the split Zeckendorf remarked sadly: 'They thought they could reform the old man—and I wish they had.' His failing was that he had been an absolute monarch for too long.

The men from Philip Hill were not the only ones to run across the freak of American real estate. Zeckendorf was an indefatigable contact man and reasoned that any of the rich British developers who hit New York might be useful to him. He met Johnny Rubens and Barney Shine, who with Alec Colman developed an 816,000 square foot office building in Boston, perhaps the soundest single British development in the US. On his second visit to New York

John Rubens, who had never met Zeckendorf before, found two bottles of whisky in his hotel bedroom. One was a present from William Zeckendorf, Senior. The other was a present from William Zeckendorf, Junior. Rubens was nervous of Zeckendorf and decided to do no business with him, and he greatly angered Zeckendorf by turning down an invitation to a lavish lunch arranged in his honour, with the Mayor of New York present, as a prelude to business. Felix Fenston was also wooed by Zeckendorf. He was in New York just to visit a friend who was ill. Zeckendorf learnt that he was in town and rang him up, eager to do business, 'What do you want to do? Do you want to buy? Or sell? Or both? It's for you to choose.' Fenston was not keen to do any of these, but Zeckendorf insisted that he came to look at a site. 'It was difficult to resist his enthusiasm,' Fenston recalled, 'and in the end he picked me up at my hotel at 7 o'clock in the morning.'

But, apart from Clore's purchase of 40 Wall Street, the other developer from England who did business with Zeckendorf was Max Rayne. In the late fifties he had taken up a modest position in Canadian real estate, which was administered by Cecilia Benattar, a highly competent native of Manchester married to a Canadian architect. In June 1962 Zeckendorf bought from Conrad Hilton the Savoy Plaza, an old wedding cake of a hotel on Fifth Avenue and 58th to 59th Streets, overlooking Central Park. In October of the same year, pushed as ever for money, Zeckendorf sold one-third of the equity of the Savoy Plaza to Max Rayne's company for $100,000; in return Max Rayne lent Zeckendorf $2·4 million as a second mortgage. The hotel was losing money, but Zeckendorf had a plausible plan for converting the building into a co-operative apartment block. In January 1963, however, President Kennedy changed the tax law on co-operatives and killed the incentive for the promoter. The hotel lost money even more rapidly and Max Rayne and Mrs Benattar, who by this time had transferred her headquarters to New York, were finding it increasingly difficult to live with Mr Zeckendorf. He was in arrears on loans from both Rayne's company and from the company owning the Savoy.

As a penalty for the default Max Rayne bought out Zeckendorf's two-thirds of the Savoy and then controlled 100 per cent of the Savoy Plaza. But it was still far from clear how to stop it losing money as a hotel or how to put it to a different use. Mrs Benattar, at this time aged only thirty-one, set about clearing the company's debts to unencumber its assets. Then the idea slowly emerged that the Savoy Plaza must be rebuilt as an office block. Suddenly the master stroke arrived, which turned this extremely sickly deal into an excellent one, and it came, typically, from the hand of Bill Zeckendorf. He approached Mrs Benattar, wanting to buy the entire project back. She was not keen, as the plan for an office building was being formed. It turned out that Zeckendorf had a tenant for the office space up his sleeve, and the tenant was none other than the world's largest industrial company, General Motors. The upshot was that Zeckendorf introduced General Motors as a tenant, and as tit for tat Max Rayne would forget the loan, now $2·3 million, provided Zeckendorf paid the interest. But Zeckendorf failed to do so and lost this handsome commission. General Motors formed a joint company with Max Rayne and agreed to occupy 750,000 of the 1,600,000 square foot, marble clad skyscraper of fifty floors. Final profitability of this $90 million project will depend on the price at which the 350,000 square feet of space not used by General Motors is leased, but the finances are helped by a long-term loan from Metropolitan Life of up to $90 million at a basic rate of $4\frac{3}{4}$ per cent. The credit of General Motors screwed the interest rate so low; Max Rayne discovered that 'General Motors would not put their name to 5 per cent paper.'

After his final split from Second Covent Garden, Zeckendorf spent a frenetic two and a half years selling off bits of his empire and trying to keep his creditors at bay. As always his deals were enormously complicated—he seemed much to prefer an intricate deal to a simple one—and only he could understand them and the intricacies of the many documents he signed. Finally his creditors tired of waiting and there exploded what Zeckendorf called 'the holocaust'. This occurred at 4 o'clock in the afternoon of May 7 1965, when the Marine Midland Trust, trustee for $4·3 million of Webb & Knapp's debentures, petitioned for a reorganisation under the Bankruptcy Act. The summer before, as he had bravely struggled to pay his bills, Zeckendorf told reporters: 'the reports of my death are greatly exaggerated'.

Two months after the petition the trustees reported 'a bleak picture' and that the records were in bad shape 'in this corporate maze'. But Zeckendorf, who had guaranteed many millions of Webb & Knapp's loans, was not personally bankrupt and continued to live in great style in a beautifully decorated nine-room pent-house overlooking the East River. He continued to deal in property, though at one remove. A month after the petition for W & K's bankruptcy a new company was formed by William Zeckendorf, Junior, and his brother-in-law. Mr Zeckendorf, Senior, was not a director and he was not a shareholder. He was consultant to the new company and he did continue to germinate deals on the telephone at the breakfast table. He also continued to drive to his office in a freakishly large grey Cadillac with WZ-1 on the number plate, using en route one of its two telephones. But in the office, as ever in Madison Avenue, things were slightly different when I visited him in December 1965. Many desks were empty, the fresh flowers had turned to plastic, and one or two things were missing. The wooden case to hold the ticker tape machine had a few wires at the bottom but no machinery.

Mrs Benattar, who emerged from her brush with Mr Zeckendorf much better than the bankers from Philip Hill, explained one of the difficulties in dealing with him: 'Zeckendorf was a man of integrity. But it was a matter of semantics. Words meant different things to him and to us.' He was also a man with phenomenal powers of persuasion. Max Rayne experienced this. He said: 'When I was really worried about the joint company with Zeckendorf, I sent over two quite unusually tough negotiators to try and contain him and see that he spent no more money. Two days later they 'phoned from New York: "Mr Zeckendorf has some other very interesting projects over here. Would you like to put up some more money?" '

*

In 1959, at the same time that Jack Cotton was letting out his premature cries of victory over his invasion of New York, other developers were making the trip to Australia. British developers made their greatest impression in that country, where there was a genuine work of pioneering to be done. Property development on post-war British lines had hardly emerged. An estate agent who helped to open up the door for the developers to pour in their money in the late fifties and early sixties told me that he had found that the Australians had a hitching rail mentality about development. Australian towns and cities had grown up around the houses and shops and banks, with rails along the street front for visiting farmers to tie their horses to; later new buildings were put up on the same individual sites, with the same frontages and narrow cores as they were in British cities until the Second World War. But one of the main obstacles to the entrepreneur was a lack of bridging finance from the banks. The rhythm of the Australian banking system is geared to an agricultural economy. The banks lend heavily to farmers against the wool clip for part of the year. With the wool sold the banks are brimming with deposits again for another few months. This seasonal flow of money is useless for property developers, who for the average office building might need to borrow from a bank for two to three years on end.

With the developer excluded for lack of money, occupiers tended to put up their own buildings after the war. Occasionally the Australian offshoots of institutions based on London, such as the Legal & General, built offices for leasing to others. Insurance companies were flush with cash and did not need to ask the banks for bridging finance. But almost always these buildings would sit on the same plot as the torn-down old building, and the yield on the investment would be a relatively meagre $6\frac{1}{2}$ to 7 per cent. Thus when they were asked to lend developers long-term finance they were lukewarm. A minor snag in the late fifties was that the then chief executive of the Australian Mutual Provident, far and away the biggest of the Australian insurance companies and the trend setter, was inclined to favour agricultural rather than urban investments.

British property men probably moved into Australia rather more cautiously than they might have done if one of the earliest big speculative schemes taken on by a British company, Taylor Woodrow, had not turned sour. This was the Western Market project in Melbourne. It is discussed in hushed tones by those respectful of their rivals' mistakes, or with glee by the brash. The scheme was slightly off-pitch, it ran into trouble with Melbourne City Council and never got off the ground. The loss to Taylor Woodrow was not great but it was a nasty setback in what was intended as a prestige operation.

The danger in Australia was the same as in other foreign countries: ignorance of local conditions. This was lessened by the strong British influence in business and by there being so little competition in this particular field. The invaders overcame the problem of short-term bank money either by lending from the parent in England or by borrowing from that ever adaptable race of bankers, the Swiss. They were helped in their timing quite unconsciously. 1959 happened to be a year of credit squeeze in Australia. This forced the hand of sellers of property. Some of the very few companies which had invested in commercial property in at all a big way, such as L. J. Hooker, were forced by the squeeze to liquidate some of their holdings.

The British developers fell upon these pickings and then set about piecing together large sites and city blocks in Sydney, Melbourne, Perth, Brisbane and Adelaide just as though they were in Holborn or Cheapside. Since there was no proven market for the end product, these men may have been propped up with the courage of the over-confident. They were certainly spurred on with the courage of the fashionable, for soon it became the accepted creed that Australia was the land of opportunity for the developer, and that the men from Mayfair would carry all before them.

Australian property men must have sensed a latent cockiness in the new competitors, for the British were unpopular in the early years. They might well have progressed even faster than they did if they had, as a matter of policy, teamed up with local operators. Some did. Second Covent Garden, Oddeninos and London County, Freehold & Leasehold all took local partners on some projects. But one incident did little to help the image of the British developer. This was an abortive foray of Alec Colman's into Sydney. Alec Colman, with his first attempted deal in Australia, made an offer of £A1·4 million to Sydney City Council for a municipal property in Martin Place. This was accepted by the Council in April 1960 and a unanimous motion was passed congratulating the Lord Mayor, the Town Clerk and the City Building Surveyor on the success of their trip overseas to discuss the sale of the land. This congratulation proved decidedly premature. Months dragged by as Colman tried to vary the terms of the sale both on planning permission and method of payment. Later the Lord Mayor of Sydney had to deliver an ultimatum to Colman. Was he going ahead or not? It finally turned out that he was not. But since this was one of Sydney's pet projects, the Colman affair received a great deal of publicity in Australia, not altogether flattering for British developers.

There were no upsets in Australia on the scale of the Zeckendorf

disaster. 'But no-one,' an agent remarked to me, 'has as yet made a
bomb. They might have done better in London.' The offices built
on spec have tended to let without much difficulty, largely to
international companies which have not had to be educated away
from the idea that an industrial company owns its own freehold.
The shopping centres built by Hammersons and by Arndale were
also modest successes. But while most companies have only
performed respectably so far, the time to draw up a balance sheet,
both for the individual firms and for the country's balance of pay-
ments, will be in ten to fifteen years' time. Although each company has invested only a small proportion of its total assets in
Australia, the cumulative contribution by the British has been a
solid one since redevelopment started on any scale around 1959;
no statistics are available, but possibly about half the new office
buildings in the main Australian cities have in recent years been
promoted by British developers. Between 70 per cent and 80
per cent of Australia's population, now 11·3 million, is to be found
in the cities and is growing more rapidly than the world average.
Provided the location of each building has been correctly judged,
the statistics should comfort Australian office developers, for the
sprawl of the urban population will ensure a high demand for their
buildings and rents should rise as leases end after ten years or so.
But the judgment of the developer will turn out much more vital
in Australia than in England. Land is a scarce commodity in England and planning authorities have necessarily been restrictive for
fear of waste and blackening of the countryside. In Australia,
which is 82 per cent the size of the United States with 6 per cent
of its population, land and location are bound to be more flexible.
In the United States the values of downtown shops deteriorated
rapidly in the fifties with the rise of suburban shopping centres.
Similarly, commercial centres in Australia could slip to the east or
the west for reasons of problems with traffic or cost of land, and
owners of today's prime offices could far more easily catch a cold
than owners in Bishopsgate or London Wall. On the other hand, if
the commercial centres do expand upwards within their present
boundaries, the British developer will continue to be a dominant
force, for a large part of the old, undeveloped freeholds are now in
British hands. The possibilities are obvious and with development in Britain suffocated by over-building and Government
restraints, competition is bound to be fierce and margins fine. One

young developer was boasting during 1966 that he would be 'Mr Australia'. The realities will tend to be far more pedestrian, and, with the Colman affair an uneasy memory, more discreet.

*

A third hunting ground for developers was Europe. Once again, it was during the years 1959, 1960 and 1961 that developers began to lick their lips at the thought of applying their prowess to the cities of the Continent. With only a few exceptions they drew a blank.

The rest of Europe was not a commerical developer's paradise like England. Most countries fiercely restricted commercial development in order to channel as much capital as possible into housing. The centre of German cities had to be rebuilt after the ravages of bombing, but the local authorities had a much greater grip on real estate than in this country and there was more building by companies for their own occupation.

The Scandinavian countries had highly planned economies with virtually no scope for speculative office or shop building. In France a combination of restrictive rules of planning, taxation and a disobliging capital market kept the commercial developer at bay. The French Government heavily subsidised private developers of flats through concessions on tax, for France's stock of housing was much more inadequate than Britain's. This led to a big demand for flats, which were usually sold freehold by the builders and often even before the building had begun. Speculators would buy flats from the promoter off the plan and sell them to the eventual occupier when the building was more nearly completed. Speculation grew so enthusiastic that new laws were introduced in mid-1963; there had been a crop of scandals involving entrepreneurs who collected deposits by selling flats off plan, but failed to build the flats.

In Brussels there was a certain amount of office building on spec, but in relative terms the British phenomenon was absent anywhere on the Continent. This naturally excited the British. But in six years in which many attempted to open up this market, there were only sporadic successes. Perhaps Joe Gold, with his slight stutter and determination to persevere, performed better than any of his rivals, largely through employing full time a specialist in European property, Dennis Hillman-Eadie. He was also helped by his brother Bernard being an architect. Joe complained bitterly that Continental architects were unbusinesslike.

Apart from the snag that the potential in Europe for their talents was far less than they imagined, the chief barrier for many developers was their attitude. Instead of buckling down to a thorough study of the different conditions in the various countries, many operators dithered around, apparently rather offended that the customs were not the same as in England. Extremely few could speak any European language. Formal letters at the early stage of a negotiation to buy some property starting, 'Dear Sir, with reference to your letter of the 18th ultimo . . .' were apt to put off their counterparts across the Channel. The laws affecting real estate varied considerably. Estate agents often acted both for the buyer and for the seller in a deal, and were paid by both sides; this was a habit for which the British, with a charming show of ethical righteousness, showed a great distaste. The Continentals sensed this feeling and were scornful in return, so that a considerable lack of sympathy was kindled. Since there were so many enquiries which came to nothing, the largest and most prestigious estate agents became highly disillusioned with British developers, as they also did in New York.

Brussels was the one city in which a modicum of work was actually carried through. Richard Costain, the contractors, took a 50 per cent share in a fourteen-storey block named Britannia House. Its partner was the biggest contractor in Belgium, Armand Blaton. All over Europe contractors often promoted development as a sideline to their normal business. A company fostered by the noble stables of N. M. Rothschild & Sons in London and de Rothschild Frères in Paris, with the confident name of The European Property Company, developed two office blocks in Brussels. But this company, which was managed by Jones, Lang, Wootton, never fully lived up to the initial high hopes for it; it was a creature of respectability, born in 1962 by institutions for institutions, when the era of the individual was fading. The sweet memory of the minting of great fortunes spurred the imitators to search for a repetition.

Belgium was the easiest country to do business in as the zealous Belgians were prepared to put up with a great deal of to-ing and fro-ing from developers in pursuit of a deal. The planning authority in Brussels was also more permissive than in most other European cities, with the result that a minor glut of office space had emerged by 1966. Then General de Gaulle came to the rescue by driving out first SHAPE and then NATO from France with his nationalism. This stimulated demand in Brussels from camp followers such as oil companies.

One hurdle, which grew more formidable as Mr Wilson's financial crisis of 1965 and 1966 worsened, was permission from the Bank of England to export capital. The Old Lady insisted on developers agreeing to send back the money or earn a certain return on capital in a shorter and shorter period. Long-term capital for property development was virtually non-existent on the Continent; investors were too well acquainted with the terrors of inflation to lend their money on a fixed return for too long. This meant that buying and building and selling as a trading operation was almost the only form of activity open to most developers. It encouraged some companies in to the tail end of the boom in flats in Paris: London, City & Westcliff and Greencoat Properties were the two which achieved most. But 'You have to be up early in the morning in Paris to keep abreast of the changes in the laws' as Lord Broughshane, the chairman of Greencoat, said.

CHAPTER FOURTEEN

Troubles at the Bull Ring and the Elephant & Castle

Two major and uncomfortably visible blunders, born of over-confidence, helped to cool the optimism generated by the property world as the boom faded away in the sixties. As the plans were unveiled to the public in 1960, the shopping centres to be built at the Elephant & Castle in south London and at the Bull Ring in Birmingham were seen as the first two examples of a revolutionary concept: a large number of shops—140 at the Bull Ring and 120 at the Elephant—all under one roof and on different levels. Here was a chance for property developers to show their sophistication. Unfortunately, sophistication was one quality which had been superfluous in the collection of a large fortune in property through the fifties and the local authorities which sponsored both the Bull Ring and the Elephant seem to have been much too ready to accept what developers offered them. As the moment of greatest danger with a saucepan of milk is at the point of boiling, so the chance of burnt fingers is most acute when an industrial boom moves towards its peak.

As they grew 113 miles apart—publicists on each side preparing to claim that theirs was the biggest self-contained shopping centre in Europe—both projects had a remarkable amount in common. Each was essentially a by-product of a road traffic plan, each was leased after a competition by the local authority to a developer, and each was initiated, quite by coincidence, in the same month, September 1959. In both cases, partly in order to cram a sufficient number of shops on the site to justify the ground rent offered by their clients, the architects designed the hybrid buildings on several levels, with a curtain-walled, rectangular office block perched on top. But the Bull

Ring, which cost £5½ million to build compared with the £2¼ million for the Elephant, was a much more complicated affair, housing Birmingham's central bus station, a car park for 550 cars, a ballroom and a large retail market of stalls operated by the Corporation.

As their births fade into the distance, these two shopping centres provide some object lessons in how not to plan, especially the experience at the Elephant. Its origin was a crude and fundamental misconception on the part of the London County Council. At a press conference in February 1956 Sir Isaac Hayward, leader of the LCC, showed off the LCC's plans for a 30-acre comprehensive development area at the Elephant & Castle. He said: 'As important and busy road and rail junctions and centres of business, shopping and entertainment, the Elephant & Castle and Piccadilly Circus have a good deal in common. . . . By imaginative and realistic planning and with goodwill and co-operation between the Council and business and trading interests, the Elephant & Castle can, I am sure, become one of the main commercial, shopping and entertainment centres of south London. With its famous name, history and traditions on which to build, the new Elephant & Castle offers opportunities one would have to go a long way to better. Here's a real chance for south London to "show them how" on the north side of the Thames.'

Sir Isaac's message was eagerly taken up by the headline writers: 'the Piccadilly Circus of south London'. South Londoners who had lived in the slums near the Elephant before it was thoroughly bombed in the war and many others had a soft spot for the Elephant. It had always been the crossroads of south London, for it was the natural meeting place of the roads and paths within the wide arc of the Thames between Lambeth Bridge and Tower Bridge. As the bridges at Westminster, Blackfriars, Vauxhall, Waterloo and Southwark were completed between 1750 and 1820, all their roads collided at the Elephant & Castle. And as terraces of houses and squalid blocks of flats poured into south London in the 19th century, the growing population converged for shops and for entertainment at this first staging post on the route south of London. By the turn of the century the Elephant & Castle was famous for its music halls, brothels, pubs and general frenzy of its night life. Between the wars it continued to thrive as the coarse climax of the long shopping streets which converged at

P

its roundabout. The largest cinema in Europe, with 3,700 seats, was built there.

The LCC was keen to re-create some of this past vitality. But the dominating feature of its plan was the road. This was diverted around two huge roundabouts, connected by an eight-lane dual carriageway, in order to cope with the traffic from six main roads. This road plan was conceived by the LCC's traffic engineers twelve years before in 1948, but the broad comprehensive scheme flourished so proudly by the LCC in 1956 smacked of a town planning solution from the early thirties. Moreover the engineers—as they were doing all over the country at the time—woefully under-estimated the explosion in the motor car population. The roundabouts were finally finished in 1964. Two years later, in mid-1966, I asked a senior town planner at the GLC how much longer the roundabouts would be able to deal with the traffic. 'In certain circumstances,' he replied, 'they are quite inadequate today.'

'What are those circumstances?'

'Every morning and every evening, in the rush hour.'

'So what will you do about it?'

'We are thinking of building a bypass around the roundabouts.'

The parcels of land left by the roads' dissection were allocated to various uses and connected by a series of subways. By 1959 the LCC was ready to deal with the biggest, Site 1. This was to be the focal point of the entire project and the site was to be offered to developers in a competition judged on a mixture of architectural, social and financial considerations. Over 300 applicants asked for details of the scheme and the LCC received 36 proposals, whose general quality and architectural standard it considered 'very high'.

It is here that the fatal amateurism in the project becomes glaring. The LCC told developers roughly what should be built on the site: a total floor area of not more than 290,000 square feet, split up between shops and offices, with the shops taking not less than 100,000 square feet. The offices were included as a safety valve. The LCC knew, from watching the experience of developers on near-by sites, that there was still a roaring demand for office space and that a profitable letting of the offices would balance to some extent the risk in the shops. But how did it hit upon these figures of 290,000 square feet and 100,000 square feet? It had made no market survey of whether Site 1 was a suitable location for a heavy concentration of shops. It had no way of checking whether the developers' proposals were realistic. It did not consider seriously whether shoppers might be put off by having to negotiate the long subways underneath the traffic; nor that the surrounding population, whose standard of living had risen hugely since before the war, might after twenty-five years have deserted to the West End or to other established south London centres such as Brixton, Lewisham or Streatham for its comparison goods like clothes. It merely decided on traditional, sentimental grounds that the Elephant must be a shopping centre again. 'We are experts on schools and on housing. We are not experts on shops. But the fact that we had 36 competitors,' I was told, 'showed that there was sufficient interest and that the location was right.' The figures for floorspace appeared to be little more than guesswork.

The five developers on the short list were Arnold Lee, Bernard Sunley, Max Rayne, a syndicate headed by Marcus Leaver and the Willett group of companies. Willett was the winner with its scheme designed by architects Boissevain and Osmond, pronounced by the LCC's planning committee as '. . . the best solution, being quite outstanding in its original conception of an arcaded multi-level shopping centre . . .'

Willett had no previous experience of developing shops. It was strange that the LCC had even allowed it to compete. Willett was a housebuilding company and estate agency dating from 1868, started by the father of the William Willett of 'Daylight Saving' fame; it had flourished between the wars on building high-class houses in Hampstead. After the war it had marked time until 1956 when Kenneth Rose, a speculative housebuilder from Birmingham, came in as joint managing director. Rose, a deceptively quiet man, shook up the family firm, then existing placidly on its residential estate agency in Sloane Square, and with another outsider as lieutenant, Bill Albery, thrust it into the development of houses and flats for sale.

Rose tried his hand at the Elephant & Castle competition as a way of taking Willett into the commercial development business, which he could see was booming, without needing too much capital tied up in sites. He decided on the architects Boissevain and Osmond, essentially a husband and wife team consisting of Paul Boissevain and his wife Barbara Osmond, after a chance meeting when Willett had sold Paul Boissevain a plot of land. For this job

Rose wanted a good 'competition' architect and knew that the firm had been placed second in the competition for the Sydney Opera House in Australia and second again in the National Gallery competition in London. But Boissevain had never designed a shopping centre.

Before committing his company in the final stage of the competition, Kenneth Rose did not commission a viability study or any detailed research to discover what volume of shops the site was likely to stand. A viability study might have cost up to £10,000 and if its conclusion was 'don't build a single shop on that site', it would have been £10,000 thrown away. Like most of the other developers in the competition, Rose accepted that the LCC knew what it was up to in its specifications. He bid £125,000 a year for the site and offered to build 200,000 square feet of shops and 100,000 square feet of offices. These figures were also necessarily little more than guesswork.

It was five years before the end product was finally built and put to the test. Meanwhile William Willett went through a crisis. Soon after the firm had been awarded the prize at the Elephant, the family shareholders had a row with Rose and Albery, who departed.

Bill Albery joined Charles Neale, another solicitor turned property man. Neale came from a family of solicitors in the City of London and became interested in property in 1952 when his firm needed new offices. From then on he devoted more time to property development than to his solicitor's practice. But he tended to cultivate the image of the pheasant-shooting City man and disown the world of property. His biggest deal was to assemble bit by bit the site for the vast, 350,000 square foot office block in Southwark Street and sell it to Charles Clore. When he took over Gorringes, the department store near Victoria Station, he remarked: 'I am not a property dealer in any way and I normally associate with bankers and financiers.'

Not long after Albery started to work for him, Neale was searching for a suitable company into which he could tip his various properties. Albery suggested William Willett and, though there was competition from Edger Investments, the shares eventually went to Neale. It meant that he also won the Elephant & Castle scheme, which he judged an attractive picking, and took back into Willett both Albery and Kenneth Rose, after a year's absence.

As a result of these manœuvres the Elephant effectively had a new sponsor in October '61, for Charles Neale was the dominant stockholder in Willett. The following year William Willett was floated as a public company, valuing Neale's personal share at over £1 million; the prospectus relied heavily on forecasts of income from the Elephant & Castle: £312,500 for 1965 and £375,000 for 1966. In the autumn of 1962 construction at the Elephant began.

Charles Neale did not live to see the Elephant finished. He died in March 1963 at the age of forty-six. Meanwhile the period of construction took longer than expected due to bad weather and delay by the LCC, and instead of being completed in June 1964, the shops were not ready to open for another nine months.

By that time it was obvious that the Elephant would prove a sticky proposition as a shopping centre—at least in its early years. Under half the shops were leased, an ominously low proportion for an opening day. Already the inevitable whisper had been running around the property business: 'White Elephant'.

What was the trouble? First of all, it had become clear to prospective retailers that the potential of the catchment area, the area from which the shops drew their shoppers, had been seriously exaggerated. It had been claimed that the centre would serve over 1 million people who lived within a 3-mile radius. This guess ignored the alternatives within the 3-mile radius. It would have been absurd, for instance, to expect the residents of Westminster to pass over the adequate shopping facilities around Victoria Street in favour of the Elephant & Castle, unless the attractions there were a compelling counter-pull to the West End. Besides, many living much nearer were well served by conventional shopping streets such as the Walworth Road, which had grown stronger in the twenty-year gap since the Elephant had last been a shopping centre. For those shoppers to change their habits, an exceptional choice of shops would have had to be offered at the Elephant.

This was not offered. About a year after the opening day, E. I. Metin, a student working in the LCC, prepared a thesis on the Elephant & Castle for his final examination at the Institute of Town Planning. From surveys he estimated that the average resident population using the centre was roughly 20,000 as well as a working population of 10,000. He considered that this total of 30,000 might grow to 37,000.

The site itself and the immediate access to it were great stumbling blocks in the way of shoppers. Surrounded by the sea of traffic from one of the busiest junctions in London on three sides and by a railway line on the fourth, the majority of shoppers were forced to use the subways. Habits die hard and it would in any circumstances have been a struggle to persuade shoppers to dive underground to reach their shops. But these subways were long, at 8 to 9 feet wide narrower than the LCC wanted due to the tight budget allowed by the Ministry of Transport, rather dark, poorly signposted and utterly devoid of any charm. E. I. Metin's survey showed that the shoppers found access to the centre highly complicated and often lost their way. As the architect Paul Boissevain remarked, 'the site is really saying no with a big NO to almost any poor pedestrian who wants to creep into the building'.

However, once on the site the design chosen for the building did not pander to the conservatism of shoppers. Rather, it was a risky challenge to traditional habits. It was undoubtedly only sensible to enclose the centre, turning the back of the shops on the roar of traffic. The building is rectangular with three levels of shops set out in an almost identical pattern one above another with broad pedestrian ways running down the centre of each long axis and across the centre of the short axis on the lower and middle floors. The floors are connected by stairs and escalators, though there is no escalator down from the upper floor. An outside ramp leads from the lower to the middle floor.

By the opening day most of the lower floor was let. Woolworths, Boots the Chemists, W. H. Smith and Tesco were important retailers to boost the developers' morale, but not their pocket, since they are powerful enough to demand concessions in rent as a tit for tat for their power of luring customers to the centre. About one-third of the middle floor was let and virtually none of the upper floor.

This situation improved only slightly in the course of the next year and a half in spite of valiant efforts by Bill Albery to drum up temporary lettings, and to offer low initial rents, capital loans for shopfitting and other incentives to tenants.

Some of the shoppers surveyed by E. I. Metin—all were interviewed on the ground floor since there were not enough people to be found on the upper floors—expressed surprise that there were any upper floors at all. Most said that they never went there. The signposting inside the centre did not cry out that there were delights to be found above the ground floor. Mothers with prams had to make a long detour outside the building to move up the ramp from the middle floor to the lower or vice versa. Without a natural flow of pedestrians, except from the main line railway station, which seemed to provide very few shoppers indeed, the upper two floors were caught in the vicious circle of too few shoppers making the effort to climb to the shops and too few shop-keepers braving the struggle to attract them. On a day when the sliding roof was closed the upper floor, with four forlorn shops let out of forty, looked more like a mysterious film set for a spy thriller than a group of shops.

After the retailers had traded for over a year, Willett was host to some disillusioned tenants, many of whom were then losing money. Radio Rentals, a 750-strong chain of radio and television shops, leased a £1,200-a-year shop on the middle floor at the end nearest the Walworth Road, thinking that the shopping centre might become an extension of the Walworth Road at that end. It did not turn out like that. Normally Radio Rentals expected to draw some 35 per cent of its customers from passing pedestrians, ignoring those who come specifically to their shop. At the Elephant they found that this percentage was minimal, perhaps only 1 per cent. Several retailers complained to me that the car parking was inadequate. Yet one normal Saturday afternoon in June 1966 (Fridays and Saturdays are the two busiest days in the centre) the park in the basement for 154 cars was less than half full. This car park was intended primarily for the shopkeepers, the plan being to construct another multi-storey park for 500 or so cars on a site across the railway line. With the existing car park not fully used, would a bigger one help? Some shop retailers and Kenneth Rose claim that it would because the centre would then attract shoppers from a farther flung area, who knew of the big park. But unless the enlarged parking rapidly drew in more tenants, which seems doubtful, the Elephant & Castle could hardly hope to compete, except for such everyday, local needs as groceries, against the global variety of the West End or the far larger established centres of shopping already established in south London. After a year and a half the developers still had not supported their enthusiasm for the car park by building it, but they claimed that the change of the road pattern by the LCC was delaying the start.

A manufacturer who turns out a product which does not sell, perhaps a line in electric fires which are badly designed and dangerous, scraps his stock and writes off his losses. For a property developer the solution is not so simple. His product is built to last for 70 to 100 years. At the Elephant the basic defects were not easy to cure. Its location was ill-chosen, access was difficult and the layout of the shops on three floors was inconvenient for those shoppers who penetrated the castle surrounded by its moat of traffic. What is needed is an imaginative rescue operation, bringing some new users to the site, to overcome the basic defects.

Willett paid dearly for its rash attempt to jump on the bandwagon of the property boom. The rent of the site costs £125,000 every year (for all its bungling at the planning stage the LCC continued to pull in the rent), and interest on the total building cost of some £2·3 million would have been £161,000 at 7 per cent. As the LCC so rightly guessed the offices, the safety valve, let easily and the 'developers' friend', the Ministry of Works, paid £120,000 a year for the eleven-storey block. But after a year only one-third of the expected rent from the shops was coming in, or £90,000. With an income of £210,000 and an annual cost of £286,000 Willett was losing a hefty £76,000 a year. It may be losing slightly less by now as the shops fill up one by one, but it may take many years before this development in its present form ceases to lose money.

It is typical of the buoyancy of the property market that Willett should not have paid for its mistake with bankruptcy. It was baled out and cushioned against its losses at the Elephant by some excellent deals elsewhere, notably the letting of its huge office block in Victoria Street to New Scotland Yard. There Willett, a subsidiary of Westminster Trust, was making a profit of £570,000 to offset against this £76,000 loss. So what Willett lost on the swings of the Elephant, it gained on the roundabout of New Scotland Yard.

*

With something of the same character as the Elephant, the Bull Ring before reconstruction was a traditional cheap and vigorous mixture of barrow boys and shops, the most celebrated of old

Birmingham's street markets. But it was less of a self-contained concentration than the pre-war Elephant, for it was adjacent to the glamorous national retailers and department stores of High Street, New Street and Corporation Street, the equivalent of London's Oxford and Regent Streets. Separated by a few hundred yards from those increasingly prosperous streets, the Bull Ring varied the conformity of the multiples' neon with a welcome down-at-heel hubbub.

The redevelopment of this area sprang as a side-issue from the Birmingham Corporation's £27 million Inner Ring Road, encircling the heart of Birmingham. This plan was conceived between the wars by Sir Herbert Manzoni, city engineer of Birmingham from 1935 to 1963. Although it had several features which ran directly counter to the modern theory of planning, the ring road was pushed ahead by the buccaneering, hard-headed officials and councillors of Birmingham and was begun in 1957. One businesslike aspect of the plan was to lease off to developers all spare slivers of land which had been compulsorily acquired for the road. Frank Price, then chairman of the Public Works Committee, later Lord Mayor of Birmingham as well as a director of Walter Flack's Murrayfield Real Estate, has recalled in an article* the beginning of this policy: 'Once we had started on the physical work of the road I saw quite clearly that if our vision of the New Birmingham was to take shape it was essential to make it as commercially successful as possible.'

The first section of the road to be built, Smallbrook Ringway, was lined with offices and shops on one side, and on the other with offices, shops and the most luxurious hotel to be built at the time outside London, the Albany run by Lyons the tea-shop people. But one comfort which the Albany lacked was quiet. The roar of traffic from its location beside a three-lane dual carriageway was overpowering and soon after the hotel was first occupied the builders had to move back in to fit the windows with double glazing.

For Birmingham Corporation, though, the policy of reducing the cost of the road by selling off leases on the roadside land was amply justified in financial terms. After initial hesitation, since this was not an established place for either shops or offices, a combination of the Birmingham architect Jim Roberts, a property

* The *Birmingham Sketch*, September 1965.

developer, Jo Godfrey of Property & General Developments, and a firm of contractors-cum-developers, John Laing, tackled the first site on the south of the Ringway. Frank Price said that 'after the publicity given to this scheme investors came pouring in'.

Jo Godfrey continued the good work for Birmingham's coffers and his own company's finances alongside the ring road with more office buildings designed by Jim Roberts. Their last and most revolutionary building for Birmingham was the slick, twenty-one-storey circular tower of offices, the Rotunda, which was slow to let as the famine of offices turned to glut but was a proud landmark for Birmingham and for Roberts, who set up his thriving practice on the highest two floors.

Meanwhile, at much the same time in 1958–59 as Godfrey and Roberts were planning the Rotunda, they were also negotiating with Birmingham for an even more ambitious project across the ring road from the Rotunda on the Bull Ring site. The ideas of Roberts fitted in well with those of the City's architect, the scheme for a vast centre of shops and market stalls was publicly discussed and published in the architectural magazines, and the details worked out in tandem between public and private enterprise. But then a great wrangle began over what price Godfrey should pay for the site. After months of haggling there was an impasse. Godfrey was prepared to offer only £50,000 a year in ground rent. Birmingham wanted £75,000 a year.

Eventually Birmingham decided to offer the site to developers by public tender and the brief to competitors was published on 11 September 1959. Unlike the LCC, Birmingham's officials did not lay down in their brief the details of the volume of shops to be built. They just set out in general terms what was needed: car park, bus station, market stalls, shops and so on. The vital decision on the number of shops was left for the developers to decide. Since Birmingham, like the LCC, had not done any serious research on the potential of the Bull Ring site as a shopping centre, it was wise to leave the decision to somebody else.

Developers were given three months in which to submit their plans; by American standards this was about half the normal time needed to make a trustworthy analysis for such a major project. One important feature of the winning scheme—to have it entirely covered over—was thought up only ten days before the closing date for entries. Laing, partner with the frustrated Mr Godfrey just down the road, won with a ground rent of £109,000 a year. Godfrey, for all his earlier deadlock with the Corporation, did compete and offered £80,000 a year for a somewhat enlarged version of his original plan. There were eleven competitors in all, less than a third of the number at the Elephant, although the Bull Ring's site had greater natural advantages. But developers were strongly orientated towards London. Both the LCC and Birmingham's officials, when they announced the result of the competitions, were insistent that they had chosen the winner for its architectural and planning qualities combined with the financial offer, and that they had not just taken the highest bid, though they did not disclose what the higher offers were.

The publication of Laing's scheme caused a minor outcry in the architectural world. Leslie Ginsberg, then head of the Birmingham School of Planning, wrote in a moderate tone in the *Architects' Journal* of 4 February, 1960: 'The scheme owes much to another project put forward earlier by Property and General Investment, which had all but been approved by the Public Works Committee, when negotiations broke down on financial grounds. This scheme had been prepared by Birmingham architect, James A. Roberts, who did all the initial donkey work including protracted negotiations with British Railways, Midland Red Omnibus and the various other interests involved, and who paved the way for the type of project now approved. Indeed, his own scheme obviously played a large part in influencing the final design which has been accepted, and the greater simplicity of his massing suggests that if he had been allowed to take it a further stage, he would have probably put forward as good a scheme as is now before us. . . . It does seem rather sad that the architect responsible for two adjoining projects could not be encouraged to go forward with this major scheme and so provide the architectural unity which is so badly needed.' An editorial in the same issue entitled 'The dangers of the secret competition' spoke of the work done before the public tender by Jim Roberts: '. . . the Corporation has, in effect, had the services of a planning and architectural consultant free of charge, and all the competitors were able to build on his work and to develop or plagiarise his published ideas. It is satisfactory to know that the scheme approved by the Corporation has much to commend it, and that it was not merely chosen because it was the most attractive financial bid. It may well have been the best scheme, but as the others were not published, the public can have no confidence that this was so. The whole affair leaves a nasty taste behind it, and the sooner the RIBA finds the way to bring competitions of this kind within the ambit of its regulations the better. Birmingham has been singularly lucky to get as good a tune as it has out of such a very poor machine.' If there was plagiarism, Birmingham was much more to blame than Laing because the specifications laid down for the competition derived directly from the abortive scheme prepared by Jim Roberts.

The Bull Ring was finished in late 1963, a year and a half earlier than the Elephant. It was a pioneer of its species. Any pioneer in business, be it in nylon or commercial television, faces a tough struggle to make a new product acceptable. But Maurice Robson, a manager as opposed to an entrepreneur, who headed Laing's property development side, was lumbered with an extra difficulty in trying to sell the Bull Ring to his customers, the retailers. It was an exceedingly complicated product. Moreover, Laing, like Willett, had jumped into this heavy £5½ million commitment largely on the strength of the developer's intuition, the acknowledged formula at that heady stage in the property boom and with insufficient research into the possible needs of the site or the possible reaction of the population to the new building.

From the outside the Bull Ring is an untidy jumble of a building. Apart from a magnificent, virile bronze bull, designed by Trewin Copplestone, and hoisted high on the end walls, it is hard to decipher the purpose of the sprawling structures. It says almost nothing to the passer-by. Undoubtedly the architects, Sydney Greenwood and Laing's staff architect, T. J. Hirst, within the limitations of Birmingham Corporation's brief were faced with a great difficulty in relating so many uses on a small site and attempting to produce a cohesive whole. Car park, office block, one of the biggest Woolworths in the country, market stalls, rows of shops and a bus station, all have been thrown together into one heavy lump. Inside, this multiplicity of uses is also a great problem and again has been unsatisfactorily solved. The shopper is faced with the choice of no less than five different layers of shops.

At the bottom of the cake is the bus station, leading in to the market hall, which is operated by the local authority on a sublease from Laing. The market hall opens at the opposite end to the bus station into an open-air market square, or rather triangle, next to St Martin's Church. This triangle is filled with stalls for vegetables or flowers, textiles and job lot lines to replace the traders who lined the streets of the old Bull Ring. A second way out of the bus station takes the shopper into a lobby from which there are escalators or stairs up to the two main floors of shops, connected to one another by more escalators and by stairs for those prepared to look for them. Alongside the lower of these two floors is the upper part of the mammoth Woolworths. Between the two is a group of small shops at one end on a level with the ring road and the entrance to the car park. And higher than the upper main floor, known as the Grand Parade, is the fifth level of shopping, leading over a bridge across the road, past more shops and into New Street Station. The other exit from the Grand Parade was across another bridge alongside an enormous rectangular Fine Fare supermarket, down more escalators to an oversized, sunken traffic island, where a tired public garden honours Sir Herbert Manzoni, under a subway the other side of the island and finally up a flight of stairs into the more normal atmosphere of the traffic-choked, pavement-squashed streets of central Birmingham.

To walk around the Bull Ring gives the impression that a highly sophisticated designer with a Meccano set, tied down to a restrictive brief, was the originator of the structure. There was a more natural reason for the five levels at the Bull Ring than the three at the Elephant: the ground fell by 50 feet from one side of the site to the other, whereas it was flat at the Elephant. But the Bull Ring's complexity gave the developers a severe headache.

Maurice Robson and his manager at the Bull Ring, Adam Hepburn, gave an unusually frank talk about the problems to the Chartered Surveyors in February, 1965. Since Laing was busy with other big developments up and down the country and intended to be a continuing force as a developer, Maurice Robson realised that it was better to discuss openly the Bull Ring's difficulties, which were in any case common gossip in the property world. And while every bit as secretive on some important details as the quietest of the developers, Laing was involved as a contractor on a wider front in housing and contracting, and its main owners, the Laings, active on official bodies.

Maurice Robson told the surveyors: 'At the very outset, our early publicity attracted a large number of tenants ready and willing to take accommodation. But after eighteen months or so had elapsed and construction work was under way they found it more and more difficult to understand how they could possibly carry on their business in such an apparently complicated maze of different levels. One or two began to fall out and, as so often happens in these cases, the rot began to set in, until we found ourselves, early in 1963, with a huge shopping centre which we knew would soon be involving us in outgoings approaching £500,000 a year, and pretty well devoid of tenants.

'Even worse than this, the drums were beating and the jungle telegraph had it that the scheme was doomed to failure . . .' Mr Robson had begun by saying that 'the RICS originally asked me to give this talk to you last winter, and I had to decline the invitation because at that time there was every prospect that the centre would be empty when the Duke of Edinburgh opened it in May of last year, and I had not the slightest desire to stand up here and talk to you about empty shops . . .'

It was at the point when the drums of the estate agents and retailers began to beat out the message of doom that Laing's experience and professionalism, greater than that of Willett at the Elephant, came into play. Robson saw that if the centre was to open as planned in November 1963 with most of the shops unlet, the vicious circle of unlet shops, not enough shoppers and thus nobody willing to take the shops might turn his £5½ million investment into a chronic white elephant. If the shops could be let before opening day, even at lower rents than would give Laing a profit in the early years, it would at least give the centre a chance.

So in the spring of 1963 Robson decided to put off the opening from November until the following May of 1964. This was not good for the morale of those who had already leased shops. Laing also added to the two firms originally hired as letting agents, John D. Wood in London and Cheshire Gibson in Birmingham, both rather inexperienced at letting shops on a national scale, a third, with much more specialised skill, Edward Erdman. At the same time the campaign to let the shops was stopped. It was to be started up again with a high-powered thrust when building was finished in the autumn and 'the maze of internal scaffolding and paraphernalia' was out of the way so that prospective tenants could see their way around. But before the campaign was reopened Robson personally asked some of the biggest retailers in the country to take space on concessionary terms in one or two key spots in the project in order to act as a magnet to pull in other traders. His great coup here was to persuade John Collier, the self-made millionaire head of the £120 million United Drapery Stores, to take a large slice of the shops at the pivot of the Grand Parade.

Robson's gamble on delay was a winner. It saved Laing from what could have been an outright disaster. By May 1964, after some tense months of hard work, some 85 per cent of the shops were let. But the rents had had to be lowered sharply. Barratts the shoe people, 'Walk the Barratt Way', took a shop, 38 feet wide by 67 feet deep, in the first letting campaign at £9,500 a year, rising to £10,500 at the seventh year and £11,250 from the fourteenth to the twenty-first year. Stylo Shoes leased a shop in a similar position almost exactly opposite Barratts which was the same width but only 37 feet deep. This difference in depth might normally give a 50 per cent lower rent. But Stylo arranged its lease in the hard push of the second campaign and its lease was at £4,000 for the first seven years and £4,500 for the remaining fourteen. Instead of 50 per cent, Barratt was paying between 137 per cent and 150 per cent more.

All the leases varied much more than is normal with a clutch of new shops, depending on how hard a bargain the particular retailer or his agent could strike. Most of them knew that Laing was desperate to have the centre let by opening day. A handful of traders leased their shops on percentage rents. The percentage rent is common in North America, but virtually unknown in Britain. The retailer pays a low basic rent, and a determined proportion of his turnover after it tops a certain level.* It has not caught on largely because it is more difficult for a developer to finance a project neatly under British methods, and because retailers who have operated through almost incessant inflation have preferred to have fixed rents as far as possible. But in their time of trouble Laing tempted a few traders in this way by offering extremely low basic rents to compensate for the uncertain prospects at the Bull Ring. John Collier the tailors and Richard (dress) Shops, both in the United Drapery group, took percentage rents. This type of lease has subsequently proved popular at the Bull Ring and all new lettings are on this principle.

The shopping public of Birmingham did not flock to the Bull

* See page 105 of *Costs and Competition in Retailing*, by W. G. McLelland (Macmillan, 1966).

Ring. It responded slowly. To start with there were private cries of woe among the traders at the relative dearth of shoppers, though there was a fair turnout on Saturdays. But in the second year trade was 30 to 40 per cent up, that is, '30 or 40 per cent up from damn all', as one trader put it. And on Saturdays there was a huge, swirling crowd before very long. This, however, showed one of the deficiencies in design. On a Saturday afternoon when the crowd was at its thickest, the escalators carrying shoppers between levels could not cope with the numbers, even though the capacity to serve customers in the shops was not yet stretched as it should be at the peak of the week. Laing has been altering the escalators. In any event shops cannot do well on little more than one reasonably good trading day a week.

What were the snags at the Bull Ring? Laing had one big excuse, which was that the link into New Street Station could not be joined through the long delays by British Rail in its complete rebuilding as Birmingham's one passenger station by a consortium of three developers. Once this was built, Laing claimed, the flow of pedestrians would be much increased and properly balanced. There are reasons for doubting this, but until the station is joined up there will be no proof on this point.

The two main faults at the Bull Ring seem to me that it was too big for its location and that it was poorly designed. Both these drawbacks could have been lessened if not avoided by greater care and research at the planning stage. One of the more ominous patterns to emerge in the early days of the Bull Ring was the flow of pedestrians out of the bus station, into the Corporation's bustling retail market on the same ground floor level, out past the open-air stalls and sweeping round under the subway into the traditional centre of Birmingham. This suggested two things. First, that the selection of shops in the Bull Ring did not satisfy any needs which the existing main streets did not already meet. Secondly, that the environment in the centre, for all its absence of traffic, its air-conditioning and canned music, did not have any particular appeal to shoppers.

The Bull Ring was more ingenious than the Elephant, it was more professionally handled, but the disfiguring birthmark with which each started life was that they were in the wrong place. These decisions of location were taken by the local authorities and accepted by over-enthusiastic developers. The Bull Ring was either too near the centre of Birmingham or too far from it: if, instead of being two hundred yards or so away, it had been sited cheek by jowl with established central pitches of the department stores and other big-time shops or perhaps in the middle of a city block surrounded by such shops, then it might have reaped more of the overspill quite naturally from the shoppers who converged on the centre from all over the vast sprawl of Birmingham, not just from the direction of the Bull Ring. If on the other hand it had been 2 to 3 miles out from the centre in some prosperous but poorly served suburb, it might possibly have attracted all the normal variety of the High Street and acted as a counter-pull for those who were unwilling to brave the traffic of the city's centre. This would have been a great risk.

The shopper and the retailer are certainly both conservative characters, loth to change their habits. At the Bull Ring Laing was offering them a revolutionary change of scene. The shopfronts showed how hard it was for the traders to adjust their ways. Almost all installed the type of glass shopfronts normal in the High Street, apparently ignoring the full air-conditioning provided. One retailer even put up a weather drip.

The whole concept of the Bull Ring, far from everyday experience, was difficult for the shopper to accept. Its atmosphere was unnatural. Whereas the Elephant has a sliding roof which can let in some daylight on fine days, the Bull Ring is totally enclosed. With its simple paved stone flooring the Elephant's arcades echoed the normal clatter of heels; at the Bull Ring the floors were of black rubber tiling, which absorbed the noise and could give an eerie feeling of unreality. With the several levels of shops, the atmosphere tended to be that of a giant, claustrophobic palace of multiple retailers, a far cry from the regularity of the High Street or the intimacy of the department store. A disenchanted local politician, Councillor Beaumont Dark, spoke in angry exaggeration in 1965: 'The Bull Ring is perfectly all right if one wants an army fortification within the city centre. As a trading area it is at present a flop.' He called it the biggest white elephant in the history of Birmingham.

But the general consensus in Birmingham of that level of opinion which interests itself in civic prides was to brandish the Bull Ring as an example of the Second City's progress. Phrases such as 'Europe's most advanced shopping centre' and 'internationally

Q

famous' fitted neatly into dignified speeches. For the daring promoter of the novelty, the pleasure of pioneering was two-edged. Winning the competition put Laing firmly on the map alongside the big-time shop developers, next to Ravenseft and Hammersons, Sam Chippindale and Barry East and Walter Flack. But as the flaws in the project became clear to the property world Laing's reputation was somewhat tarnished. It was also an extremely expensive affair for Laing. Just how expensive is obscure. At the Bull Ring the money was put up on sale and leaseback by Pension Fund Securities, the alias for Imperial Chemical Industries' pension fund. This method of financing makes it impossible for the researcher to build up a rough financial picture of the project, in the way that it is possible, for instance, with the empire of Harry Hyams. However, Laing was clearly in the red at the Bull Ring, probably deeper in the red than Willett at the Elephant. My estimate suggests that the loss will have been between £50,000 and £100,000 a year for at least the first five years. Given the acute competition for the shopper's purse building up in the conurbation of Birmingham, it will be a tough task to make the Bull Ring profitable even after that. But Laing is strenuously tackling the task of promoting the centre and making it more attractive and the trend of turnover in the shops has at least been in the right direction.

*

Paul Boissevain visited the United States before he designed the Elephant & Castle. Sydney Greenwood visited the United States before he designed the Bull Ring. The promoters of both projects stressed the North American parentage of their 'one stop' shopping centres. But in the euphoric climate of the British property market in 1959, they were able to ignore one of the cardinal rules of North American development. It is not possible in the United States or Canada for a developer to find the finance for a shopping centre without first signing up with a department store or similar tenant who would be prepared to rent a big chunk of the floor space. This act of faith gives the financier some proof that he is putting up money for a sound project. British banks, insurance companies and pension funds did not have sour memories of real estate in the thirties after the Great Slump as the American financiers did, and almost everything, however improbable, had turned out well in the post-war years, so they overlooked this rule of caution. But, if it had been kept, it is probable that neither centre would have been built in its present form.

In Southwark and in Birmingham the local authorities achieved one prime objective: a handsome price for their land. But in their wider aims they failed. The empty shops on the two upper floors of the Elephant were no asset to the amenities of Southwark, nor did they pay rates. The commercial troubles of both centres showed that the land was not being used to the best advantage. Possibly the Elephant was more suited to an office block and the Bull Ring to a far bigger car park above a retail market.

Laing learnt the lessons from their mistakes at the Bull Ring. In several excellent subsequent projects, some of them mentioned in the next chapter, it was noticeable that they stuck closely to the central core of the towns' traditional area and to one level of shops.

CHAPTER FIFTEEN

White Elephantiasis

AT conception and in the first year or so of construction at the Bull Ring and the Elephant & Castle, all was puff and glory. Success was taken for granted. But long before it became apparent that such assumptions were ill-founded, the admiring publicity given to the announcement of these two projects had indirectly encouraged the short-lived and occasionally disastrous spate of shopping developments in the early sixties.

In chapter 9 I showed that development of shops in the provinces passed through a quiet phase in the years 1955 to 1960, relative to the roaring activity in London's offices; and that one reason for this was that the supply of land was hard to buy in big enough quantities. It was in part the very attraction and simplicity of office development which kept many property men out of provincial shops. But at the end of the fifties a series of factors switched attention towards High Streets up and down the country. The rapid build-up in the number of developers competing for the fortunes to be extracted from office development depressed profitability, or at least appeared to do so; given the time scale of each project it was not possible to know the return on money invested in a development until some three years or so after the site was bought. The cost of land rose so quickly in the late fifties and early sixties that experienced developers shook their heads in gloom. But as it turned out rents in London more than kept pace with the cost of land and the average profitability of well-placed London office developments has never really altered significantly in the entire post-war period.

Simultaneous with the nervousness of office developers looking for an alternative medium around 1959 and 1960 was the growing eagerness of many local authorities to woo the developer and his money to their towns. This quaint combination of the entrepreneur and the town clerk effectively defeated the fundamental problem of land shortage, since the local authority, as described in the case of Jarrow, would compulsorily buy the developer's raw material for him and lease it to him.

Before 1959 local authorities often had the greatest difficulty in persuading developers to risk their money in the few large-scale shopping projects being planned, though within a few years they were to be deluged with offers. Bradford's officials began to replan the central area in 1946. They concentrated on the small flat area, like the bottom of a basin, around which Bradford is centred, in its fold in the Pennines. The physique of this phenomenon of the woollen trade had hardly changed since its most flourishing, mid-Victorian years—except for the worse; it had become blacker, grimmer and, in parts, decayed during the inter-war depression and the Second World War.

Towns which had not been damaged by bombs were not generally allowed to use public money for buildings other than housing or schools. Although these towns could buy the land with a combination of money from the Government and the local authority, they had to bring in private capital to finance the shops and offices. It took Bradford several years to persuade developers to invest in the Broadway area, the bottom of the basin. They were understandably nervous because this was not traditionally a shopping area, in spite of its being the focal point of the town. But the more important factor was that town centre development was hardly recognised in the property world, had not yet become fashionable at the time, roughly 1955 to '59, when Mr Wardley was doggedly canvassing for developers: Mr Wardley was the city engineer, city surveyor and town planning officer of Bradford all rolled into one. He first tried to persuade national retailers to build their own shops individually on lease from the corporation. They were not prepared to take the risk of plunging capital into an untried location. Then, under the lead of one firm, a group of retailers banded together to build a section of the development in co-operation, in order to bolster one another's confidence and be sure of making an impact. But their confidence was not strong enough and this plan failed at the eleventh hour. Mr Wardley then turned to developers. Here again a number of fruitless negotiations and false starts raised and dashed Bradford's hopes of a brand new city centre. Eventually Hammerson, one of the Big Six in shop development, was prepared to sign on the dotted line; it began to negotiate in October 1956, but the deal was not settled for over two years. An announcement of the project was made in May 1959. On Hammerson's side it involved a potential investment of £1.4 million. But the pessimism of the market was so great about schemes of this sort and size that Hammerson was able to insist on escape clauses. The scheme was chopped up into four stages. Hammerson was allowed two years to finish each stage and then a period of one year in which to consider its option to continue with the next stage. In this way the scheme could have taken twelve years, but in fact it was built and the shops and offices let within five. Because there had been no rivalry to take on the development in the first place, Bradford was forced to grant a lease on what later appeared highly generous terms, so that Hammerson earned a return of 16 per cent on its investment. This implied that it could recoup by way of mortgage, not only the cost of £1.4 million, but an extra £840,000 besides. Later, Hammerson built some more shops on the periphery of the main scheme.

That financial yield on Hammerson's development in Bradford was remarkably high. Of course no-one was to know that when the agreement was clinched and announced in 1959, or for another five years. Even so, within a year or two, in 1960 and 1961, the terms on which developer/local authority schemes were agreed became far more favourable to the local authority. The number of candidates prepared to take on central area redevelopment, and the prices they were prepared to offer, rose dramatically. When Leeds offered by tender a piece of land to be developed as a shopping centre in early 1960, only one company put in a bid and the tender was cancelled. Four months later the tender took place again and there were nine offers. (The end result of that tender, the Merrion Centre, is discussed later in this chapter.)

Apart from the awareness created by publicity given to Bradford, the Bull Ring and the Elephant & Castle, and apart from the restrictions and competition in office development, an uncertain combination of other factors stimulated ambitious projects in the provinces. Some were ephemeral reasons to do with business sentiment. The golden fifties had tended to induce in some property men a vague feeling of infallibility; property shares soared up by leaps and bounds on the stock market during 1959, and the Conservative victory in the autumn consolidated the mood of optimism.

This naturally fitted in with a willingness to undertake developments of the much greater individual size which town centre work demanded. The trend towards more grandiose schemes was psychologically in tune with the times.

Retail trade was also in a buoyant phase, especially that darling of retail growth in the early sixties, the supermarket. The figures for grocery supermarkets in the decade 1956 to '66 as estimated by the Supermarket Association of Great Britain was:

	Numbers	% Increase
1956	100	—
1958	175	+ 75
1960	367	+111
1962	996	+171
1964	1,628	+ 63
1966	2,500	+ 53

Proportionately, expansion in the numbers of supermarkets was greatest in 1960 to 1962, the years in which property developers were busiest in provincial shops, and even busier, more significantly, in laying plans to develop even more shops. By the middle sixties, as plans began to turn into shops in increasing volume, supermarketeers and retailers generally were slowing down their expansion in numbers of outlets.

Towards the end of the fifties local authorities were in just the mood to reciprocate the keenness of the developer to develop. Until then building activity had been concentrated on housing, schools and factories and offices, with relatively little new building of shops, except in badly bombed cities. But the local authority seldom approached urban renewal with the sole intention of providing shops. They were more often prompted by the simple need to have decaying and obsolete buildings replaced in the centre of a town, and to tackle problems of traffic. In Bradford a combination of these two factors sparked off the central redevelopment. Shops and offices happened to be the most profitable way for the corporation to finance the renewal. But Bradford's plan, started as long ago as the late forties, was understandably crude in its attempt to cope with the traffic. Cars rushed around the shops and other new buildings on the traditional pattern—only in greater volume and rather more efficiently than before.

Bradford was under way when the study of Traffic in Towns, the Buchanan Report, was commissioned in June 1961, and, as it said when it appeared in July 1963: '. . . we know now, by bitter experience, that the motor vehicle is in conflict with the present structure of towns . . .' This knowledge was a spur to local authorities to redevelop the centres, the most congested areas, of their towns, where the road patterns had been fixed in the last century.

Again, from the local authorities' side, there were vague, indefinable pressures encouraging central area redevelopment, quite apart from the glaring problems of worn-out buildings and obtrusive vehicles. Local councillors and officials often saw partnership with developers as a convenient method of financing civic improvements. It was easy for the objective to stray from strict considerations of planning and aesthetics, to the tempting side issue of the greater glorification of a particular town. Once private developers were brought in on a large enough scale to tap a profitable commercial vein, other municipal benefits could flow from the revenue or capital which he provided. These tended to be extra car parking or a modern hotel, or an indirect subsidy for public buildings such as libraries or even a new town hall or a swimming pool.

From 1959 onwards a great aura of prestige began to attach to the words 'town centre development', both in the world of property developers and the stock market and in the world of local authorities. In the same way that competition rapidly escalated among developers to take on these bigger shopping centre projects, so the local governors were more and more keen to initiate them. This enthusiasm was parallel to the great rush and rivalry of Victorian worthies to build bigger and better town halls and public buildings. Professor Asa Briggs, in a fascinating account* of the rivalry between Leeds and Bradford and the saga of Leeds Town Hall, describes the opening in 1851 of the St George's Hall in Bradford. The mayor, Samuel Smith, had proudly detailed in his speech that 'We are eleven feet wider than the hall at Birmingham, and about as much longer. We are exactly the same width as Exeter Hall, London, with greater length, a loftier ceiling . . .' A similar feeling of rivalry was one motive behind a good many shopping centre schemes promoted in the early sixties and it was an extremely dangerous influence: two neighbouring towns were quite capable of claiming that part of their shopping public came from an

* One of the studies in *Victorian Cities* (Odhams Press, 1963).

overlapping area, and both would encourage the developer to put up too many shops.

By the end of 1963 some seventy schemes were being vetted by the Ministry of Housing and Local Government, compared with roughly fifteen at the end of 1959; each Comprehensive Development Area, the preliminary to Compulsory Purchase Orders (see page 128), had to be approved by the Ministry. Reliable statistics on this subject are almost non-existent, but Mr R. B. Morgan of the Co-operative Wholesale Society drew up a list* in 1965 of developments either being built, or far enough advanced for the developer to have been nominated. It was not exhaustive, but it showed almost 500 schemes—some big cities had several—and over 100 developers at work. In only eighteen instances was the local authority acting as its own developer. Mr Morgan continued to gather material for a further list and in the year after the first list was published, he had added another 200 projects.

Probably many of these schemes are unrealistic and others, for a variety of reasons, will never pass the planning stage. It was estimated that if all the shops being planned at the end of 1963 had been built, this country's retail outlets would have catered for the shopping needs of a population of 150 to 200 million. But that threat of massive over-supply gradually receded because of the elastic time scale in urban renewal. Two extreme cases already described are the Aldwych, first planned in 1836 and finished in 1923, and the Monico saga. Town centre development is an extremely long drawn out and complicated process. From the start of planning to the end of building can hardly take less than three years, and, if it is a mammoth one, it might be as much as seven to ten years. In that long period of gestation it is easy for ideas on planning, for costs of construction, and for the economic climate to have altered significantly. The time scale greatly heightens the risks, both for the local authority and the developer.

At the time when ideas and schemes were being proliferated most intensively by planners and developers, roughly the years 1959 to 1963, there was little completed shopping development to use as a yardstick. The centres of bombed cities like Hull or Coventry had been rebuilt, and the new towns had grown up with

* From the *Property Developer & Investor*, published by the Association of Land and Property Owners and the National Federation of Property Owners in conjunction with the *Estates Gazette*.

shopping centres. But both those were special cases, for one important element was missing: competition. Not competition among
developers to carry out the work, though even that was not enthusiastic, but competition from other existing shops. Almost all
the redevelopments dreamed up in the early sixties were of old
town centres where the new traders would have to battle against
those already entrenched; the project was seldom so large in relation to the town that, as in Jarrow, virtually all the existing shops
were wiped out. The plans of '59 to '63 were also hatched under
the popular illusion—among the public, municipal worthies and
developers themselves—that property developers seldom made
mistakes. The atmosphere was anti-caution.

From 1964 and 1965 onwards caution began to creep in. The
very speed at which the plans were multiplying and the evident
increase in competition, sometimes from patently green development companies, was one warning signal. Another was the difficulty for all to see of some completed shopping centres. Middlesbrough, Victorian cradle of the iron industry, was host to a scheme
which promised to have many characteristics of a white elephant.
This was promoted by a company based on London, Metropolitan
Railway Surplus Lands. Founded in 1933 with the purchase of
buildings on either side of the Metropolitan railway line, MRSL
was a public company with the Docker family as the largest single
shareholder; Sir Bernard Docker inherited the chairmanship from
his father, who started the company. It was run by a courteous and
intelligent businessman of the old school, Billy Balch, a distinguished president of the Royal Institute of Chartered Surveyors;
he introduced a much needed line of non-pomposity. Until
the end of the fifties MRSL used to give the impression simply of a
competently managed landed estate and the other side of Mr
Balch's activities, speculative housebuilding, always performed
consistently. But, like many others, Balch and MRSL were unable
to resist climbing on to the bandwagon of development, not always
with happy results.

The problem child in Middlesbrough, the Dundas Street
precinct, consisted of 37 shops in a straight arcade, a curtain walled
office block of 56,000 square feet sitting at right angles across the
middle, and a large car park for 300 cars underneath. It was finished
at the end of 1963. But for the air of desolation shed by the emptiness of 80 per cent of the shops for the first two years after

completion, Dundas Street, and especially its office block, might have been a pleasant contrast to the drab Victorian utility of Middlesbrough's streets. No doubt, when this £1½ million project was just finished, the locals would have echoed a phrase used in 1866 as the Middlesbrough Exchange was built at a cost of £28,000: 'a pile of buildings which would do credit to any town'. But by early 1966 Dundas Street, with its rows of apparently unwanted shops facing one another, must have been a nagging sore in the town's flank. It is never pleasant to have signs of failure in one's midst.

The trouble with Dundas Street was partly its location. It was reasonably well placed in the angle between two of the main shopping streets—Linthorpe Road and Corporation Street—but it was not boldly enough linked to either of these and one end of the arcade led to a back street of little importance or interest. This meant that there was no strong natural flow of pedestrians through the precinct, an almost vital attribute for a shopping centre. But a greater trouble was that MRSL paid too much for the land in relation to realistic rents. This was aggravated by a deal with the Ministry of Works, which owned a piece of the site and sold it in return for leasing the entire office block at a rent of 9s. a square foot. It is hardly economic to build an office building of several floors for that rent, and an attempt to compensate for this was made by raising the rents for the shops.

After a year or so, with few retailers leasing the shops, rents were lowered. Once a shopping centre is empty for a while the scepticism of retailers tends to snowball; the aura of white elephant sticks. No trader wants to be the first to risk his money and his reputation in a place which the shopping public may associate with a flop. The problems of Dundas Street were aggravated also by the general knowledge in the retail world that another shopping centre was being planned close by in a slightly better location. After changing estate agents MRSL managed a respectable recovery in 1966 and 1967. Although there is many a slip between 'agreement to let' and a letting, Mr Balch, by then chairman of MRSL, was able to tell his shareholders in June 1967 that he had 'better news of Middlesbrough. . . . We have now let or agreed to let 23 of the 37 shops. . . .' In my view it may still be some years before all the rest of the shops find tenants, before the development is profitable to MRSL, or before it is a definite asset to the town.

Much the most common drawback with the shopping centres

which failed to catch on was simply that they were in the wrong place. This was the case with the Bargates Shopping Centre in Burton-on-Trent, developed by Hammerson. It was about a quarter of a mile from the best retail pitch, standing back from the road in the shape of a three-sided square, with a car park behind. When I visited this development in the autumn of 1965 about half the thirty-one shops were empty. By early 1967 twelve shops were still empty, and it had then been opened for almost three years.* Three retailers had closed up and left, an ominous sign. Unless he can relet the shops the trader has to continue to pay his rent, so that it takes a hard experience to force him out.

In a clean-limbed way the Bargates Centre looks appetising. It is a bright, well-proportioned addition to the beer town, and has an imaginative garden in its forecourt. But it seems doubtful that it will be a successful retail trading centre for a long time. A plan promoted by Burton Town Council will help to ensure that it is not. With Laing as developer, leasing the land from the council, a big shopping centre is to be built in the backland immediately behind Station Street and New Street, a logical place for more shops. That should fully provide for Burton's shopping needs and it was perhaps unwise of the Council to have given planning permission to Hammerson for Bargates. For Hammerson the project was no great disaster. The capital laid out was only £350,000, which is a fleabite to a group with a £90 million development programme. But in real estate any flop is most unhelpful for a property company's reputation; it sits there in an unpleasantly permanent way, advertising to the world its defects—in this case that Hammerson had been too greedy and had tried to put too many shops on a poorly-located site.

Laing is also the developer of an intelligently placed scheme in Leeds. The hottest shopping area in Leeds is broadly grouped around a rectangle of streets, with the Headrow on the north, Briggate running north and south, and Boar Lane on the south side. Briggate is one of the busiest streets for shopping in the country. Laing's £1·7 million scheme fell into a section of the larger rectangle, behind the junction of Briggate and Boar Lane. The development was set off by the merger of the *Yorkshire Post* with the *Yorkshire Evening News*, for the *Evening News* no longer

* The progress of the shopping centres described may conceivably have altered significantly since the time of writing. I doubt it.

needed its printing works in Trinity Street, running north from Boar Lane, parallel with Briggate. The multiple retailers, often highly critical of the siting of new shopping centres, so much approved of this scheme that five prestigious names decided to extend their main road shops backwards into Laing's precinct and jointly co-operated in making the planning application. The five were Marks & Spencer, Montague Burton, the Leeds Co-op, H. Samuel, the jeweller, and C. & A. Modes. The blessing of these powerful operators seems to underwrite the success of the project, soon to be launched.

Leeds has a population of 514,000 compared with Burton's 51,000. There was a faint similarity between the situation in the two central areas. Laing was bringing in a challenger to an existing centre, which was again slightly off pitch. This is the Merrion Centre, situated just to the north of the Headrow and thus outside the golden rectangle. The developer was Town Centre Securities, a company run by Arnold Ziff and his brother Neville. The Ziffs were one of many Jewish families which escaped from the continental pogroms at the end of the last century and settled in Leeds; there were 15,000 Jews in Leeds in 1900. The Ziffs came from Lithuania at much the same time as, for example, the Sieffs of Marks & Spencer. Arnold's father and uncles started and ran a chain of shoe shops in the North Country, Stylo Shoes, and he and his brother expanded it to a chain of 140 shops by 1964, the year in which it took over the 155-shop Barratts Shoes.

This background of retailing gave the Ziffs suitable experience for property development. Town Centre Securities was started in the spring of 1959. Arnold Ziff is frank about his motives, which were the same as many others who jumped into development once the boom was well under way. 'We saw Cotton and Clore and the others making millions. It's not all that difficult. Why shouldn't we? That was how we felt.' They were rich to start with, so that they did not have the usual initial problems over finance. By the autumn of 1960 Town Centre Securities was floated with a value on the market of £250,000. In that year the Ziffs also tendered for the Merrion scheme and their bid was the only offer received when Leeds first put out this 7-acre site to tender. They competed again among the nine others in the second tender. 'The City Engineer rang me up,' said Arnold Ziff, 'and told me that "we like your scheme but we don't like the ground rent you've offered". "We can talk about that, can't we?" I said. So I went down to the Town Hall and we came to a compromise.'

Apart from 100 shops, the Ziffs proposed an hotel and a huge car park for 1,100 cars, the largest multi-storey car park in the country—the City liked both those ideas—a market hall full of stalls, a cinema, a Mecca ballroom, a discotheque, a public house, a garage, two blocks of offices and a 42-lane bowling alley. Its advertisements called it 'Truly a city-within-a-city'. At the design stage Arnold Ziff had told his architect that the Merrion Centre must have at least 100 shops. The first plan showed only 90. Twice Ziff sent the architect away to fit in a few more. Finally he returned to say that he had managed to make 98, 'but I've squeezed in all that I can'. 'O.K.,' said Ziff, 'but leave me the plans.' He then drew in four extra shops at the back of the main building and the architect was very cross. 'But those shops did excellent trade,' Ziff recalled proudly.

The Merrion Centre, opened in 1963, had a lukewarm reception from retailers. After two years all but about fifteen shops were let, which was reasonable enough, and in financial terms Town Centre certainly scored well. One embarrassing blot was that MacFisheries leased two adjacent shops but soon closed up and moved out. However, many other retailers were happy. One snag with the site was that a cold, grey area of shabby street divided the Merrion from the bustle of the Headrow. Once that patch has been redeveloped and the link to the Headrow is improved, trade at Merrion's shops should rise to a level at which all the retailers are happy.

One serious defect in the design of the Merrion Centre was an unpleasant invention of modern architecture: the wind tunnel.* This phenomenon, technically known as a 'rolling eddy', is caused by tall slab buildings. The wind hits the flat surface of a tower block, dives down to the ground rather faster than its original speed, and shoots along faster still at about the level of a shopper's knee in the opposite direction to the natural wind. Sometimes it can be diverted upwards again by an adjacent building so that it rejoins the prevailing wind in an almost circular process. The Merrion Centre, whose 'rolling eddy' was caused by a thirteen-storey slab block, was not alone with its problem. A worse case was in a shopping centre in Croydon, the Croydon Centre. This

* See Insight in the *Sunday Times* of 3 July 1966.

had a twenty-two-storey office block at one end, which set off a veritable gale among housewives' skirts on a windy day. That was one reason for the particularly slow letting of the eighty-five shops in the Croydon Centre. Others were its siting and competition from the better placed Whitgift Centre (see page 189). The solution at the Croydon Centre was to build a roof over the shopping precinct, which was a rectangular shape with a courtyard in the middle, years after the building was originally finished. In Leeds some of the more militant retailers put pressure on Arnold Ziff to do the same thing, and after protesting for a while that the problem

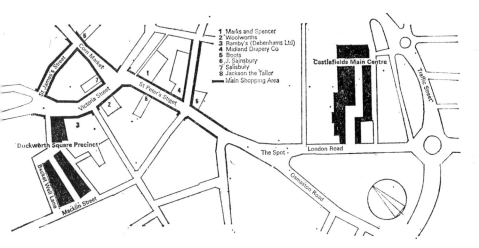

1 Marks and Spencer
2 Woolworths
3 Ramby's (Debenhams Ltd)
4 Midland Drapery Co
5 Boots
6 J. Sainsbury
7 Salisbury
8 Jackson the Tailor
━━ Main Shopping Area

THE CENTRE OF DERBY, AND ITS TWO WHITE ELEPHANTS

was largely of the retailers' imagination, he agreed to do so. 'Rolling eddies' did not exist until the building regulations after the war allowed developers to build above 80 feet. As blocks grew taller, architects were unaware of the rough weather conditions that might be created for the luckless pedestrian. In London the malignant eddy can be experienced alongside the Shell Tower at the South Bank, at the Elephant & Castle and by the Stag Brewery development at Victoria.

The most intractable problem of new shopping centres, their location, could be found in an extreme form in Derby. Here there was not one, but two independent cases of white elephantiasis. The map above roughly indicates the best frontages in Derby's main shopping streets. Both the unfortunately named Main Centre and the Duckworth Square precinct suffered from the same disability: they were not close enough to these choice frontages. In the case of Duckworth Square the land was assembled by a Mr David Duckworth and sold as an embryo project to Town & City Properties, one of the major shop developers. At an all-in cost of some £350,000 Town & City then developed a group of twenty-eight shops around a paved courtyard with two floors of car parking above the shops. Another seven shops, part of the scheme, were placed at the entrance to Becket Well Lane from Victoria Street, providing a faint link between the precinct and the bustle of Victoria Street. (These shops were built on the site of a chapel, which was replaced above the shops, a monument to Midlands realism.) But the link was not nearly strong enough and, worse, the precinct itself led to a back street of houses, stone cold as far as shopping was concerned. The design of Duckworth Square was forbidding, with the surrounding floors of car park above gloomily cutting out some of the light. Its appearance, at least in its first three years, was not helped by lack of tenants. Fifteen of the twenty-eight shops in the main precinct were unoccupied at the end of that period. It is hard to envisage a recovery in the fortunes of this project.

Castelfields Main Centre was debatably even worse positioned than Duckworth Square. After the Spot, the intensity of the shopping along London Road tails off quite markedly. But the design of this other precinct, finished about a year before Duckworth Square, was much more pleasant; the agents for Duckworth Square complained that their precinct was dragged down through being the second on the scene since retailers were wary of precincts in Derby by that time. Main Centre was also started off by two individuals, Mr Alfred Isaacs and Mr Lewis Lewis-Evans, but they continued to own some shares in the project after they sold a slice of the developing company to Sir Robert McAlpine & Sons, the contractors. As part of the deal McAlpines put up the finance, around £1 million. In Main Centre there are fifty-three shops, a large supermarket and two small towers of offices, 50,000 square feet in the two. Four years after opening Main Centre still had twenty empty shops, although an early brochure had boasted in estate agents' euphemism: 'for few remaining shop units and offices apply . . .' Of the twenty empties six were fateful blanks where retailers had already come and gone. At the opposite end from London Road the Main Centre enticed the shopper to two exits, but they gave on to nothing more attractive than a car park and some stretches of Derby's rubbled wasteland. Clearly the prospect of this end will improve in due time; a municipal car park is to be built at one side. But, given that there is a longish walk from the London Road end of Main Centre to the clusters of multiple shops in the middle of Derby, a car park alone, of whatever size, will not do the trick.

The argument is sometimes produced: 'These were private enterprisers, risking their own money, and they have to some extent come unstuck. Surely that is the end of the matter? Why worry further?' Apart from the economic waste, which as a cumulative figure for the country could be considerable and could be avoided by clever planning on the part of the local authority, there are social side effects of white elephantiasis. The most damaging is perhaps on the morale of a town, and the smaller the town the worse it is. The sight of empty shops is deeply dispiriting, something like the sight of unemployed hanging around streets. A glut of shops, unlike toothpaste or most other products, cannot be stored and then unobtrusively disposed of. Secondly, when the shops are in the form of a precinct and not in a traditional row along a street front, they seem inevitably to attract vandalism. An area which is supposed to be renewed and vital can very soon degenerate into neo-slum. Thirdly, failed development in a town tends to hinder any further commercial schemes. In Cleckheaton, a small town with a population of 39,000 near Halifax, the grass was growing lustily from the bottom of tired grey hoardings along the unused front of ten out of fifteen shops in the main street several years after they had been finished by the developer, Second Covent Garden Property. Cleckheaton probably needed some more shops, but that scar in the main street made other developers hold back from building them in the right place. The permanence of an unlet building can be rigid.

It is easy to be critical of local authorities for allowing poor development. But there are many excuses. Redevelopment on any scale is a business of great complication. It is hard to expect most individual authorities of small to medium size to have the necessary skills or experience among their officials, still less the wisdom of final decision on the subject among their councillors. A radical,

R

major redevelopment might only hit a town once every four generations. Developers and their advisers were dealing with the same problem from the other side of the fence all the while. The private side was bound to be favourite to outpoint the public side in negotiation. To counter this advantage, the local authorities had two safeguards. If a Comprehensive Development Area had to be declared, the blessing of the Ministry of Housing was necessary and a Ministerial enquiry on the scheme itself was usual. But this tended to be a rather negative process. Guidance from the Ministry before that stage was reached was essentially permissive; three Planning Bulletins, all fairly platitudinous and optimistic in tone, were issued to local authorities in 1962 and 1963 on town centre development. They should have been riddled with many specific caveats.

The other safeguard was that local authorities could employ expert consultants to advise them on redevelopment. This too had its snags. Usually the consultants were a firm of estate agent/surveyors, or architect/surveyors. Sometimes the method of paying these consultants led to abuses. They might be paid a nominal fee or no fee at all, and instead when some developer was chosen to carry out a project on a lease from the local authority, it would be stipulated that the firm of architects or estate agents must be retained to design the buildings or to let them once finished. They would thus reap their fees from the developer. But the distressing corollary of this system of payment was that it was in the interest of the consultants to recommend development even if it was not necessary, and, moreover, development on the biggest scale that was plausible.

One puzzle in all town centre schemes was how to measure future demand for shops. The boom in town centre plans brought into being a relatively new professional man: the practising urban economist. Some developers, accustomed to rely on hunch, commonsense and experience, were deeply sceptical of this breed, but were quite prepared to use them for window dressing on occasions. If the economist came up with a conclusion which agreed with the developer's idea, his work would be used. Otherwise it would be jettisoned. The surveys produced by economists certainly tended to vary so considerably in their methods as to remind the onlooker of the old saw that the views of six economists on one subject would produce at least seven opinions.

In an article in *Urban Studies** one economist, Harvey R. Cole, himself threw a pailful of cold water on his own profession: 'At present there is some general recognition that the main variables in estimating future shopping space requirements are population and income, but the way in which these are projected and the relative weight given to each vary so much from one consultant or planning officer to the next that it is literally a lottery what answer is produced for any particular town. Indeed, to a great extent the choice of adviser will determine the recommendation more than the basic facts. . . .'

Harvey Cole pinpointed an engaging absurdity produced by county planning staff in assessing the future shopping needs of Hereford. In a thorough survey it projected rather too slavishly the performance of individual trades in the years 1950–61 into the unknown period up to 1981. This threw up the conclusion that 40 per cent of all extra retail space in Hereford in that period should be allocated to hairdressers.

One worrying and naïve selling point commonly used at one time by developers was to draw concentric circles around a town and argue that since a certain number of people lived within the radii they would shop at the centre of the circle. In America economic analysis of shopping trends is a much more sophisticated and accepted business. One of the leading firms of real estate consultants, Larry Smith & Co., set up a branch in London and a partner there, Mark Norton, said in a paper† on shopping centres:

'One of the most popular misconceptions about regional shopping centres is, I believe, that they are a fine location for selling convenience merchandise, by which I mean food, hardware and chemist's items. Our own experience indicates that this is simply not the case.

'I would like to quote an excerpt from the Ministry of Housing's letter on the Haydock Park planning appeal:

' "Indeed, the strongest objection to the present proposal is not that Haydock would compete with Liverpool and Manchester but that, in order to do so successfully, it would have to make

* *Urban Studies*, June 1966, Volume 3, No. 2, published by Oliver & Boyd.

† Delivered to the Middlesex branch of the Royal Institution of Chartered Surveyors on 12 October 1965.

some 50 per cent of its sales in convenience goods which could be bought in existing centres of any size."

'Against sales volume projections made in this appeal the developer's suggestion would mean that at Haydock Park about £15 million worth of convenience merchandising would be sold annually. Normal conversion ratios for well-managed convenience stores indicate that £15 million of annual sales would be equivalent to about 400,000 to 450,000 square feet of convenience retail space at Haydock Park. There is not one successful shopping centre in the world today with even 100,000 square feet of convenience retail space. . . .'

In the examples at Burton-on-Trent, Middlesbrough and Derby, developers had privately bought pieces of land and had been granted planning permission by the local authority to build shopping centres. The developers had been forced on to dud locations by the high cost of land in the prime area and by the natural reluctance of incumbent retailers to sell. That was the developers' fault. Although it was sometimes technically tricky for a local authority to refuse a valid planning application, the energetic and resourceful authority could certainly do so if faced with a budding white elephant. But many local authorities have looked very superficially at the commercial implications of commercial schemes. When the alternative is blight or gross misuse of land, economics are just as important as aesthetics.

When the local authority is the owner of the land and an initiator of development, clearly its responsibility for the economics is greatly increased, even though it may bring in a developer and his capital for his final twist of skill and intuition. Given the long cycle of a major town centre redevelopment, the number of cases where the authority can be seen to have slipped up on economics is limited. But I have little doubt that more cases will come to light over the next few years. Doncaster is a town which already has a young white elephant, conceived by the town in conjunction with a developer, and it may be that this will be seen as a classic of poor planning in years to come.

The map opposite shows in rough outline the orientation of Doncaster's most bustling shopping streets. The multiples cluster closest along the valuable front of French Gate, Baxter Gate, High Street and St Sepulchre Gate. There has been some overspill into Hall Gate—the Bell brothers from Newcastle have cunningly

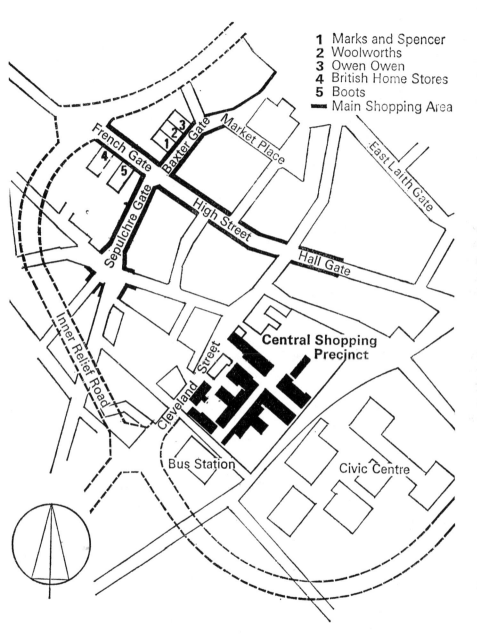

Legend:
1 Marks and Spencer
2 Woolworths
3 Owen Owen
4 British Home Stores
5 Boots
— Main Shopping Area

French Gate
Baxter Gate
Market Place
East Laith Gate
Sepulchre Gate
High Street
Hall Gate
Inner Relief Road
Cleveland Street
Central Shopping Precinct
Bus Station
Civic Centre

CENTRAL DONCASTER AND ITS SO-CALLED
'CENTRAL SHOPPING PRECINCT'

driven a precinct through from Hall Gate into the secondary shopping street of East Laith Gate—and back along Silver Street and round into the Market Place. The drawback to this traditional pattern, which had grown up from Doncaster's beginnings as a Roman town, was the usual one that these streets took the brunt of the traffic in the town, a heavy load even after the M.1 passed by the outskirts. To attack this congestion the Corporation called in architect Frederick Gibberd and planned an inner relief road around the centre. At the same time a scheme for a 15-acre quarter was drawn up with the hope of embellishing Doncaster with a civic centre and a trim new shopping centre, the twin ambitions of many a local authority, the one often intended partly to pay for the other.

Doncaster, on the advice of Gibberd and Goddard & Smith, one of the more thrusting among firms of estate agents, chose a crude method of selecting a developer for their land. They auctioned it. There are variations on this system. But the variation picked by Doncaster was to commission Gibberd to draw up an extremely loose plan of the shopping centre and then allow Goddard & Smith to invite developers to gather in an auction room and bid for the privilege of developing the land. This process of invitation was seldom discriminating. With Doncaster the winner was a company which had little experience of town centre development. Although the vogue for financial tenders has abated, the dangers of such competition—over-development and shoddy architecture—are intense in an industry of limited knowledge and with great social and aesthetic undertones. Not long before these four shopping acres of Doncaster were auctioned in May 1963 the then chief planning officer of Coventry, Mr Arthur Ling, poured cold water on this superficially neat method of financial competition: 'I think we should treat our towns as places where people live and not just lots for sale at an auction.' The militant ratepayer might reply that the local authority's duty is to sell or lease at the best possible price the land which it has to dispose of. The counter argument to that is that in the interests of the community the best possible price for a given piece of land is not necessarily the highest price.

At £108,500 a year the highest bidder for the would-be pride of Doncaster's shoppers was a Mr Asher Lewis Shane, or rather his private company, the pompously named Equitable Debenture & Assets Corporation. As the hammer fell in Goddard & Smith's auction rooms in the rich pastures of St James's Square, London, Doncaster found itself wedded to a developer who had at that point been in the business full-time for a mere three years. Asher Shane hailed from South Wales, came to London in 1935 and qualified as a solicitor. Shane did a lot of work for his clients on property, but it was not until 1960 that he decided to devote himself to property on his own account. Shane was one of property's many instinctive optimists and he came in on the tail end of the boom when optimism was still the winning philosophy.

The auction for Doncaster roused great passions in the property world, not least among those developers who offered far less than £108,500 a year and disliked the system. Property Investments Consolidation, one company which complained on every possible occasion about competitive financial tenders, put in a submission to Doncaster, 'understanding' acidly that Goddard & Smith had carried out very considerable research on the possibilities of the shopping centre on behalf of Doncaster. But they had not been given access to the report. Many mutterings of gloom about the chances of the Shane scheme were made while it was being built.

Shane threw an open party, caustically dubbed by retailers as The Gin Party, for any estate agents or retailers who cared to visit his precinct when it was finished in the autumn of 1965. But the end result in terms of the number of shops let was not impressive. Woolworths took a large store and so did Tesco. Apart from those only some twelve of the other seventy-three shops had tenants trading by the spring of 1967. Admittedly, Doncaster had exceptional problems during 1966, with several of its factories plagued with sackings and an unemployment rate way above the national average at 6 per cent. But had those seventy-three shops been genuinely needed, they should have been easily let before or after a short-lived local recession. As it was the investment of around £1·2 million must have been causing Mr Shane's company a severe loss and Doncaster's planners a bad bout of heart-searching. It was also causing Doncaster and its ratepayers a severe loss. By the middle of 1967 it had not received its originally expected £182,000 in rent from this site, known locally as Golden Acres.

What had gone wrong? An article on Doncaster in the *Economist*'s survey of Yorkshire, 'The Road from the Mills' (4 March 1967), summed up, 'It looks as though too many shops have been provided too quickly, and though this may be all right by 1985 or some such date, things look pretty awful in the meantime.' Too many, and too far from the heart of the traditional shopping. The main link between the old and the new is Printing House Street, running from St Sepulchre Gate to Cleveland Street parallel with High Street, but that has only a minor array of shopkeepers and the walk is long enough from the junction of Baxter Gate and High Street thoroughly to put off a housewife with basket. The apparently curious decision of Woolworths to open up in the new precinct was swayed by its liking for concessionary rents, and by its inability to expand its existing store, which was hemmed in on one side by Marks & Spencer and the other by Owen Owen. But there was an alternative to Shane's scheme, for Sam Chippindale's Arndale was busy building a lusty competitor during 1966 and 1967. This was grouped around the corner of French Gate and St Sepulchre Gate, and will include the Boots and the British Home Stores marked on the map. This will greatly strengthen the existing traditional centre and has weakened and will weaken further the newcomer sponsored by the Corporation. In retrospect it seems highly irrational of Doncaster to have given planning permission to both these schemes almost simultaneously. It would surely have been far better to have allowed only Arndale to build and at the same time devised some scheme for draining the traffic out of the important shopping streets. The Shane scheme and the temporary blight which it is imposing might then have been unnecessary.

Public indignation and emotion has to some extent been directed at the aesthetic aspects of developers' work in provincial cities and towns. Usually this protest is heavily loaded with preservation for the sake of preservation and so one-sided as to pass by as eccentric. For instance Mr James Lees-Milne wrote in the *Sunday Times* of September 20 1964 an article entitled 'The Ruin of Our Cities'. Its tone was rabid: '... speculators ... are hungrily buying up the centres of our cathedral cities and market towns for astronomical sums which individual freeholders simply cannot resist. Reluctant sellers are tempted or cajoled into submission. Sometimes the most recalcitrant are finally driven into submission by the appalling devastation left around them. . . . Eventually all the buildings of the area, good, bad and indifferent are swept away and replaced with chain-stores, supermarkets and blocks of flats devoid of distinction and all looking alike.' Later it added, 'There are people today amassing stupendous fortunes by systematically destroying our historic cities.' This last remark was hardly valid by the time the article appeared.

It would have been more constructive if the critics of developers had looked more closely at the economics of the new buildings. Some old and attractive buildings have been mistakenly pulled down, but it is even worse that new buildings, which are inadequately used or not used at all, should replace them. One alternative suggested to the trials of redevelopment by mixed enterprise is that the local authority should do the entire job themselves. Relatively few have tried so far, held back by their order of priorities and problems of finance. In only 18 of the 500 or so schemes discovered by Mr Morgan in 1965 were the local authorities playing developer. The vital need to hit the commercial nail on the head in shopping development is always likely to open up a dangerous weakness in schemes promoted by local authorities. There is now a sufficient fund of experience in reputable firms of estate agents that the authority can hire know-how, but it is bound to lack the decisiveness of a private developer and may stray disastrously from the commercial commonsense which personal financial involvement imposes.

In the new town of Seacroft, three and a half miles north-east of Leeds, the housing committee of Leeds sponsored a central development at a cost of £1½ million. This was officially opened by the Queen in October 1965 with many expressions of mutual congratulation, an ominous overtone of the Duke of Edinburgh's official unveiling of Birmingham's Bull Ring. Seacroft's shops were slow to let. At the time of opening only 17 of the 76 shops were trading; by July 1967, 82 shops had been built and 55 were open. The total population of Seacroft in 1966 was 25,500 with a target of 60,000 by 1981. If the planners deliberately provided more shops than were immediately needed, that was a commercial howler for empty shops have a depressing effect on trade at the outset and this in turn frightens off a second inflow of retailers. Far better, even though it may be more expensive, to build a centre in stages. Two other elementary slips in the planning of Seacroft's centre were to place a fish-and-chip shop on the corner site at the entrance to one of the precincts, and to have a pub along an entire side of the central square. A corner site is far more suitable for a retailer such as a dress shop, which relies heavily on window display, than for a restaurant. Similarly, it is breaking all the rules to fill the most valuable frontage of a main square with the 'dead' walls of a pub, which does not need this pitch as most retailers do. These may seem trivial points to a planner, aiming for the ideal on paper, but they are of great importance if the objective is the commercial success of the project. It will only be full of shoppers and vital if it is commercially successful. The experience of Seacroft hardly suggests that the local authority as an alternative to the private developer is all roses.

But the dilemma of too many shops was not confined to one particular formula of redevelopment. A surfeit of boarded-up gaps in shells of newly built shops could be seen in Margate and Manchester, Shrewsbury and Garforth, Bangor and Portsmouth, Colne and Ipswich. The problems flowing from over-optimism should by now be realised. Because of the long periods between initiation, construction and completion in the case of developer/local authority schemes, some developers may discover before they start to build that they have agreed to pay the local authority over the odds. At Barrow-in-Furness Hammerson parted company acrimoniously from the local authority, in November 1965. The developer had already built the first stage, a small office block and a handful of shops at a cost of £160,000, and had been on the point of signing a lease for a further, much larger project. The co-operation ended abruptly with Hammerson accusing the town council of delaying to such an extent that the commercial viability of the scheme had been impaired. Naturally the town council interpreted the breakdown differently.

Whatever the stumbling block at Barrow, other problems of this sort are probably yet to emerge. In a far-sighted paper read to the Chartered Auctioneers and Estate Agents Institute in December 1963, a prominent estate agent, Trevor Donaldson, spoke of some of the dangers of auctions, 'The typical form of lease and contract put out at these auctions is a far-sighted and comprehensive document, but I defy anyone to foresee all the problems which will arise in a large development such as we are talking about and I predict that many of these "water-tight" contracts will "go bad" before the developments themselves are completed.' This fear may apply to contracts made in other ways, not just after auctions.

Later in the same talk Donaldson gave a more general warning. 'Property developers will no longer be property developers unless they develop property, and with so many developers about they have little choice but to compete boldly for schemes which, by old standards, are almost incapable of assessment. Comprehensive re-development is with us and seems likely to remain and developers have little option but to compete if they wish to remain in business. I believe many of them will go broke in the process, but the process will be slow and perhaps not apparent to the onlooker.' So far no developer of any size has gone broke, but the odd signs of strain can be detected below the surface. In Preston, for example, in early 1966 a ten-storey office block with eleven shops around its ground floor passed from the ownership of a small developer, Calgary and Edmonton Land, to the building contractor, Tersons, which put it up. It had been finished for around two years but was virtually unlet. Named Crystal House, it was known in the property world as Crystal Ball House. This was an unhappy case of the local authority owning a site—it was the Old Town Hall site—and letting it off at auction to the highest bidder, who turned out to have been excessively sanguine. In this instance Goddard & Smith organised the auction. After a year and a half Tersons had managed by altering the rents to let most of the offices and four out of eleven shops.

By September 1966, two months after the 'July measures' of economic squeeze and freeze, the Government was officially recog-nising the potentially serious situation on the redevelopment front. In a circular to all local authorities setting out new rules for controlling 'planning' investment, the Ministry of Housing and Local Government noted that loan sanctions had risen from £24 million in 1962–63 to nearly £50 million in 1965–66. The cost of land bought in advance of requirement had jumped from £8 million in 1962–63 to £19 million in 1965–66. The circular said: 'It is imperative to secure that the preparation and execution of develop-ment schemes goes forward in an orderly manner so as to make the most effective use of resources within the limits of what the country can afford. There are at present several hundred town centre redevelopment schemes at various stages of preparation and im-plementation. These vary considerably in their realism, soundness and prospects of implementation. Moreover proposals of individual towns are prepared in isolation and often take little account of proposals being put forward by neighbouring authorities. In total the proposed provision of facilities in town centre schemes up and down the country greatly exceeds the need and possibility of execution. Over-optimistic redevelopment schemes which fail to be carried out result only in blight.' It added later, 'Proposals which skilfully combine management measures, and the conservation of the distinctive atmosphere and character of town centres with some limited redevelopment, are more likely to be approved than grandiose rebuilding schemes.'

This chapter has shown a gloomy side of shopping developments. There are also many excellent schemes which I have not mentioned. But the problems are highlighted by the failures, not the successes, and the problems have not been sufficiently recognised or debated in public. Much greater discussion and investigation of the subject is needed, especially since there are more problems such as those at Doncaster yet to come to light.

CHAPTER SIXTEEN

What Next?

THE era of the property tycoon as the arch-symbol of capitalism is over. Forces of competition and taxation have ended the days when an individual could rapidly amass a fortune with a few well-chosen deals or developments. As with other extreme phases of commercial history, there was something faintly absurd about many of the events in the property boom. Oddenino's, a company largely owned and run by a hotelier-cum-developer named Instone Bloomfield, bought St Luke's Printing Works in Covent Garden in February 1960 'for investment and development'. It paid the previous owner, the Bank of England, £900,000. A few months later a planner in County Hall included the printing works in the grand design for Covent Garden after the flower and vegetable market had moved out. After two years of negotiation the London County Council paid Oddenino's £1·5 million for the property. Oddenino's made an effortless profit of £600,000.

Although the era of the gold rush may be spent, property needs to be rebuilt and virgin land to be developed. The property developer and his property companies will survive. What seems certain is that they will be increasingly open to the whim of Government interference, though many developers would hardly consider that possible after the changes in tax, building control and planning legislation of the last few years. Paradoxically, restriction from the State will increase the attraction of operating in commercial property for the bigger, better organised companies which can cope with the complexities of an unabating flood of legislation. Land is a commodity whose supply does not expand. In a relatively populous country—at 583 people per square mile the United Kingdom is the fifth most thickly inhabited industrialised country in the world—the Government is bound to be more and more restrictive in its role as the Great Planner. There will always be variations from district to district; values close to Whitehall would slide if the Government and the Civil Service was moved to the Yorkshire moors, as the *Economist* once suggested. But on balance a tight control of building will tend to raise the demand for existing buildings and those new developments allowed through the net. This is one difference between real estate in this country and America. The American planning authorities, with 11½ times as much land per head, are much more prepared to let rival shopping centres be built on either side of a city and allow the customers to decide which is the more useful. If one was a flop, the authorities would not restrict supply until demand was forced towards a basically unsatisfactory product, as the Government has in effect done with its office ban to some office buildings in the London area.

This unnatural protection from the chill of competition may yet save some of the shopping centres described in the last chapter, and more misjudged efforts now being built. It should not be too late for the Government to rouse public opinion to the dangers of the fairly widespread mistakes made by developer and local authorities hand in hand. The object of this would not be to gloat, but to alert the councillors and officials of other towns who may be on the point of advocating or permitting similar follies. It is amazing how closely the pattern of error has been repeated from town to town. If only one dud shopping centre were to be prevented, action would have been worthwhile; one town would have been saved from a nagging patch of long-term blight.

The first step would be for the Government, presumably through the Ministry of Housing and Local Government, to publish some detailed statistics of the shop development scene all over the country. These would be extremely easy to collect. The date of building and the state of letting could be given for each town and city, with appropriate summaries. This would act as a general alert. It would be useful, too, to have a blow-by-blow account of what has gone wrong in, say, Derby or Doncaster. A case study or two in layman's terms might mirror the problems of planning in many another borough. It would certainly be of interest to the ratepayer, who suffers directly and indirectly from poor planning.

Regionalism, an increasingly fashionable theory in recent years, may be in part a solution to the low quality of much post-war planning. It is probable that some variety of regionalism will be recommended by the Royal Commission on local government under the chairmanship of Sir John Maud which is due to report in the middle of 1968. The size and parochialism of local planning authorities have bedevilled many decisions. It was the Town and Country Planning Act of 1947 which gave the prime responsibility on planning to county councils, county boroughs and urban and rural district councils. This pattern was highly democratic in intention, but there was inevitably a conflict between democracy and good planning. With such a large number of towns each administering their own plans there was never enough talent among permanent officials to go round. The concept and practice of town planning was relatively new, yet the Ministry of Housing and Local Government played a permissive role as overlord. This left wide scope for inexperience or incompetence.

Planning authorities have also overlapped, both vertically and horizontally. There has often been a conflict of interest between, say, district councils and the superior county councils, so that the end result has been some mediocre compromise. More perilous has been the rivalry between neighbouring authorities to encourage or sponsor overlapping services. Shopping centres are the easiest candidates to promote in competition. Because X has a spanking new shopping centre, so must we have one 10 miles away in Y. Decisions set off by that sort of emotion have been taken without proper enquiry into the degree of new shopping facilities needed, or the extent to which the two towns might both be trying to attract identical customers from the hinterland between the two towns. The Ministry of Housing's own circular of September 1966, quoted at length in the last chapter, implicitly gave a strong indictment of the structure of planning: '. . . proposals of individual towns are prepared in isolation and often take little account of proposals being put forward by neighbouring authorities. In total the proposed provision of facilities in town centre schemes up and down the country greatly exceeds the need and possibility of execution. . . .'

It must be tempting to leave the host of small authorities as they are and patch their decisions together through better co-ordination from above. The Labour Government has already taken a faltering step towards regionalism through the establishment of eight regional councils and boards for England, one for

Scotland and one for Wales. However, this has been only a tentative move since these bodies were set up by the central Government, through the Ministry of Economic Affairs, and they function largely as advisers to the Ministers. They lack bite. The next stage in my view should be that powers of planning should be entirely taken out of the hands of existing local authorities. The new planning bodies would cover much larger areas than at present, in order to take local decisions in better perspective and to give each body a larger and better qualified staff. Thus Cornwall and Devon might be administered as one largely rural unit, and the major towns of South Wales, Swansea, Cardiff and Newport, lumped together into one largely urban unit.

A prime objective in the new system should be to encourage speed in planning and to cut down on appeals. In 1965 there were 443,387 planning applications in England and Wales, of which 78,452 were refused. In England only, in February 1967, 7,209 appeals were pending and appeals by enquiry were taking as much as thirty-eight weeks to be settled; this period dropped on average to twenty-seven weeks under written procedures for settlement. Planning and redevelopment are bound to become more complicated and subtle, but if private developers are to continue to play a part in development, the more efficient the machinery of planning, the more likely are they to be attracted.

In spite of their unsavoury public reputation as a class, commercial property developers do not in general object to the justice of the legislation imposed on their industry in recent years. Indeed, the principles underlying the Land Commission of 1967, the main item, are almost universally accepted: that there should be a development levy on values created by decisions of the local authority, and thus the community, and that the Commission should operate in the real estate market in order to lubricate the supply of land for development. (However, the property world did quarrel fiercely with the Government over the mechanics through which those principles should be applied.)

In retrospect, the development levy, now an established fact of life which is never likely to disappear, can be seen as one area affecting property where the Conservatives failed in their thirteen years of power from 1951 to 1964. The 100 per cent tax on development values attempted by the Labour party in the Act of 1947 was clearly a mistake of degree, in that it severely sapped the incentive for the seller to sell or the developer to develop. But it was perhaps an even greater mistake on the part of Mr Macmillan to have abolished the charge completely in 1953. Apart from its being widely accepted as a just tax, its abolition was over the years extremely harmful to the image of property developers. Had Macmillan reduced the rate from 100 per cent to, say, 25 per cent, the public would have seen that as development marched forward, it too was sharing in the spoils of the greater values created. The role of the developer would have seemed much less objectionable. On other fronts the Conservative record on real estate is hardly impressive; building controls should arguably never have been removed completely by Mr Birch in 1954, so that the boom in offices could have been spread out over a longer period and regulated more carefully; the Rent Act of 1957, outside the scope of this book, is not claimed even by Mr Sandys' admirers to have been a successful piece of legislation; Conservative governments were slow off the mark on tax reform, especially with capital gains tax. Had the Conservatives been more enlightened in all these areas, the public might well have regarded developers more as it did any other manufacturers. The Trades Union Unit Trust, when plunging into the capitalist delights of ordinary shares in 1961, might well not have banned property shares for three years.

Property development will tend more and more to embrace large areas of land and to need huge sums of money. This is a side effect of the trend to comprehensive planning, and it will mean that the proportion of commercial rebuilding carried out in some form of co-operation between private developers, local authorities and the Land Commission will still increase. What is essential is that a greater amount of information than is at present available should be given to the public about the detailed terms of this co-operation. Local authorities should be obliged to publicise the details of every contract concerning land which they make with private operators. This does not happen universally. It is all the more important at a time like this, when contracts made by over-optimistic developers may be altered to the apparent disadvantage of the local authority. At the same time local authorities should be forced to provide meaningful statistics about their holdings in real estate, which in the case of the bigger authorities are vast. When Birmingham's Conservatives started to sell off some of Birmingham's long-held freeholds in the autumn of 1966, a policy curiously

s

out of keeping with orthodox ideas on planning, those who enquired what was the city's total ownership of land in terms of acres and value were told that the figures were not readily available and would be hard to produce. The GLC's answer would have been the same. It would be much better for the public interest if normal commercial principles of accountancy applied to the estates of these rich landlords. Financial secrecy can hide inefficiency.

Similarly, the central Government should help by producing better statistics to help the town planners. There has recently been some energy devoted to bringing statistics on trends in population, traffic, level of purchasing power and so on more up to date, but there is a long way to go. The Inland Revenue could help to provide planners and the real estate market with a great deal of useful information if it chose to collate and publish the huge reservoir of facts about real estate values which flow to it through tax returns. So far the Revenue has taken the archaic line that this information is confidential. But no-one would suggest that each fact should be published, rather that the totals and the trends broken down into area and types of property should be freely available. In few markets are reliable facts so hard to come by as in land. The Land Commission could certainly help to cast some light here, or at least could prod other bodies such as the Inland Revenue to do so.

As the scale of property development continues to increase, so will property developers and their companies change. The day of the individual entrepreneur with flair has passed. This is not to say that the individuals who built up some of the mushrooming post-war companies will not continue to do so successfully for some time to come. Harry Hyams, for instance, can look forward at the age of thirty-nine to three decades or so at the head of the Oldham Estate Company. But, as it is hard to envisage a tiny car company in the United States growing into a challenger to General Motors or Ford, so there are unlikely to be embryo property companies today which will rank alongside the giants in ten years' time. Profit margins are lower, opportunities are fewer, and the faint singeing of fingers in provincial shops will make lenders less indiscriminate to the small man.

Another brash, pioneering industry will become staid, respectable and institutionalised. If the profession of property could do so also, the reputation and the operation of the world of property would improve in leaps and bounds. The one important prelude to this would be for all the professional societies connected with real estate to join together into one, raising the standards to conform to the best in any of the constituent societies, and then gradually raising the code of conduct. This need is realised by many inside the profession, but parochial interests have so far prevented a grand marriage being consummated. If the petty jealousies aroused by the mechanics of amalgamation can be overcome, a unified body could be extremely powerful and influential. Beyond this, it seems possible, as Sir Henry Wells, now chairman of the Land Commission, suggested in his farewell speech as president of the Royal Institution of Chartered Surveyors, that various professions might form themselves into joint partnerships. Solicitors, accountants, architects and surveyors or estate agents all overlap to some extent and might be much more useful to the public in one firm.

Unless the laws of taxation are changed, the relative importance of pure property companies on the private side of the development fence is likely to decline over the years. The change to corporation tax in Mr Callaghan's 1965 budget penalised companies which pay out all their earnings by way of dividend. The structure of a publicly quoted property company more or less obliges it to pay out all its earnings. There are ways to lessen the impact of this tax, but many companies will not do so and it will weaken their contribution to development.

Building contractors and insurance companies, huge, impersonal organisations, will increasingly take up the running along with a few of the largest property companies with easy access to big money from the capital market. Building contractors have always been close to developers and are likely to participate more often themselves, as their counterparts do in other countries. As development calls for greater and greater funds, insurance companies may find themselves in something of a monopoly position and they may have to be tempted with high profit margins to lose their shyness of the risks in direct involvement; only a handful have so far plunged heavily into development. Local authorities will themselves assume the role of complete developer more often.

In 'Traffic in Towns' Professor Buchanan and his group suggested that the future of redevelopment in the centres of big cities would embrace areas as large as half Oxford Street and 148 acres to the north. In such chunks even the resources of individual insurance companies would be inadequate. When that stage arrives consortia of developers will have to be formed. Then the more institutional character of developers will come into its own. As the merger of Jack Cotton with Charles Clore showed in an extreme form, or the many efforts over the last eighteen months to merge smaller property companies which have been frustrated by quarrels over who was to be chairman, individualistic, first-generation businessmen do not make comfortable bedfellows. But the insurance companies and contractors and impersonal property corporations will line up happily into the faceless, fund-raising consortia of the future.

Appendix 1*

Name	First Profession	Name of Main Company
Bampton, Kenneth	Estate agent	Bampton Property Group
Bell, John	Housebuilder	North British Properties
Bernstein, William	Furrier	Fortress Property
Black, Sir Cyril	Estate agent	Beaumont/London Shop
Blausten, Cyril	Estate agent	Simo Properties
Blausten, Leonard	Estate agent	Simo Properties
Bloch, Sidney	Solicitor	Hallmark Securities
Bloomfield, Instone	Property dealer	Oddenino's Property
Bourner, George	Estate agent	British Land
Bridgland, Sir Aynsley		Haleybridge Investment Trust
Broackes, Nigel	Insurance clerk	Trafalgar House
Brown, Nathan	Engineer	Nathan Brown Estates
Chamberlain, Walter	Housebuilder	Corinthian Investments
Chippindale, Sam	Estate agent	Arndale Property Trust
Clark, Robert	Solicitor	Stock Conversion
Cleary, Fred	Estate agent	Haslemere Estates
Clore, Charles	General dealer	City & Central Properties
Cohen, John		Rodwell Group
Cohen, Lord, of Brighton	Estate agent	Atlas Homes
Colman, Alec	Estate agent	E. Alec Colman Investments
Corob, Sidney		Corob Holdings
Cotton, Jack	Estate agent	City Centre Properties
Cowan, Sydney	Housebuilder	Samuel Properties
Cussins, Philip	Building contractor	Cussins Properties
Diggens, Ronald		Allnatt (London)
Dolland, Arthur	Solicitor	Dolland Group
East, Barry	Estate agent	Town & City Properties
Edgson, Stanley	Estate agent	Central Commercial Properties
Ellis, Charles	Heating contractor	Croydon Centre Developments
Farrow, George		Peachey Property
Fenston, Felix	Estate agent	Metropolitan & Provincial Props.
Flack, Walter	Estate agent	Murrayfield Real Estate

Name	First Profession	Name of Main Company
Fox, Cecil	Tailor	Stem Properties
Freedman, Louis	Estate agent	Ravenseft Properties
Freshwater, Osias	Estate Agent	Freshwater Group
Glover, Gerald	Solicitor	Edger Investments
Gold, Joe	Estate agent	Centrovincial Estates
Goldschlager, Lorant	Banker	Thames Estates
Hagenbach, Arnold	Multiple baker	Arndale Property Trust
Hammerson, Lew	Mackintosh maker	Hammerson Property
Harris, Bob	Furrier	Harris & Co.
Harris, Harry	Furrier	Harris & Co.
Harrison, Gabriel	Housebuilder	Amalgamated Investment
Hemens, Arthur	Estate agent	London Shop Property
Hines, Johnny	Estate agent	Town & Commercial
Hunnisett, Charles	Jeweller	South Bank Estates
Hutley, Anthony	Estate agent	Peachey Property
Hyams, Harry	Estate agent	Oldham Estate
Hyams, Philip	Cinema owner	
Hyams, Sydney	Cinema owner	
Joseph, Maxwell	Estate agent	Union Property
King, Roy		Roy King Properties
King, Sam	Schoolmaster	Regional Properties
Knight, Lawrence	Estate agent	Sovereign Securities
Leaver, Marcus	Estate agent	Allied Land
Lee, Arnold	Solicitor	Imry Property
Leigh, Kennedy	Merchant	Kennedy Leigh Property
Levy, Joe	Estate agent	Stock Conversion
Lewis, Cecil	Estate agent	Burlington Estates
Littman, Joe	Furrier	Aldford House (Park Lane)
Lottenberg, Jacob	Silk merchant	Lynton Holdings
Luck, Laurence	Estate agent	Charterbridge Corporation
Lyon, Ronald	Builder	Ronald Lyon Holdings
Manousso, Luke	Estate agent	Maybrook Properties
Marler, Leslie	Estate agent	Capital & Counties Property
Maynard, Fred	Estate agent	Ravenseft Properties
Messer, Sam	Estate agent	Mansion House Chambers
Miller, Eric	Estate agent	Peachey Property
Mitchell, Sir Godfrey	Building contractor	George Wimpey/Oldham
Morrison, Jack	Retailer	Amalgamated Securities
Mouray, Maurice	Dress retailer	City & Town Buildings
Myers, Bernard	Tailor	Rodwell Group
Myers, Sefton	Estate agent	Rodwell Group
Neale, Charles	Solicitor	Willett Group
Newton, Gerald	Retailer	Country & New Town
Oppenheim, Henry	Property owner	City Wall Properties
Oppenheim, Meyer	Furniture retailer	Argyle Securities
Orchard-Lisle, Aubrey	Estate agent	

Name	First Profession	Name of Main Company
Overall, Douglas	Estate agent	Sterling Estates
Palumbo, Rudolph	Property dealer	Rugarth Investment Trust
Pearlberg, Beatrice	Dental surgeon	Ve-ri-best Manufacturing
Perry, Albert	Builder	Estates Property Investment
Potel, Robert	Solicitor	Star (Greater London)
Radziwill, Prince Stanislas	Aristocrat	Metropolitan & Provincial Props.
Rayne, Max	Coat manufacturer	London Merchant Securities
Rind, Sylvia	Shop assistant	Greenhaven Securities
Ronson, Gerald	Furniture maker	Heron Holdings
Rose, Jack	Estate agent	Land Investors
Rose, Philip	Estate agent	Land Investors
Rubens, John	Accountant	Central & District Properties
Samuel, Basil	Estate agent	Great Portland Estates
Samuel, Sir Harold	Estate agent	Land Securities
Samuel, Howard	Estate agent	Great Portland Estates
Sebba, Sam	Solicitor	Warnford Investments
Sherman, Archie	Estate agent	Metrovincial Properties
Shine, Barnett	Skirt manufacturer	Central & District Properties
Spiro, Moss	Solicitor	Fly Over Investments
Sputz, Otto	Engineer	Parway Land
Sunley, Bernard	Building contractor	Bernard Sunley Investment Trust
Tobin, Leonard	Solicitor	Lintang Investments
Tovey, Douglas	Estate agent	
Walton, Issy	Property dealer	Scottish Metropolitan
Wates, Norman	Building contractor/ housebuilder	Wates
Wingate, Harold	Chemist	Chesterfield Properties
Wingate, Maurice	Property dealer	Wingate Investments
Winham, Francis	Estate agent	Western Ground Rents
Witting, Dudley	Estate agent	Chancery Lane Properties
Wohl, Maurice	Property owner	United Real Property
Yablon, Ralph	Solicitor	Town & Commercial
Ziff, Arnold	Shoe retailer	Town Centre Securities

* This appendix clearly needs a heavy qualification. Although the bulk of the information on which the list is compiled comes from public documents such as prospectuses or records at Companies House, the gross value of a man's shares at, say, £1·5 million does not necessarily mean that his net worth is over £1 million, because he may have other commitments. It is not possible to draw up a list of millionaires and prove the fact in each case. But I believe that this list, within a margin of error of some 10 per cent either way, gives a fair estimate.

Appendix 2

3rd October, 1966

Charles Clore, Esq.
22 Park Street
London, W.1

Dear Mr Clore,

Following my conversation on the telephone with your secretary last Friday, I am writing some of the questions which I would have put to you in an interview.

1. Going back to pre-war days, I was told by someone who claimed to have been told the story by yourself that you bought the lease of the Prince of Wales Theatre in 1934 almost by chance: that shortly after you returned from South Africa you happened to drop into an auction room: that no other bidders had appeared at the scheduled time, and that, for lack of competition you decided on the spur of the moment to buy the lease on the Prince of Wales.
   Is this story true? It seemed to me to have the ring of how things tend to happen in life.

2. Were you involved to any extent in the development of real estate before the war? If so, what type of properties, and where?

3. Apart from Charles House, how many other 'lessor' schemes did you develop? How many square feet has Charles House? Who was the architect?

4. Which of your property developments are you proudest of?

5. Did you buy the site for the Hilton with or without planning permission for a hotel? In which year did you buy the freehold?

6. Would you claim to have foreseen the full extent of the post-war property boom?

7. Do you consider that your talents have been best used in property development or in some of the other industries in which you have been involved?

Yours sincerely,
Oliver Marriott,
Business News

22 Park Street
Park Lane
W.1
4th October, 1966

Miss Jane C. Purser
Secretary to
Mr Oliver Marriott,
The Sunday Times,
200 Gray's Inn Road, W.C.1

Dear Miss Purser,

Mr Clore has asked me to reply to your letter of the 3rd October.

He has made it a rule not to give interviews, as apart from the constant risk of being misquoted, he finds that to give an interview to one member of the press, means, that he has to give interviews to all the others or offend them.

I can however, help you with regard to your questions:

1. Mr Clore bought the leasehold interest in the Prince of Wales Theatre in 1930 and then proceeded to acquire the other interests. He finally acquired the freehold and was able to rebuild the theatre in 1937.

2. Before the war, Mr Clore was involved in a number of developments, principally of industrial premises.

3. After the war, it was only possible to get licences to build where the premises were pre-let; in consequence, the earlier post-war development schemes were lessor schemes.

4. Mr Clore cannot pin-point any particular development of which he is most proud, as the facts vary in each case; e.g., he is very proud of a little-publicised development in Southwark Bridge Road, which in fact is one of the largest office developments in London but was built in record time for occupation by the Ministry of Transport. He does not believe in any great architectural triumphs which end up in bankruptcy.

5. The Hilton site was bought without planning permission, although it was fairly clear from the advice he received that planning permission for an Hotel would be given, the only problem being the ultimate permitted size.

6. Mr Clore feels that he foresaw the full extent of the post-war property boom as this happens historically after every period of restriction.

7. This is a subject of which Mr Clore feels there are others more qualified than he to answer.

I hope the above answers are of some help to Mr Marriott.

Yours sincerely,
L. Gelman
Secretary

Appendix 3

Office Floorspace (to nearest 100 square feet) permitted in new buildings, rebuildings and extensions, 1948–63

Year	Annual Totals (sq. ft)
1948 (half year)	2,109,900
1949	3,550,800
1950	3,331,300
1951	1,696,800
1952	2,368,700
1953	3,002 100
1954	5,650,100
1955	5,868,300
1956	3,655,500
1957	4,710,300
1958	4,198,300
1959	4,336,500
1960	4,283,500
1961	4,439,900
1962	2,907,600
1963	2,063,800
Total 1948–63	**Grand total 58,173,000**

* The area covered is the 1961 Census Central Area.

Appendix 4

STATISTICS OF QUOTED PROPERTY COMPANIES*

Year	Number of marks received in each year†	Number of quoted property companies	Total market value of all quoted property companies‡ £m
21 February, 1939§	—‖	35	30
Years to 31 March			
1958¶	15,902	111	103
1959	101,531	120	247
1960	169,044	146	437
1961	133,128	149	638
1962	183,519	169	800*
1963	149,431	179	775
1964	108,391	183	730
1965	82,443	175	670
1966	57,586	166	664
1967	53,538	164	603

* Derived mainly from Statistics Relating to Securities Quoted on the London Stock Exchange, published by the London Stock Exchange.

† As it is only voluntary that any particular deal should be 'marked', or recorded, this gives only an indication of trend.

‡ At 31 March in each year except for 1939.

§ From *Monthly Investment List*, published by Straker Brothers Ltd.

‖ Marks not then compiled.

¶ No separate property section before this date.

* Only a relatively small part, say £120 million or so, of the increase in value from £103 million in 1958 to £800 million in 1962 would be attributable to the extra 58 companies quoted in that period.

Appendix 5

LIST OF SOCIETIES WITH ESTATE AGENCY*
(in order of foundation)

Name	Date of foundation	No. of full members	Letters used	Remarks
Royal Institution of Chartered Surveyors	1868	18,000	FRICS ARICS	The oldest and largest body
Chartered Auctioneers' and Estate Agents' Institute	1872	8,600	FAI AAI	Amalgamation in 1912 of two Institutes. (1872 is foundation date of the oldest body)
Rating and Valuation Association	1882	2,000	FRVA ARVA	
Chartered Land Agents' Society	1902	1,300	FLAS QALAS	Originally for resident land agents, most of whom were chartered surveyors
Incorporated Society of Auctioneers and Landed Property Agents	1924	3,500	FALPA AALPA	Originally formed as home for those who could not comply with chartered societies commercial rule
Faculty of Architects and Surveyors	1924	2,000	FFS AFS FFAS AFAS	1,800 are surveyors, 200 are architects
Incorporated Association of Architects and Surveyors	1925	3,100	FIAS AIAS FIAA AIAA	First set of letters refers to surveyors: other to architects
Institute of Auctioneers and Appraisers of Scotland†	1926	Nearly 400	FIA (Scot) AIA (Scot)	Mainly livestock auctioneers, but some managers, valuers and estate agents
Valuers Institution	1928	4,200	FVI AVI	An amalgamation in 1953 of the Valuers Institution and Valuers Association (1936): also incorporates the National Association of Auctioneers
Guild of Surveyors†	1950	800	FG of S AG of S LG of S	Formed for otherwise unattached surveyors
Institution of Business Agents†	1954	100	FIBA AIBA	Specialists in business transfer side of estate agency
National Association of Estate Agents†	1962	1,200 claimed	MNAEA	Formed to oppose 1963 Bill in that form
Federation of Local Associations of Estate Agents†	1965	17 assocns	—	A group of local associations formed to ginger up the national societies. 45 more associations interested

* As at the beginning of 1966.
† It is possible to join these bodies without taking an examination.

Appendix 6

SELECTED FIGURES FROM THE TOTAL INVESTMENTS
OF BRITISH INSURANCE COMPANIES*
(000's omitted)

Year	Mortgages	Ordinary stocks and shares	Real property and ground rents	Total
1927	£112,144 10·7%	£36,237 3·4%	£56,759 5·4%	£1,051,047
1937	£171,839 10·3%	£150,019 9·0%	£103,744 6·2%	£1,671,567
1947	£157,724 6·2%	£271,921 10·6%	£148,749 5·8%	£2,560,991
1957	£689,328 13·4%	£885,571 17·2%	£441,887 8·5%	£5,149,215
1960	£927,039 14·0%	£1,416,916 21·4%	£614,932 9·3%	£6,610,642
1965	£1,654,968 16·2%	£2,293,338 22·5%	£1,047,562 10·3%	£10,195,747

* Compiled by the British Insurance Association.

Appendix 7

GOVERNMENT OFFICE ACCOMMODATION*

(millions square feet net)

Zone	Crown Freehold	Leased	Requisitioned	Total
At:				
December 1965				
London Central	3·1	6·3		9·4
London Other	2·9	5·1		8·0
Total London	6·0	11·4		17·4
Elsewhere	13·1	10·9		24·0
Grand Total	19·1	22·3		41·4
At:				
December 1955				
London Central	3·0	6·2	0·1	9·3
London Other	2·9	2·9	0·1	5·9
Total London	5·9	9·1	0·2	15·2
Elsewhere	10·3	10·6	0·3	21·2
Grand Total	16·2	19·7	0·5	36·4

* Supplied by the Ministry of Public Building and Works.

Appendix 8

Type of space	Number of square feet and estimated price per square foot	Estimated income £
Offices	130,000 at 60s.	390,000
	370,000 at 80s.	1,480,000
Shops	120,000 at 30s.	180,000
Showrooms	160,000 at 20s.	160,000
Industrial	216,000 at 10s.	108,000
Garage for 900 cars at £200 a space		180,000
77 flats at £500 each		38,500
	a total gross income per year of	2,536,500

Valuing this income to give a yield of 6⅔ per cent,
or 15 years' purchase of rents, gives a value to the
project of   £38,000,000
less an estimated gross cost of land and construction of   £16,000,000

leaves a net equity value of approximately   £22,000,000

Appendix 9

(See the note at the foot of this Appendix)

(i) PORTFOLIO OF THE OLDHAM ESTATE COMPANY

A *Name of subsidiary or associated company*	B *% of capital held by Oldham*	C *Properties involved*	D *Lender of bridging or/and permanent finance*	E *Type of development (figures in sq. ft)*
1. Anthow Investments	90	Mohican House, Southwark	Wimpey	Offices. 40,000
2. Blackmore Press	95	Orbit House, Blackfriars	Co-operative Ins.	Offices. 114,000
3. Causeway Invs	100	Anneuel House, Finchley	Wimpey	Offices. 36,000
4. Calvalcade Props	100	77–83 (odd), Upper Richmond Rd, Putney	Co-operative Ins. and Wimpey	Offices. 40,000
5. Chiltern St Inv.	46·5	Kellogg House, W.1	Pearl Assurance	Offices. 94,000
6. Command Property Investments	100	41–2 London Wall, E.C.	Co-operative Ins. and Wimpey	Offices.?
7. Compact Property Investments	100	Southern House, Croydon	Co-operative Ins.	Offices. 200,000
8. Component Props	100	Henley Cable Works, North Woolwich	Co-operative Ins. and Wimpey	Factory. 314,000
9. Drapers Gdns Prop.	100	1–10 Drapers Gardens & 8 Copthall Ave, E.C.	Co-operative Ins.	Offices, 180,000 and Bank
10. Dynamic Properties	100	ICT House, Fulham High St	Co-operative Ins.	Offices. 62,000
11. Eastbourne Terrace Investment	100	Telstar House, Eastbourne Terrace, W.2	Co-operative Ins. and Wimpey	Offices. 88,000 Shops & Pub.
12. Five Old Burlington Street	100	583 Fulham Rd & 2–10 (even) Argon Mews, Fulham	Co-operative Ins.	Offices. ?
		16, 18–22 Ack Lane & 13 Bramhall Lane South, Bramhall, Cheshire	Wimpey	?
13. Glanprime Inv.	100	4, 6, 8, 10 Whitehorse Rd, Croydon	Wimpey	Offices. 58,200
14. Holborn Hall Inv.	90	South corner of Gray's Inn Rd & Clerkenwell Rd, W.C.1	Co-operative Ins. and Wimpey	Offices. 36,500 Shops. 22,500
15. Ilmahoc Invests	90	Kingston Bridge House, Hampton Wick	Co-operative Ins.	Offices. ?

F	G	H	J	K	L
Cost from recent balance sheet* £	Estimated total cost if different from F £	Let or unlet	Estimated value fully let† £	Estimated net equity value of Oldham's share £	Remarks
L.C. 275,000	300,000	Unlet	980,000	610,000	Building completed
L.C. 560,000	—	Let	1,571,000 (dir. val.)	940,000	Let to Ministry of Works
F.C. 235,000	270,000	Let	740,000	470,000	Let to Central Elec. Gen. Board
F.C. 361,000	370,000	Let	750,000	380,000	Let to International Computers & Tabulators
F.C. 817,000	—	Let	2,250,000 (dir. val.)	660,000	Let to Kellogg
F.C. 120,000	—	Unlet	—	—	A small, old property, perhaps the kernel of some far distant redevelopment
F.C. 1,873,000	—	Let	4,125,000	2,250,000	Let to British Transport Board
F.C. 329,000 L.C. 48,000	—	Unlet	—	—	As a factory, an oddity in the Hyams pattern
L.C. 3,017,000	3,200,000	Let	10,500,000	7,300,000	Let to National Provincial Bank
F. & L.C. 448,000	—	Let	831,000 (dir. val.)	383,000	Let to International Computers & Tabulators
L.C. 620,000	1,650,000	Unlet	3,100,000	1,450,000	Building completed. Has a neighbour on same site (see no 26)
F.C. 128,000	—	?	128,000 (dir. val.)	—	A small, old property
F. & L.C. 80,000 C.C. 260,000	—	?	—	—	Development not known
F.C. 197,000 C.C. 450,000	670,000	Unlet	1,200,000	530,000	Building completed
F.C. 330,000	750,000	Unlet	1,700,000	855,000	Building under construction
F.C. 325,000	—	Let	769,000 (dir. val.)	400,000	—

* The balance sheets are in most cases dated 31 March 1966. F.C. stands for freehold cost, L.C. for leasehold cost, and C.C. for capital commitments.
† Dir. val. stands for directors' valuation.

T

A	B	C	D	E
Name of subsidiary or associated company	% of capital held by Oldham	Properties involved	Lender of bridging or/and permanent finance	Type of development (figures in sq. ft)
16. Marathon Props	90	Early Bird House, Eccleston Square, S.W.1	Co-operative Ins. and Wimpey	Offices. 78,000 Bank & 129 Flats
17. Nerico Invests	92·5	Island Site bounded by Carey St, Portugal St & Searle St, W.C.2	Westminster Bank	Offices. 193,000
18. New Kingsway Improvements	75	Space House, island site bounded by Wild St, Keeley St, Kemble St, & Kingsway, W.C.2	Scottish Widows	Offices. 195,000 Shops. 42,000
19. New Whetstone Developments	100	Every Ready House, Whetstone	Co-operative Ins.	Offices. 80,000
20. Oldham Estate (N'n Investments)	85	211–15 Dalton Road, Barrow-in-Furness	—	—
21. Oldham Estate (St Peters)	100	Comprehensive Development Area No. 1, Oldham	—	Shops, etc.
22. Oldham Estate (Shop Sites)	100	Six different shopping sites in Cheshire (2), Yorkshire (2), Lancashire and Slough	—	Shops, etc.
23. Pivot Properties	100	Royex House, London Wall, E.C.	Co-operative Ins.	Offices. 96,000
		Girls High School site, Croydon	Westminster Bk. and Wimpey	Offices. 454,000
24. Sovmots Invests	100	Centre Point, St Giles' Circus, W.C.1	Westminster Bk. Co-operative Ins. and Wimpey	Offices. 202,000 Shops. 50,000 Flats. 50,000
25. Sovneath Invest.	100	A large part of Denmark St, or Tin Pan Alley, W.C.1	Wimpey	Offices, Shops and Flats
26. Westbourne Terrace Investment	100	Neighbouring site to Telstar House but facing Westbourne Terr. (see no. 11)	Co-operative Ins. and Wimpey	Offices. 62,000
27. Whipmayes Invest.	95	Arcadia Works & House, and Greater London House, N.W.1	Co-operative Ins. and Wimpey	Offices. 400,000
28. Whympeas Invests.	100	41 Eastcheap, E.C.	Co-operative Ins. and Wimpey	Offices. 19,000
		3–27 Railway Approach, 3–9 London Bridge Street, & 2–6 Joiner Street, S.E.	Westminster Bank and Wimpey	Offices. 146,000 Shops. 9,000

F Cost from recent balance sheet* £	G Estimated total cost if different from F £	H Let or unlet	J Estimated value fully let†	K Estimated net equity value of Oldham's share £	L Remarks
F.C. 1,238,000 C.C. 750,000	2,000,000	Unlet	2,920,000 (offices only)	830,000	Offices completed but flats delayed by Victoria Line
F.C. 2,721,000 C.C. 1,400,000	4,200,000	Unlet	10,100,000	5,450,000	Building under construction
L.C. 4,579,000 C.C. 550,000	5,300,000	Unlet	11,760,000	4,850,000	Building completed. This is the only known Hyams project financed by Scottish Widows which has wisely taken 25% equity cut
L.C. 903,000	—	Let	1,480,000	577,000	Let to Ever Ready
F. & L.C. 126,000 C.C. 43,000	—	—	—	—	—
L.C. 224,000 C.C. 1,550,000	1,800,000	Unlet	2,200,000	400,000	Local company makes good. This is just the first phase of a huge central area scheme
F.C. 102,000 C.C. 151,000	—	Unlet	—	—	—
L.C. 970,000	—	Let	3,965,000 (dir. val.)	2,995,000	Let to Royal Exchange Ass.
L.C. 266,000 C.C. 4,000,000	4,400,000	Unlet	9,800,000	5,400,000	Building under construction
L.C. 1,592,000 C.C. 3,200,000	5,000,000	Unlet	16,700,000	11,700,000	Pride of the Hyams empire
F. & L.C. 470,000	—	—	—	—	This plan which would have snuffed out Tin Pan Alley was stopped by the Nov. '64 office ban
L.C. 20,000 C.C. 620,000	700,000	Unlet	2,200,000	1,500,000	Despite Seifert's protests and the façade falling down during development, the LCC forced Oldham to give this block the same façade as the rest of Westbourne Terrace. It has plastic ornamental work
F.C. 3,732,000	4,000,000	Part let	10,400,000	6,080,000	Old Carreras factory converted into office block and modernised. 3 floors let to Continental Oil
F.C. 194,000	230,000	Unlet	550,000	320,000	Old building modernised
F.C. 1,556,000 C.C. 1,500,000	3,200,000	Unlet	6,160,000	3,584,000	Building just completed

59,914,000

A Name of company	B % of capital held by Hyams	C Properties involved	D Lender of bridging or/and permanent finance	E Type of development (figures in sq. ft)
1. Approach House (Putney)	15·6	Approach House, Putney	Co-operative Ins.	Offices
2. Argent House Property Investment	22·8	Woolworth House, N.W.1	Co-operative Ins.	Offices
3. Central Milano Development & Investment	?	?	?	?
4. Commodore Props	95	Clyde Works, Grove Road, Chadwell Heath, Essex	Mrs Hyams and Moss Spiro	Factory
5. Farm St Props	100	The Old Rectory (and Elm Cottage), Chipstead, Surrey	?	House, cottage and farm
6. Fortuna Invests	31·5	Bath Club, St James' St, S.W.1	Pearl Assurance	Offices
7. Glasshouse Yard Investment	50	Therese House, 29–30 Glasshouse Yard, Finsbury	Co-operative Ins.	Offices
8. Norfolk Place Props (Nottingham)	50	12–14 Dean St, Newcastle and Head Post Office, Nottingham	Church Commissioners for England and Westminster Bk	Offices
9. Parcourt Props	67·5	13–19 (odd) Upton Road and Exchange Road, Watford	Myton and Hambros Bank	Offices. 63,000
10. Post-War Invests	70	Astronaut House, Hounslow Road, Middlesex	Co-operative Ins.	Offices
11. Urbsitus (London)	50	Union Carbide House, Grafton Street, W.1	Co-operative Ins.	Offices

F Cost from recent balance sheet* £	G Estimated total cost if different from F £	H Let or unlet	J Estimated value fully let† £	K Estimated net equity value of Hyams' share £	L Remarks
F.C. 215,000	—	Let	458,000	41,000	—
L.C. 803,000	—	Let	2,200,000	320,000	Hyams' minority interest was recently bought out
?	?	?	?	?	The name of this company, but nothing else, might confirm the rumour that Hyams owns an office block in Milan‡
F.C. 240,000	?	?	?	?	See remarks under Oldham No. 8
Rectory 12,000 Farm 27,000	—	—	—	—	One of Mr Hyams' residences
L.C. 1,000,000	1,200,000	Unlet	2,000,000 (dir. val.)	252,000	An old club modernised
L.C. 151,000	—	Let	450,000	149,000	—
?	?	?	?	?	—
F.C. 608,000	630,000	Unlet	1,420,000	533,000	Building completed
L.C. 180,000	—	Part let	1,000,000	574,000	Building completed
L.C. 310,000	—	Let	840,000	265,000	An early Hyams, discussed in chapter 1

2,134,000

‡ No trace can be found of any company owning the Westbury Hotel, Brussels, of which Harry Hyams is known to own at least part.

These calculations are necessarily all approximate estimates. However, they have been checked at several points with professionals. Although I have had no help from the companies concerned, I would be surprised if the total figures are not within 10 per cent, one side or the other, of the truth. This is, needless to say, not a technical document.

The broad conclusion, given that Harry Hyams owns 40¼ per cent of Oldham Estate—an identical proportion to Wimpey's—is that Hyams' share of Oldham is potentially worth £24,100,000. It will be appreciated that many of the buildings are not let and that some are not finished; thus this calculation is very much a forecast. But, as explained in chapter 8, I take the view that the longer these office blocks remain empty, the more valuable they are likely to become. The only complication in the sums is long-term capital gains tax and the effect of this is impossible to assess. It is unlikely to be very great.

Adding the £24,100,000 from (i) and £2,134,000 from (ii) puts a total figure of £26,234,000 on the net worth of the investments of Mr Hyams analysed here. Given that he must have realised at least £1 million worth of holdings in real estate, the fortune of Harry John Hyams can be conservatively assessed at £27 million.

Index

NOTES